Unlocking Quantum Information Technology

This book explores the dynamic intersection of quantum computing and management strategy, offering an exploration of this cutting-edge technology's potential impact. From its inception to its current state, this book traces the evolution of quantum computing, providing readers with a contextual understanding of its development. It illuminates the transformative power of quantum computing and its implications for business and management practices. Through case studies and expert analysis, readers gain insights into how quantum computing can revolutionize data analysis, optimization, and cybersecurity. The chapters in this book equip managers and entrepreneurs with the knowledge and foresight needed to capitalize on the opportunities presented by the quantum computing era.

Unlocking Quantum Information Technology will be beneficial to a mixed audience of specialists, analysts, scholars, researchers, academics, and students in fields of business and management, especially those interested in quantum computing technology, machine learning, and artificial intelligence technology.

The chapters in this book were originally published as a special issue of *Technology Analysis & Strategic Management.*

Davide La Torre is Full Professor in Applied Mathematics and Artificial Intelligence at SKEMA Business School at Université Côte d'Azur, Nice, France. Affiliated with prestigious institutions worldwide, he holds national professorship qualifications in Applied Mathematics, Computer Science, and Economics. With over 220 publications, his research spans mathematics, artificial intelligence, economics, and medicine, influencing academia globally. Throughout his career, he has held various leadership roles, including Departmental Chair, Program Director, and Associate Dean, in numerous institutions across the globe.

Faisal Shah Khan is a mathematical scientist with a global track record in advancing quantum computing and quantum communication technology across academia, government, and industry. He has authored peer-reviewed scientific papers on topics that include quantum logic circuits, quantum game theory, and optimization using quantum computers and has been an invited speaker at international conferences including the Arab-American Frontiers Symposium sponsored by the US National Academies of Sciences, Engineering, and Medicine. He has served as a senior consultant to the Dubai-based multinational DP World. He is passionate about artificial intelligence and data science and is actively engaged in the quantum computing and AI startup ecosystem, demonstrating a strong entrepreneurial interest. He is Adjunct Professor at SKEMA Business School USA and a research fellow at Rethinc. Labs, a division of the Kenan Institute of Private Enterprise, UNC Kenan-Flagler Business School.

Unlocking Quantum Information Technology

Opportunities for Business and Management

Edited by

Davide La Torre and Faisal Shah Khan

Routledge
Taylor & Francis Group
LONDON AND NEW YORK

First published 2025
by Routledge
4 Park Square, Milton Park, Abingdon, Oxon, OX14 4RN

and by Routledge
605 Third Avenue, New York, NY 10158

Routledge is an imprint of the Taylor & Francis Group, an informa business

British Library Cataloguing-in-Publication Data
A catalogue record for this book is available from the British Library

ISBN13: 978-1-032-83570-9 (hbk)
ISBN13: 978-1-032-83574-7 (pbk)
ISBN13: 978-1-003-51002-4 (ebk)

DOI: 10.4324/9781003510024

Typeset in Myriad Pro
by codeMantra

Publisher's Note
The publisher accepts responsibility for any inconsistencies that may have arisen during the conversion of this book from journal articles to book chapters, namely the inclusion of journal terminology.

Disclaimer
Every effort has been made to contact copyright holders for their permission to reprint material in this book. The publishers would be grateful to hear from any copyright holder who is not here acknowledged and will undertake to rectify any errors or omissions in future editions of this book.

Contents

Citation Information

The following chapters in this book were originally published in the *Technology Analysis & Strategic Management*, volume 33, issue 11 (2021), except Chapter 7, which was published in volume 35, issue 7 (2023). When citing this material, please use the original page numbering for each article, as follows:

Chapter 1
Quantum-sapiens: the quantum bases for human expertise, knowledge, and problem-solving
Steve J. Bickley, Ho Fai Chan, Sascha L. Schmidt and Benno Torgler
Technology Analysis & Strategic Management, volume 33, issue 11 (2021), pp. 1290–1302

Chapter 2
Temporal work by consultants in nascent market categories: constructing a market for knowledge in quantum computing
Oona Hilkamo, Anne-Sophie Barbe, Nina Granqvist and Amber Geurts
Technology Analysis & Strategic Management, volume 33, issue 11 (2021), pp. 1303–1316

Chapter 3
Exploring landscapes of quantum technology with Patent Network Analysis
Syuan-Yi Jiang and Shin-Liang Chen
Technology Analysis & Strategic Management, volume 33, issue 11 (2021), pp. 1317–1331

Chapter 4
The centrality and innovation performance of the quantum high-level innovation team: the moderating effect of structural holes
Yue Yang, Yi She, Jin Hong and QingQiu Gan
Technology Analysis & Strategic Management, volume 33, issue 11 (2021), pp. 1332–1346

Chapter 5
A bibliometric analysis of quantum computing literature: mapping and evidences from scopus
Jiaxing Wang, Lihua Shen and Wuyuan Zhou
Technology Analysis & Strategic Management, volume 33, issue 11 (2021), pp. 1347–1363

Chapter 6

Asleep at the wheel? Responsible Innovation in quantum computing
Philip Inglesant, Carolyn Ten Holter, Marina Jirotka and Robin Williams
Technology Analysis & Strategic Management, volume 33, issue 11 (2021), pp. 1364–1376

Chapter 7

Reading the road: challenges and opportunities on the path to responsible innovation in quantum computing
Carolyn Ten Holter, Philip Inglesant and Marina *Jirotka*
Technology Analysis & Strategic Management, volume 35, issue 7 (2023), pp. 844–856

Notes on Contributors

Dr Anne-Sophie Barbe is a post-doctoral researcher at the School of Business at Aalto University, Espoo, Finland. Her research mobilizes organization theory and economic sociology to investigate the social dynamics underlying the construction of technological markets. Her research has been published in *Technological Forecasting and Social Change*.

Steve J. Bickley is a PhD student at the School of Economics and Finance at the Queensland University of Technology, Brisbane, Australia. His current research focuses on modeling complex human systems.

Ho Fai Chan is a postdoctoral research fellow at the School of Economics and Finance at the Queensland University of Technology, Brisbane, Australia. His research lies in the areas of Science of Science (SciSci) and Scientometrics.

Shin-Liang Chen is a postdoctoral associate at the Department of Physics in National Cheng Kung University, Tainan, Taiwan. He is currently also a visiting scholar at Dahlem Center for Complex Quantum Systems at the Free University of Berlin, Germany. He received his PhD at the Department of Physics in National Cheng Kung University, Tainan, Taiwan. Before that, he received his MS at the Department of Physics at National Sun Yat-sen University, Kaohsiung, Taiwan. His research interests cover quantum information, quantum entanglement, and quantum nonlocality.

QingQiu Gan is a PhD student at the School of Management at the University of Science & Technology of China and Department of Information System, City University of Hong Kong. Her research interests are in technology commercialization and blockchain.

Dr Amber Geurts is a researcher at the Department of Strategy & Policy of TNO at the Netherlands Organisation for Applied Scientific Research. Her research focuses on key (enabling) technologies such as AI and quantum as well as mission-oriented policies and data-driven foresight. Before joining TNO, Dr. Geurts conducted her post-doctoral research at Aalto University, Espoo, Finland. Her research has been awarded several grants and has been published in various outlets including *Advanced Science*, *Technological Forecasting and Social Change*, *Journal of Cross-Cultural Psychology*, and *Journal of Economic Issues*.

Professor Nina Granqvist has engaged with the field of quantum phenomena for well over a decade, with her research on nanotechnology awarded with key prizes in her field. The focus of her research is how new ideas and technologies move from margins to mainstream, with a particular focus on market emergence. Her research has been published in the top management journals, including *Academy of Management Journal*, *Organization Science*, *Organization Studies*, and *Journal of Management Studies*.

Oona Hilkamo is a doctoral candidate at the School of Business at Aalto University, Espoo, Finland. She has an MSc in Technology from Aalto University School of Science, Espoo, Finland. Her doctoral research focuses on the social-symbolic construction of emerging technologies and markets, focusing on narratives, storytelling, and visual sensemaking practices.

Jin Hong is currently Full Professor of School of Economics at the Hefei University of Technology, China. He mainly focuses on innovation and entrepreneurship management, organizational behavior and human resources management, and regional sustainable development.

Dr Philip Inglesant is a research associate at the Department of Computer Science at the University of Oxford, UK. He is researching responsible innovation in online algorithmic systems and formerly in the Networked Quantum Information Technologies hub.

Syuan-Yi Jiang is a PhD candidate at the Chair of Innovation Economics at Technische Universität Berlin, Germany. She received her MBA at the Graduate Institute of Technology Management at National Chung Hsing University, Taichung, Taiwan, in 2016. After that, she was a research assistant at Engineering and Technology Promotion Center in National Cheng Kung University, Tainan, Taiwan, during 2016 and 2017. Her research interests comprise innovation management, patent analysis, and standard analysis.

Professor Marina Jirotka is Professor of Human Centred Computing at the University of Oxford, UK. She leads a team that works on responsible innovation, in a range of ICT fields including robotics, AI, machine learning, quantum computing, social media, and the digital economy

Faisal Shah Khan is a mathematical scientist with a global track record in advancing quantum computing and quantum communication technology across academia, government, and industry. He has authored peer-reviewed scientific papers on topics that include quantum logic circuits, quantum game theory, and optimization using quantum computers and has been an invited speaker at international conferences including the Arab-American Frontiers Symposium sponsored by the US National Academies of Sciences, Engineering, and Medicine. He has served as a senior consultant to the Dubai-based multinational DP World. He is passionate about artificial intelligence and data science and is actively engaged in the quantum computing and AI startup ecosystem, demonstrating a strong entrepreneurial interest. He is Adjunct Professor at SKEMA Business School USA and a research fellow at Rethinc. Labs, a division of the Kenan Institute of Private Enterprise, UNC Kenan-Flagler Business School.

Sascha L. Schmidt is Professor and Director of the Center for Sports and Management (CSM) at WHU – Otto Beisheim School of Management, Dusseldorf, Germany. The "Future of Sport" is one of the Sascha's key research areas.

Yi She is a PhD student at the School of Management at the University of Science & Technology of China, Hefei, China. His research interests are in multinational investment, institution, and innovation performance.

Lihua Shen is a senior researcher in the Library of Zhejiang University, Hangzhou, China. Her main research interests include library and information science.

Carolyn Ten Holter is a social scientist by training and is part of the Human Centred Computing research group at the Department of Computer Science at the University of Oxford, UK. She has over twenty years' experience in the private sector and is currently investigating responsible innovation in quantum technologies.

Benno Torgler is Professor of Economics at the School of Economics and Finance and the Centre for Behavioural Economics, Society and Technology at the Queensland University of Technology, Brisbane, Australia. His primary research interest lies in the area of economics, but he has also published in journals with a political science, social psychology, sociology, and biology focus.

Davide La Torre is Full Professor in Applied Mathematics and Artificial Intelligence at SKEMA Business School at Université Côte d'Azur, Nice, France. Affiliated with prestigious institutions worldwide, he holds national professorship qualifications in Applied Mathematics, Computer Science, and Economics. With over 220 publications, his research spans mathematics, artificial intelligence, economics, and medicine, influencing academia globally. Throughout his career, he has held various leadership roles, including Departmental Chair, Program Director, and Associate Dean, in numerous institutions across the globe.

Jiaxing Wang is a postdoctor in Zhejiang University of Technology, Hangzhou, China. Her main research interests include computer science and artificial intelligence.

Professor Robin Williams holds a personal chair in Social Research on Technology at the School of Social and Political Science at the University of Edinburgh, UK, where he is Director of the Institute for the Study of Science, Technology and Innovation (ISSTI). Professor Williams has developed an interdisciplinary research programme into the social shaping of technology. His personal research has focused upon the design and use of Enterprise Systems, eCommerce and eHealth, and more recently mobile and web 2.0 technologies.

Yue Yang is an MD student at the School of Management at the University of Science & Technology of China, Hefei, China. Her research interests are in social network analysis and innovation performance.

Wuyuan Zhou is a researcher in Zhejiang Academy of Science and Technology Information. His main research interests include scientometrics, competitive intelligence, and intellectual property.

Preface

This edited book serves as a comprehensive resource, gathering contributions that delve into various facets of the strategic management of quantum information technology. In today's dynamic digital landscape, businesses are in a constant quest for innovative solutions to gain a competitive advantage, enhance operational efficiency, and unlock new avenues for growth. At the forefront of this technological evolution lies Quantum Information Technology (QIT), offering transformative capabilities that have the potential to redefine entire industries and revolutionize business operations.

QIT leverages the principles of quantum mechanics to fundamentally transform how information is processed, communicated, and safeguarded. Beyond its applications in computing, QIT encompasses a spectrum of domains. Quantum communication, for instance, offers unparalleled levels of security by harnessing quantum phenomena such as entanglement and uncertainty. Quantum sensing facilitates ultra-sensitive measurements with diverse applications spanning from medical diagnostics to environmental monitoring. Additionally, quantum cryptography provides unbreakable encryption methods, ensuring the confidentiality and integrity of sensitive data in an increasingly interconnected world.

For businesses, the integration of QIT presents a multitude of opportunities for transformation across various sectors. Whether it's optimizing supply chain logistics, leveraging advanced data analytics, expediting drug discovery processes, or revolutionizing financial modeling, the potential applications of QIT are vast and far-reaching. Embracing QIT enables businesses to unlock new efficiencies, enhance decision-making processes, and stay ahead in an increasingly competitive landscape. This edited book serves as a valuable resource for exploring the strategic implications and practical implementations of quantum technology in driving innovation and shaping the future of business. This is well presented in the first chapter of this book dedicated to QIT for business transformation.

In the chapter written by Bickley et al., the authors delve into the potential impact of theories inspired by quantum physics and quantum information, often referred to as "quantum-inspired" in the academic literature, on expert systems and knowledge engineering. Within this contribution, the authors demonstrate the benefits of integrating quantum logic and computation into the utilization of expert knowledge. They highlight advantages such as the ability to efficiently pose imprecise queries across vast and complex computational landscapes. This efficiency is achieved by leveraging quantum concepts like superposition, entanglement, parallelism, and interference to establish and manipulate networks of quantum qubits.

In the chapter authored by Hilkamo et al., the authors conduct an inductive analysis of quantum computing to investigate how management consultancies undertake temporal work within such contexts. Through their analysis, they uncover that management consultancies undertake three distinct types of temporal work, contributing to the construction of a knowledge market. The findings of the authors illuminate the proactive intermediating role played by management consultancies in emerging market categories, enabling them to capitalize on nascent markets such as quantum technology from their earliest stages.

In the chapter authored by Jiang and Chen, the authors employ innovation ecosystem and social-technical system theories to address existing research gaps. They achieve this by conducting a patent network analysis, which offers insights into various analytical aspects. These include identifying focal actors, delineating main technological clusters, and tracing technological trajectories within the domain. Notably, quantum science research typically involves the collaboration of high-level innovation teams, underscoring the intricate and collaborative nature of advancements in this field.

In the chapter written by Yang et al., the authors delve into an examination of the network characteristics of "quantum innovation teams" and their influence on innovation performance. They aim to unravel whether occupying a central position within the network benefits high-level innovation teams and whether there exist interactions between structural attributes within the network. This exploration sheds light on the dynamics of collaborative networks in the context of quantum innovation, offering insights into the intricate interplay between network structure and innovation outcomes.

In the chapter authored by Wang, Shen, and Zhou, the authors present a thorough and extensive examination of the global progress in quantum computing development. Initially, they survey the most recent research focal points within the realm of quantum computing. Subsequently, employing various bibliometric metrics, they conduct an analysis encompassing the current state of development, prevalent research trends, technological trajectories, and the respective contributions of authors, institutions, and countries within the field from 2016 to 2020. It is anticipated that the findings of this analysis will furnish a quantitative foundation for scientific research endeavors and decision-making processes within the domain of quantum computing.

In the chapter authored by Inglesant et al., the authors introduce and apply the concept of Responsible Innovation (RI) within a significant quantum computing endeavor. With quantum computing poised at a pivotal juncture, transitioning from laboratory experimentation to commercial viability, this phase presents a unique opportunity to observe and shape the trajectory of this transformative technology. The authors offer reflections on how this transition serves as a valuable case study, providing valuable insights for policymakers and stakeholders involved in Responsible Innovation across emerging technologies.

In the chapter written by Carolyn Ten Holter et al., the authors investigate researchers' perceptions of RI and their understanding of societal impacts of quantum technologies and sought to gauge the challenges of embedding RI across a multi-disciplinary, large-scale enterprise such as the UK quantum programme. The work demonstrated some of the difficulties involved in embedding RI approaches and in creating a dialogue between innovators and societies.

The content within this book is relevant to various themes that hold significance for business leaders and managers. These themes encompass areas of interest such as innovation, strategic management, organizational development, and emerging technologies. By exploring these topics, readers can gain valuable insights into contemporary challenges and opportunities facing businesses in today's dynamic landscape. Moreover, we anticipate that the insights provided will serve as a foundation for stimulating further discussions and inquiries, ultimately fostering deeper understanding, and facilitating informed decision-making processes within the realm of business leadership and management.

The Guest Editors
Dr Faisal Shah Khan and Dr. Davide La Torre

Introduction: Quantum information technology for business Transformation

Faisal Shah Khan and Davide La Torre

ABSTRACT
In today's rapidly evolving digital landscape, businesses are constantly seeking innovative solutions to gain a competitive edge, drive efficiency, and unlock new opportunities for growth. Quantum information technology stands at the forefront of this technological revolution, promising transformative capabilities that have the potential to redefine industries and reshape business operations. Quantum information technology harnesses the principles of quantum mechanics to revolutionize the way information is processed, communicated, and secured. Quantum technology extends beyond computing alone. Quantum communication offers unparalleled levels of security through the utilization of quantum principles such as entanglement and uncertainty. Quantum sensing enables ultra-sensitive measurements with applications ranging from medical diagnostics to environmental monitoring. Moreover, quantum cryptography provides provably secure encryption methods, ensuring the protection of sensitive data in an increasingly interconnected world. For businesses, the integration of quantum information technology presents a myriad of opportunities for transformation across various sectors. From optimizing supply chain logistics and enhancing data analytics to accelerating drug discovery and machine learning algorithms and revolutionizing financial modeling, the potential applications of quantum technology are vast and far-reaching. In this chapter we present an overview of the most important applications of Quantum Information Technology for Business Transformation.

1. Introduction

Let us revisit a moment in ancient history that relates dramatically with the recent past and, indeed, the present. This is the moment when Heron of Alexandria invented a steam engine as a curiosity. Heron's "toy" was a metal sphere containing water, with opposite angular nozzles attached to it. The sphere was mounted on an altar so that the sphere could rotate freely, and a small fire could be lit underneath it. The heat from the fire would convert the water to steam, which would shoot out from the nozzles, making the sphere rotate. Heron's toy was the first known instance of a steam engine. Heron lived circa 300 years before the common era (BCE). His toy was a proof-of-principle that steam could be harnessed for mechanical motion. It took almost two thousand years before steam engines scaled up and became economically useful during the industrial revolution in the form of steam ships and locomotives (trains), among other things. Why did it take so long for the practical use of steam and the industrial revolution to come about? Should not Heron's proof-of-principle be enough to motivate the industrial revolution and subsequent economic growth two thousand years earlier? Answers to these questions have been sought out in detail by historians, for example, Yuval Noah Hariri (2017). The common denominator of historians' research is that incremental results or proofs-of-principle like those of Heron's can go a long way when strategically managed. This has been repeatedly proven since the dawn of the industrial age, for instance, the development and commercialization of heavier than air flight. This point is further supported by the unfortunate events of the world wars of the previous century. Strategic management is the reason technology scales economically and disrupts societies.

Strategic management of technology requires a multi-faceted vision that accounts for a society's past and ties it into the present and the future. There is no reason to assume that this vision was lacking in the time of Heron. However, one can argue that what was lacking in ancient times were dependable communication lines, something that the Mongol Khans set up over 1500 years after Heron in the form of the world's first commercial postal service across their vast contiguous Mongol empire. Effective transmission of information is the bedrock of strategic management of technology, and this requires political and social stability, something the Mongol empire would provide long enough for other administrators to adopt and improve. Today, information and communication technologies have come a long way. Electronic forms of these technologies have produced the modern digital world of the late twentieth century, implementing and improving the implementation of other technologies. Strategic management of technologies has made their ubiquity and longevity possible but at the cost of making jobs obsolete. However, the same strategic management replaces obsolete jobs with new opportunities, giving rise to a finer spectrum of economic growth that has not been seen before in history before the industrial revolution. This trend continues today in the early decades of the twenty-first century, with Artificial Intelligence protocols and Machine Learning algorithms transforming societies by replacing humans with AI in certain economic sectors (medicine, self-checkout, etc). And the next paradigm shift in information technology, quantum information technology, is rapidly commercializing today, requiring urgent attention to the strategic management of this technology by business leaders and policy makers.

2. Quantum information technology

Quantum information technology, often referred to as quantum tech, exploits the intricate phenomena of quantum physics, including entanglement, interference, and genuine randomness, to yield tangible advantages surpassing those of traditional computing and information systems (Bova, Goldfarb, and Melko, 2021). The genesis of quantum tech lies in the profound realization that information is inherently physical, with its very essence grounded in the principles of quantum mechanics. Quantum physics, the seminal theory elucidating the behavior of atoms and molecules, emerged from groundbreaking experiments conducted in the early 1900s. Quantum communication constitutes the scientific endeavor aimed at engineering hardware and devising protocols capable of harnessing the inherent randomness intrinsic to quantum entities such as photons and electrons. Concurrently, quantum computation focuses on the development of hardware capable of manipulating the quintessential features of quantum mechanics, including superposition and entanglement. These quantum physical properties form the foundations upon which quantum computers operate, offering unparalleled computational power and the ability to solve a range of complex problems exponentially faster than their classical counterparts. The advent of quantum technology marks a pivotal moment in the annals of scientific and technological progress, with its transformative potential poised to revolutionize numerous facets of human endeavor. Two seminal events from the twentieth century serve as heralds of the impending quantum age, paving the way for a paradigm shift in computing and information sciences.

3. Quantum money

In 1968, Stephen Wiesner proposed the use of the truly random nature of quantum physical objects to solve the problem of creating money that cannot be counterfeited (Wiesner 1983). What is often misunderstood is that non-quantum physical systems are incapable of creating true randomness. What one sees as random data being generated by a physical system, from the toss of several coins, for example, is in fact chaotic behavior of the system in which the coins interact with the surrounding air molecules. This interaction is chaotic, that is, small changes in the initial way the coins are tossed produce large changes in the data generated at the end of the experiment. This makes the data appear random, whereas in reality, the data are simply chaotic and hard to predict. A dedicated adversary with a suitably powerful computer would fare well in attempting to discern patterns in such data. With the ever-increasing commercial availability of cheap computing power, it is a matter of best practice to assume that such algorithmic encryption schemes, many devised in the 1980s or before, have been compromised (by dedicated nation-state actors or black hats). This is where Wiesner's quantum money comes in. Certain physical properties of quantum systems are inversely correlated. This feature is called conjugate pairs. For physical properties that form a conjugate pair (like momentum and position of an electron), the more precisely one gathers information about one property implies that information gained about the other property will be least precise. This feature of quantum physical systems is known as the Heisenberg uncertainty principle (Heisenberg 1927). Wisener's quantum money utilized the Heisenberg uncertainty principle to ensure, in theory, that a counterfeiting attempt would always fail. Wisener assigned serial numbers to the electronic currency bills, where each digit in the serial was generated by following a protocol to gain precise information about one physical property of a conjugate pair in a quantum system. Now, if a counterfeiter knows what the protocol is, he still must guess, with a (true) 50–50 chance, which one of the two physical properties in the conjugate pair was used to generate the digit's value in the serial number. Half the time, he will learn the value exactly, but half the time with no precision at all. For a serial number of only 10 digits, the probability of counterfeiting a bill of quantum money is 0.00097, that is, 1 success out of every 1024 attempts. For serial numbers of length 20, a successful outcome is once every 1,048,576 attempts or 0.00000095 of the time (Khan and Aburaed 2019). Tamper-proof quantum systems are immune to hacking by analyzing patterns (Williams, Britt, and Humble 2016). Wiesner's quantum money set the stage for using quantum randomness as a resource for securing cybersecurity infrastructures with quantum tech and gave rise to rapid gains in the knowledge of harnessing true randomness sourced from quantum physical objects like photons. This, in turn, has produced the first generation of commercially available quantum communication technology of quantum key distribution.

4. Quantum key distribution

Expanding upon the Wiesner's original concept of quantum money, Bennet and Brassard formulated a groundbreaking communication protocol in 1984 aimed at facilitating the secure exchange of encryption keys for subsequent communications (Bennett and Brassard 1984). This protocol addressed a long-standing challenge known as the "chicken-or-the-egg" problem, wherein two parties seeking to communicate securely over long distances must first establish a secure encryption key without the necessity of meeting in person. The essence of quantum key exchange, akin to quantum money, lies in the transmission of quantum bits (qubits) of information between the communicating parties. If intercepted by a third party, these qubits only afford the interceptor a probabilistic estimation of the information contained within. Crucially, any attempt to intercept or eavesdrop on the quantum data inevitably disturbs its quantum state, immediately alerting the communicating parties to the potential compromise of their communication channel. This inherent feature allows for the detection of any unauthorized access or tampering with the transmitted information, prompting the parties to reset and initiate the exchange process anew. Bennet and Brassard's seminal protocol, commonly known as BB84, revolutionized the field of secure communication by leveraging the principles of quantum mechanics to establish a robust and provably secure method for exchanging encryption keys. Building upon this foundation, Artur Ekert proposed an additional quantum protocol for key exchange in 1991, subsequently referred to as E91 (Ekert 1991), further expanding the repertoire of quantum technologies for secure communication and cryptography.

5. Quantum computing

In 1973, Charles Bennett made a significant breakthrough by demonstrating that computers could theoretically achieve logical reversibility, meaning that the logical circuitry implementing any computation could be faithfully run backward (Bennett 1973). This discovery paved the way for the concept of physical reversibility, suggesting that the heat generated by such circuitry could be minimized to infinitesimally small levels. The realization of reversible computing on a technological level holds immense promise for mitigating environmental impacts, particularly in terms of heat generation. As a result, one of the notable advantages of quantum computers, especially in the context of climate change, is their potential to operate with minimal heat generation in principle. The advent of reversible computing has catalyzed the emergence of a rich body of knowledge focused on leveraging quantum entanglement-generated correlations for enhanced computational speeds and optimizing outcomes in competitive environments through the use of quantum computers. This advancement represents a significant stride towards harnessing the power of quantum mechanics for more efficient and sustainable computing solutions.

Quantum computing is fundamentally different than conventional or classical computing, as some of the landmark results in the field mentioned in Section 6 show. To explain this difference between classical and quantum computing without delving into technical details, we paraphrase Charles Bennett's analogy in which he states that classical computing is to quantum computing as wheat is to classical computing. While it may seem odd at first to compare electronic technology to a grain, the context provides clarity. In the mid-1800s, the English engineer Charles Babbage conceived a mechanical device composed of levers, gears, and storage compartments that would perform mathematical operations and perform calculations. In short, Babbage designed a mechanical computer which had the distinction at the time of being *Turing-complete*, that is, a general-purpose computer, a notion that would not be formalized until the 1940s by Alan Turing. Babbage's computer, known as the *analytical engine*, incorporated the notion of memory storage, and this was achieved by using grains of wheat (or any other grain) to pass through the computer's architecture of levers, gears, and other flow control mechanisms and stored in the aforementioned compartments. Electronic computers achieve similar results by using "grains" of electronic information or *binary digits* (bits).

It does not take too much imagination to see that information processing by the analytical engine via wheat grains is far inferior to information processing via electronic signals (digital or analogue). For one, wheat grain would have a higher propensity to cause blockage in the computers mechanisms as well as being susceptible to spoiling over time and under attack by pests. Babbage's computer would have been very faulty and noise intolerant. Hence, as Bennett says, electronic computers are far superior to wheat-based computers, and quantum computers are superior to electronic computers by a similar order of magnitude, if not many more.

6. Better results, faster calculations, public-key encryption, and quantum artificial intelligence

Building up in the ideas of Charles Bennett, Ingarden established a formal theory of Quantum Information in 1976 (Ingarden 1976). His ideas were further given a computation perspective by Feynman in his famous 1982 lecture (Feynman 1982) in which he proposed the simulation of a complicated quantum physical system using a simple one. This was essentially the formulation of universality of a quantum computer, that is, the idea that a quantum computer can solve all mathematically formulable problems, similar to the result of Turning on the universality of Turing machines as computers. These observations of Feynman's were built up on by others, notably by Deutche, Josza, Grover, and Shor, to show that quantum computers offer a new computational paradigm that can speed up certain calculations dramatically. For instance, the famous Deutche-Josza quantum algorithm (Deutsch 1985; Deutsch and Jozsa 1992), designed to run on quantum computers, can evaluate a class of functions in one execution versus conventional computers that require as many executions as there are variables in the function. In a similar spirit Shor (1994) developed a quantum computational algorithm that would break public-key cryptosystems in time exponentially faster when executed on a quantum computer than the time it would take to break these cryptosystems using classical computers. Roughly speaking, this means that it would take a classical computer 2^100 seconds to break a public-key cryptosystem whereas the same task would be completed in 100 seconds on a quantum computer. To get a proper appreciation of the difference in magnitude of the execution times, note that 2^100 seconds = 40,196,936,986,301,367,800,000 years! It goes without saying that 100 seconds is a trivial time-to-task, meaning that once implemented on a quantum computer Shor's algorithm will make all current cybersecurity protocols using public-key cryptography useless. Finally, Grover (1996) established that it is possible to speed up searching of items in a database considerably (a quadratic speedup) on a quantum computer, again implying that security protocols that assume that searching is a slow process would be useless as soon as quantum computers become available. Of course, on the other hand, problems whose solutions require a fast search of databases will benefit greatly from Grover's algorithm. Machine learning algorithms for pattern-matching and reinforcement learning algorithms belong to this class of problems. Quantum computers, therefore, are ideally suited for implementing high-quality artificial intelligence platforms. Indeed, the topic of quantum machine learning and quantum artificial intelligence is of great interest to both scientific and business communities. Biamonte not only gives a nice overview of quantum machine learning (Biamonte et al. 2017) but also points out that challenges remain in both quantum hardware and software with respect to implementation. Many of these challenges remain in place today. A more recent review of quantum machine learning comes from Peral-Garcia et al. (Peral-Garcia) where the authors present a review of the literature published on the topics between 2017 and 2023 with the goal of identifying, analyzing, and classifying the different types of algorithms used in quantum machine learning and their applications. Despite writing this review seven years after Biamonte's review, the authors opine that major improvements in quantum hardware are needed before the potential of quantum machine learning algorithms can be realized in a meaningful way.

7. Quantum games and optimal trading

In the years following the groundbreaking discoveries concerning quantum computers, scientists have unveiled yet another astonishing advantage: the potential for quantum computers to yield economic benefits that are mutually advantageous for both individuals and society as a whole. This revelation has catalyzed the emergence of a fascinating field known as quantum game theory (Khan et al., 2018), aimed at investigating the application of quantum computing technology to enhance the outcomes of strategic interactions among "players" in various domains, such as trading and finance (Khan and Bao, 2021). The implications of quantum game theory are profound as it offers solutions to fundamental dilemmas inherent in social and economic contexts. By leveraging the computational power and unique properties of quantum mechanics, quantum game theory holds the promise of revolutionizing decision-making processes and optimizing outcomes in scenarios characterized by strategic interactions and conflicting interests. Perhaps most notably, the application of quantum game theory on a global scale could usher in a transformative era for the global economy, marking a pivotal moment in history where humanity transitions towards a "circular economy". In such an economy, conflicts are economically prohibitive, and the age-old dilemmas surrounding the trade-off between individual benefits and societal welfare are effectively resolved. This paradigm shift has the potential to reshape socio-economic dynamics and propel humanity towards a more sustainable and harmonious future.

8. Quantum technology 1.0

Over the past 15 years, quantum communication and computation technologies have reached a significant milestone by transitioning beyond the realm of research and into commercialization. These technologies are rapidly advancing towards scalability and affordability, marking a transformative phase in the field. Among these advancements, quantum communication technology, particularly quantum key distributions, stands out as the most commercially mature and accessible. This emergence of what we term "quantum technology 1.0" is revolutionizing the information technology industry. Key players in this arena include companies such as D-Wave Systems, IonQ, Honeywell, IBM, and Rigetti, all of which have developed hardware capable of quasi-quantum computation. However, it's important to note that the level of quantum technology developed by each company varies and is continuously evolving. Here's a brief overview of the quantum technology developed by these companies:

- **D-Wave:** The Canadian company D-wave stands out when it comes to practical applications of quantum computing. Its quasi-quantum hardware has been studied extensively from solving industrial problems point of view, with problems coming from financial, scheduling (airline, traffic control), and pharmaceutical industries. The problems that are amenable to solution on this platform are discrete optimization problems. When formatted to run on D-wave's platform, these problems appear as quadratic unconstrained binary optimization (QUBO) problems. D-Wave's quantum annealing platform has been shown to solve a Markowitz financial portfolio optimization problem in 20–200 microseconds, compared to between 3 and 5 s on a conventional laptop using a genetic algorithm (Elsokkary et al. 2017). This is a speedup by factors of 10,000–100,000! Similar results can be found in Orús, Mugel, and Lizaso (2019); Cohen, Khan, and Alexander (2020); Stamatopoulos et al. (2020). Scheduling discrete optimization problems are ubiquitous in scheduling. Problems of optimal routing (airline, trash collection, delivery service), traffic flow, and control of traffic signals are all scheduling problems. Quantum annealing has been studied as a solution to solving difficult scheduling problems. Authors of Hussain et al. (2020) consider the problem of optimal traffic signal control on highways using quantum annealing, and in Neukart et al. (2017), authors look to identify optimal flow of traffic using the same quantum tech. Quantum annealing has also been used extensively to test optimal staffing of medical staff in hospitals (Ikeda, Nakamura, and Humble 2019), and during the ongoing COVID-19 pandemic, hospitals dealing exclusively with COVID-19 patients (Das et al. 2020). As the results appear promising, it is no doubt going to be the case that quantum annealing will play a fundamental role in planning and mitigation of future outbreaks and, indeed, in the field of epidemiology more generally. The Pharmaceutical industry is an expensive industry, with extensive testing required to find just the right mix of chemicals and molecules to find medication of the right efficacy. Modeling and simulation in this industry are of limited use as molecular dynamics get extremely involved and difficult to compute on conventional computers very quickly. In this manner, this industry should expect to benefit most from Feynman's idea of simulating a complicated quantum system with a simpler one. And indeed, benefits of quantum annealing as a solution to some of the complex molecular dynamics occurring in the pharmaceutical industry have been explored. In Fox, Branson, and Walker (2021), the authors show how the problem of codon optimization can be solved on quantum computers, with D-wave being the preferred one in terms of performance. D-wave has a dedicated program to develop the use of quantum annealing in pharmaceutical industry and life sciences, as evidenced in D-wave System (2021).

- **IonQ:** IonQ has gained prominence for its innovative trapped-ion quantum computing methodology, which relies on harnessing individual ions as qubits, the elemental building blocks of quantum information processing. In IonQ's paradigm, precision laser beams are employed to manipulate the quantum states of these ions, thereby facilitating the execution of complex quantum algorithms. Notably, IonQ has achieved substantial advancements in enhancing the fidelity of its qubits and extending coherence times, critical parameters that directly influence the performance of quantum computing systems. The company's notable achievements include demonstrating quantum advantage in select computational tasks, signifying its capability to outperform classical computing approaches in certain scenarios. IonQ is actively engaged in furthering the scalability of its quantum systems, aiming to expand their capacity and functionality to tackle a broader range of computational challenges. Through ongoing research and development efforts, IonQ is poised to continue pushing the boundaries of quantum computing, unlocking new possibilities for transformative applications in diverse fields.
- **Honeywell:** Honeywell adopts a trapped-ion methodology akin to that of IonQ, where individual ions serve as qubits. Employing sophisticated control and manipulation techniques, Honeywell's quantum systems excel in producing high-fidelity qubits and extending coherence times. The company has showcased its proficiency in managing sizable qubit arrays and has attained quantum volume metrics comparable to those of top-performing quantum systems available today. Honeywell's quantum technology is strategically oriented towards addressing computational challenges in optimization, materials science, and other domains where complex computational tasks abound. Through its innovative approach and focus on practical applications, Honeywell is actively contributing to the advancement of quantum computing technology.
- **IBM:** IBM has long been recognized as a trailblazer in the realm of quantum computing, distinguished for its utilization of the superconducting qubit methodology. At the core of IBM's quantum systems lie superconducting circuits, meticulously cooled to ultralow temperatures to facilitate the attainment of quantum coherence. Over the years, IBM has spearheaded the development of a spectrum of quantum processors, including notable iterations such as the IBM Quantum Experience, IBM Quantum System One, and IBM Quantum Hummingbird. With each successive iteration, IBM has diligently increased the number of qubits while concurrently enhancing performance metrics. An integral facet of IBM's quantum initiative is the provision of cloud-based accessibility to its quantum systems through the IBM Quantum Experience platform. This innovative platform serves as a gateway for researchers and developers across the globe, affording them the opportunity to delve into the intricacies of quantum computing. By democratizing access to quantum resources, IBM is fostering a collaborative ecosystem conducive to exploration, experimentation, and innovation in the quantum domain.
- **Rigetti:** Rigetti adopts a unique hybrid strategy in the realm of quantum computing, melding superconducting qubits with classical computing resources to harness the strengths of both paradigms. While Rigetti's quantum systems leverage superconducting circuits akin to IBM's methodology, they also integrate classical control systems to enhance scalability and adaptability. This hybrid approach enables Rigetti to optimize the performance of its quantum systems while maintaining flexibility in their operation. A distinguishing feature of Rigetti's quantum initiative is its Quantum Cloud Services platform, which provides users with convenient access to the company's quantum processors. Through this platform, researchers and developers can execute quantum algorithms and conduct experiments with ease, fostering collaboration and innovation within the quantum computing community. Rigetti is actively engaged in ongoing efforts to enhance qubit performance, extend coherence times, and refine error correction techniques. By focusing on these critical aspects, Rigetti aims to facilitate the scaling of quantum systems for practical applications across diverse domains. Through continuous research and development, Rigetti remains committed to advancing the frontiers of quantum computing and unlocking its transformative potential.

Overall, these companies are at the forefront of quantum computing research and development, each contributing unique approaches and technologies to advance the field.

While these systems provide some quantum computational advantages, they fall short of delivering the full potential promised by quantum algorithms like Shor's and Grover's. Nonetheless, even this incremental advantage proves beneficial in specific contexts, such as the green energy production industry. In the domain of quantum communication and quantum key distribution technology, companies like ID Quantique lead the way, with Toshiba and Samsung also offering solutions.

9. Quantum technology: toward the next-generation "quantum 2.0"

We classify all the previously mentioned devices as belonging to the "quantum 1.0" category. This classification is pivotal in distinguishing them from the envisaged "quantum 2.0", which entails devices actively involved in generating, manipulating, and detecting quantum states of matter through phenomena such as superposition and entanglement. Moreover, quantum 2.0 will see scaling up of quantum computing one step closer to consumer-level applications. The latest development in this regard is the initial scientific report by D-Wave claiming the solution of a problem on their quantum computer that a classical supercomputer would take millions of years to complete (King et al, 2024). An experimental quantum computer currently in development by Google has demonstrated the capability to solve problems at speeds orders of magnitude faster than even the most powerful supercomputers available today (Gibney, 2019). Similarly, Chinese scientists have reported achieving remarkable feats with their quantum computer, solving specific problems in a mere two hundred seconds compared to the estimated 2.5 billion years it would take for today's top-tier supercomputers (Ball, 2020). These advancements bring us significantly closer to the realization of using quantum computers to break through most of the public-key encryption schemes relied upon in today's cybersecurity infrastructure, a promise initially put forth by the groundbreaking work of Grover and Shor in the 1990s. Conversely, the inherent true randomness offered by quantum objects presents an opportunity to generate unhackable communication keys, ensuring the provable security of long-distance key exchanges against hacking attempts by both conventional and quantum computers. Notably, Chinese scientists are at the forefront of advancing quantum communication technology, as evidenced by their efforts in deploying communication backbones across China that facilitate high-quality quantum key distribution-based communication on a large scale (Chen et al., 2021). Furthermore, initiatives led by Chinese, European, and American entities aim to enable quantum key distribution-based communication between satellites through open space (Pultarova, 2021).

As we look towards the future, the next iterations of quantum technologies will undoubtedly be optimized for performance in alignment with the fundamental principles of quantum physics and engineering. As a result, the next generations of quantum technologies are poised to become as ubiquitous as today's mobile devices and personal computers. This widespread integration of quantum technology into everyday life will present both opportunities and challenges for researchers, entrepreneurs, and managers alike. Therefore, strategic management of these revolutionary resources is imperative to fully realize their socio-economic potential.

10. Killer-applications of quantum computing 2.0

As quantum computing hardware becomes more robust and noise-free, we can expect their applications to follow a trajectory similar to that of conventional computing technology possibly, at an even faster pace if lessons from the commercialization and application development of conventional computers are heeded. This means that existing application domains of computing can be upgraded to include quantum computing solutions. In particular, once cloud-based quantum computers become more scalable and noise-free, we can expect to see increased efficiency and new, higher-quality solutions to existing problems. Several industries have been actively studied as killer-application domains of quantum computing, prominent ones being supply chain and logistics and finance. In supply chain optimization, sea and airport operations, in particular, have been studied extensively for optimization. For example, in (Stollenwerk), Stollenwerk et al. studied how the quantum computing platform provided by D-Wave could be used at a busy airport like Frankfurt to minimize the transit time of 170,000 passengers shuttling between 278 gates. A similar study was done in 2023 by Chai et al. (Chai) that explored a related gate-assignment problem using IonQ's quantum computing platform. For sea ports, D-wave's quantum computing platform has been used to study the feasibility of improving operations at Los Angeles and Dubai ports by the companies SavantX and Dark Star Quantum Lab. While the results of these studies will not be deployable in an impactful way until quantum computing hardware becomes more robust, interest in such studies remains high as the lessons learned can help port industries be ready for the coming quantum computational revolution. In the field of finance, studies of applications of quantum computing continue to grow. As mentioned earlier, many studies have been conducted on using quantum computers to identify optimal investment portfolios. Likewise, the identification of arbitrage opportunities remains an area of interest. For example, in Rosenberg (2016), the authors used D-Waves quantum computer to look for arbitrage opportunities in FX markets. A comprehensive summary of the current state of affairs in quantum computing for finance can be found in Herman et al. (2023).

While studies like the ones mentioned here are crucial for preparing early adopters to take advantage of quantum computing when it becomes practically useful, also necessary are efforts in exploring killer applications of quantum computers that will make quantum computers indispensable to the individual consumer and not just the early adopters and industrial giants. An example of a such a killer application comes from the history of personal computing (PC) in the form of the very first spread sheet program, VisiCalc, developed to run on the Apple II. While spreadsheet programs were certainly in use on electronic computers for decades, VisiCalc was the first one custom made to run on a personal computer and give the individual consumer the ability to create value from technology. More recent examples of killer applications would be a combination of hardware and business model such as the internet and YouTube, and smart phones and social media platforms. Note that even a cursory study of these examples will show the important role that strategic management has played in the development of these killer applications.

Similar strategic management is necessary for the development and incubation of application domains for quantum 2.0. Inspired by how the internet disrupted the trading scene in 1997, we envision a *quantum trading* platform that, when incubated and managed appropriately, can disrupt internet-based trading. Based on the idea of quantum games and optimal trading discussed briefly in Section 7, quantum trading is an internet-based trading platform that allows connectivity with a quantum computer. In simple, two player scenarios, it is well known that the player who utilizes quantum features to make trades with a trader who uses only classical trading strategies can unilaterally steer the market in a direction that favors him. However, when both players make trades using quantum computational features, instead of seeing a cancelation of the quantum advantage, we see it manifest in a way that both players benefit. In particular, we see that the market tends to steer away from a mass-sell market that is disadvantageous to both players. A quantum trading platform with a small number of traders is entirely feasible to set up and test today as we transition from quantum 1.0 to quantum 2.0. Given the difficulty of developing and implementing self-policing global policies to mitigate pollution and climate change, a more optimal quantum trading platform around carbon credits, waste trading, and related blue and green financial instruments may just be the right tool to circumvent these difficulties.

Finally, we close with the mention of another potential killer application of quantum computing 2.0 born from quantum game theory: quantum generative adversarial networks quantum (GANs). GANs are machine learning architectures in which two deep learning networks engage in a zero-sum game (Hazra and Anjaria). One network, the generator, produces fake data and attempts to trick its opponent into thinking the data are real; the opponent, the classifier, attempts to classify the data as real or fake. The strategies of the players in GANs are determined by the parameter set of each network. After repeated plays of the game, an equilibrium is reached (guaranteed by Nash's theorem in probabilistic or "mixed" games) that describes the best responses each player makes to his opponent and therefore an upper limit of the ability of either player to achieve their goals. It may be that in a certain game setting, the classifier identifies fake data more often, and in a different setting, the generator deceives the classifier more often. In quantum GANs setting, where it is sometimes possible for the quantum player to have a quantum advantage (Llyod and Weedbrook), a quantum GANs generator might always be able to deceive the classifier, or the classifier might always be able to catch the fake data generated. Since large language models like ChatGPT are GANs, one imagines a "quantum ChatGPT" in which a quantum computational component provides a quantum advantage to the generator who can produce unlimited amount of fake data without being ever detected. While this application of quantum computing 2.0 would surely be more attractive to nefarious actors, it is still something that future business leaders would need to be at least aware of and take relevant mitigative actions.

References

Ball, P. 2020. Physicists in China Challenge Google's 'Quantum Advantage'. *Nature* 588: 380.

Bennett, C. H. 1973. Logical Reversibility of Computation. *IBM Journal of Research and Development* 17 (6): 525–532.

Bennett, C. H., and G. Brassard. 1984. Quantum Cryptography: Public Key Distribution and Coin Tossing. *Proceedings of IEEE International Conference on Computers, Systems and Signal Processing* 175: 8. New York.

Biamonte, J., P. Wittek, N. Pancotti, P. Rebentrost, N. Wiebe, and S. Lloyd. 2017. Quantum Machine Learning. *Nature* 549: 195–202.

Bova, F., A. Goldfarb, and R. Melko. 2021. Quantum Computing Is Coming. What Can It Do? *Harvard Business Review*. https://hbr.org/2021/07/quantum-computing-is-coming-what-can-it-do.

Chai, Y., E. Epifanovsky, K. Jansen, A. Kaushik, and S. Kühn. 2023. Simulating the Flight Gate Assignment Problem on a Trapped Ion Quantum Computer, preprint at https://arxiv.org/pdf/2309.09686.pdf.

Chen, Y. A., Q. Zhang, T. Y. Chen, W. Q. Cai, S. K. Liao, J. Zhang, K. Chen, et al. 2021. An Integrated Space-to-Ground Quantum Communication Network Over 4,600 Kilometers. *Nature* 589: 214–219.

Cohen, Jeffrey, Alex Khan, and Clark Alexander. 2020. Portfolio Optimization of 60 Stocks Using Classical and Quantum Algorithms. https://arxiv.org/pdf/2008.08669.pdf.

D-wave System. 2021. Quantum in Life Sciences: The Future Is Now. https://www.dwavesys.com/media/knedq0pb/ dwave_life-sci_overview_v2.pdf.

Das, K., S. Zaman, A. Sadhu, A. Banerjee, and F. S. Khan. 2020. Quantum Annealing for Solving a Nurse-Physician Scheduling Problem in Covid-19 Clinics. https://www.researchgate.net/publication/344047176_Quantum_annealing_for_solving_a_nurse-physician_scheduling_problem_in_Covid-19_clinics.

Deutsch, D. 1985. Quantum Theory, the Chruch-Turing Principle and the Universal Quantum Computer. *Proceedings of the Royal Society of London A* 400: 97–117.

Deutsch, D., and R. Jozsa. 1992. Rapid Solutions of Problems by Quantum Computation. *Proceedings of the Royal Society of London A* 439 (1907): 553–558.

Ekert, A. 1991. Quantum Cryptography Based on Bell's Theorem. *Physical Review Letters* 67 (6): 661–663.

Elsokkary, N., F. Khan, D. L. Torre, T. S Humble, and J. Gottlieb. 2017. Financial Portfolio Management Using D-Wave Quantum Optimizer: The Case of Abu Dhabi Securities Exchange. *IEEE High Performance Extreme Computing Conference, 2017 IEEE High Performance Extreme Computing Conference (HPEC '17): Twenty-First Annual HPEC Conference.*

Feynman, R. 1982. Simulating Physics with Computers. *International Journal of Theoretical Physics* 21: 467–488.

Fox, D. M., K. M. Branson, and R. C. Walker. 2021. mRNA Codon Optimization on Quantum Computers. https://www.biorxiv.org/content/10.1101/2021.02.19.431999v1.

Gibney, E. 2019. Hello Quantum World! Google Publishes Landmark Quantum Supremacy Claim. *Nature* 574: 461–462.

Grover, L. 1996. A Fast Quantum Mechanical Algorithm for Database Search. *Proceedings of the Twenty-Eigth Annual ACM Symposium on Theory of Computing. STOC '96*, 212–219. Philadelphia, Pennsylvania, USA: Association for Computing Machinery.

Hariri, Y. N. February 21, 2017. *Homo Deus: A Brief History of Tomorrow*. Harper. Illustrated edition.

Hazra, T., and K. Anjaria. 2022. Applications of Game Theory in Deep Learning: A Survey. *Multimedia Tools and Applications* 81: 8963–8994.

Heisenberg, W. March 21, 1927. "Über den Anschaulichen Inhalt der Quantentheoretischen Kinematik und Mechanik." *Zeitschrift für Physik* 43 (3–4): 172–198.

Herman, D., C. Googin, X. Liu, Y. Sun, A. Galda, I. Safro, M. Pistoia, and Y. Alexeev. 2023. Quantum Computing for Finance. *Nature Review Physiscs* 5: 450–465.

Hussain, H., M. B. Javaid, F. S. Khan, A. Dalal, and A. Khalique. 2020. Optimal Control of Traffic Signals Using Quantum Annealing. *Quantum Information Processing* 19: 312.

Ikeda, K., Y. Nakamura, and T. S. Humble. 2019. Application of Quantum Annealing to Nurse Scheduling Problem. *Scientific Reports* 9: 12837.

Ingarden, R. S. 1976. Quantum Information Theory. *Reports on Mathematical Physics* 10 (1): 43–72.

Khan, F.S., Abura'ed, N. How Quantum got Gamed. Digitale Welt 3, 42–45 (2019). https://doi.org/10.1007/s42354-019-0168-9

Khan, F. S., and N. Bao. 2021. Quantum Prisoner's Dilemma and High Frequency Trading on the Quantum Cloud. https:// arxiv.org/pdf/2104.04663.pdf. Front. Artif. Intell., 03 November 2021 Sec. Artificial Intelligence in Finance Volume 4 - 2021 | https://doi.org/10.3389/frai.2021.769392

Khan, F. S., N. Solmeyer, R. Balu, and T. S. Humble. 2018. Quantum Games: A Review of the History, Current State, and Interpretation. *Quantum Informaiton Processing* 17: 1–42.

King et al, 2024. Computational Supremacy in Quantum Simulation. Pre-print available at https://arxiv.org/pdf/2403.00910.pdf.

Llyod, S., and C. Weedbrook. 2018. Quantum Generative Adversarial Learning. Physical Review Letters 121 (4): 040502.

Neukart, F., G. Compostella, C. Seidel, D. V. Dollen, S. Yarkoni, and B. Parney. 2017. Traffic Flow Optimization Using a Quantum Annealer. *Frontiers in ICT* 4: 29.

Orús, R., S. Mugel, and E. Lizaso. 2019. Quantum Computing for Finance: Overview and Prospects. *Reviews in Physics* 4: 10028.

Peral-Garcia, D., J. Cruz-Benito, and F. Garcia-Penalvo. 2024. Systematic Literature Review: Quantum Machine Learning and Its Applications, *Computer Science Review* 51: 100619.

Pultarova, T. 2021. UK Company to Start Sending Secret Quantum Keys with Satellites in 2023. https://www.space.com/arqit-quantum-key-distribution-space. Review of the History, Current State, and Interpretation. *Quantum Information Processing* 17: 309.

Rosenberg, G. 2016. Finding Optimal Arbitrage Opportunities Using a Quantum Annealer. White Paper http://1qbit.com/files/white-papers/1QBit-White-Paper-%E2%80%93-Finding-Optimal-Arbitrage-Opportunities-Using-a-Quantum-Annealer.pdf.

Shor, P. 1994. Algorithms for Quantum Computation: Discrete Logarithms and Factoring. *Proceedings 35th Annual Symposium on Foundations of Computer Science*. 124–134. IEEE Computer Society Press.

Stamatopoulos, N., D. J. Egger, Y. Sun, C. Zoufal, R. Iten, and N. Shen. 2020. Stefan Woerner Option Pricing using Quantum Computers. https://arxiv.org/pdf/1905.02666.pdf.

Stollenwerk, T., Lobe, E., Jung, M. (2019). Flight Gate Assignment with a Quantum Annealer. In: Feld, S., Linnhoff-Popien, C. (eds) Quantum Technology and Optimization Problems. QTOP 2019. Lecture Notes in Computer Science(), vol 11413. Springer, Cham. https://doi.org/10.1007/978-3-030-14082-3_9

Wiesner, S. 1983. Conjugate Coding. *ACM SIGACT News* 15: 77–78.

Williams, B. P., K. A. Britt, and T. S. Humble. 4 January 2016. Tamper-Indicating Quantum Seals. *Physical Review Applied* 5: 014001.

D-Wave Systems | The Practical Quantum Computing Company (dwavesys.com)
IonQ | Trapped Ion Quantum Computing
Quantum | Honeywell
IBM Quantum Computing
Quantum Computing | Rigetti Computing
ID Quantique - The home of Quantum-Safe Crypto

Quantum-sapiens: the quantum bases for human expertise, knowledge, and problem-solving

Steve J. Bickley, Ho Fai Chan, Sascha L. Schmidt and Benno Torgler

ABSTRACT
Despite the great promises and potential of quantum computing, the full range of possibilities and practical applications is not yet clear. In this contribution, we highlight the potential for quantum theories and computation to reignite the art and science of expert systems and knowledge engineering. With their grounding in uncertainty and unpredictability, quantum concepts are able to expand theoretical and practical boundaries of research and exploration. We demonstrate the advantages of using quantum logic and computation when applying expert knowledge such as the ability to ask imprecise (inherently probabalistic) queries and do so efficiently through large and complicated computational spaces by leveraging quantum concepts such as superposition, entanglement, parallelism, and interference to sustain and manipulate networks of quantum qubits. This, we argue, can provide non-insignificant computational speedups and enable more complex data representations and analysis. We then point the keen reader towards three practical applications and provide some evidence for their quantum advantages – Scientific Discovery, Creativity and Breakthrough Thinking, Complex Systems, and Future of Sports – that we regard as largely unexplored in popular accounts of quantum theory; as such, we suggest these are low hanging fruit for the more-immediately feasible applications of quantum technologies.

1. Introduction

Simply defined by Siler (2005), 'expert systems are computer programs, designed to make available some of the skills of an expert to non-experts' (xii). In this sense, expert systems involve the transferral of expert human knowledge, experience, intuition, and reasoning to computers which may then be used to automate, train, and/or support complex human decision-making processes. Expert systems can result in considerable cost reductions, increased productivity, quality, and consistency, and reduction of uncertainty in decision-making systems. They also help to capture scarce industrial/organisational knowledge (Turban 1988).

Despite a wealth of complex computational models and increasing numbers of expert decision-support systems, human experts are still highly sought after and used extensively to support serious, consequential decision making efforts as well as helping solve smaller, more everyday types of problems (Stehr 2011). As Sriboonchitta et al. (2019) suggest, the best results are achieved when we ask imprecise rather than precise queries – those which experts typically ask – and we can leverage quantum theories to do so.

This paper explores the relationship between concepts in quantum theories to those of expert systems, creativity, problem solving, and scientific discovery. In doing so, we seek to uncover potential avenues for future theoretical and applied research outside of those usually mentioned in popular reports of quantum technologies. In the first section, we introduce quantum theory, mechanics, information theory, logic, and computation. Next, we question the current relevance of human expertise, reasoning, and decision making in the era of AI and quantum. In the last section, we provide three domains that – in our estimation – present fruitful opportunities for the application of quantum concepts and point the keen reader towards further reading along this path. In particular, an extended pre-print version of this paper (Bickley et al. 2021) highlights in detail three interesting areas of investigation – scientific discovery and breakthrough thinking, complex systems, and future of sports – which sit outside the typical areas considered for quantum applications.[1]

2. Quantum theories

In the classical sciences, systems are assumed to have mostly well-defined properties.[2] If all relevant pre-conditions are known, specific outcomes will occur time and time again, subject of course to any randomness driven by some known or unknown stochastic processes. In other words, systems and their behaviour are deterministic or probabilistic in nature. Quantum theory accepts the unpredictability of precise outcomes and recognises randomness as a fundamental concept in many complex systems (Peres 2002), in a similar sense to classical probabilistic theories focused on modelling situations and decision making under uncertainty. Quantum theories are generally seen to better explain 'cases of decisions under strong uncertainty, when utility theory fail (p.749)' (Yukalov, Yukalova, and Sornette 2018), whilst retaining predictive capacity as opposed to the more descriptive analyses of classical probability theories. Ultimately however, placing greater focus on the evidence of irregularity and randomness has contributed to a deeper understanding in many fields across the hard and soft sciences alike (Mirowski 1990).

While randomness is not unique to quantum theory, classical stochastic processes fall short of accounting for certain complex natural and human phenomenon such as the conjunction fallacy (i.e. an agent assigns a probability of two events occurring together that is greater than the probability of one event occurring alone) demonstrated famously by Tversky and Kahneman (1983). Tversky and Kahneman explained this via representative heuristics on their account that classical probability theory is not appropriate for understanding such judgements. Without resorting to heuristics, quantum theories recognise the contextuality dependence of the probability assessment and provide mathematical foundations which unlock unique benefits for the representation and evolution of context (i.e. the context in which measurement of a quantum observable takes place) (Ashtiani and Azgomi 2015).

The mathematical formalism of quantum theory can be used to estimate the probabilities of certain events (e.g. a stock market crash, the emission of solar flare, or the position of an atom in space) (Englert 2013). Rather than precise predictions, quantum theories provide insights into more imprecise queries, similar to those made by experts (Sriboonchitta et al. 2019). Born's rule (1926) provides the link between mathematical formalisms and observed (measured) phenomena (events). The defining features of said events include localisation in time and space, irreversibility, and random realisation (Englert 2013). Before we move any further, we provide our definitions for these quantum features and other quantum concepts in Table 1.

Table 1. Definitions of Quantum Concepts.

Concept	Definition
Space-Time Localisation	An event having an approximate location in physical space and historical time (Haag 2013).
Irreversibility	When an event is irreversible 'it leaves a document behind, a definite trace' (Englert 2013, p. 2).
Random Realisation	The unpredictability of an event due to the inherent randomness in which one of many possible events (each with a certain probability of occurrence) is eventually realised and not owing to missing or incomplete information (Englert 2013).
Linearity	A function which satisfies the properties of additivity and homogeneity.
Entanglement	The values of certain properties of one system are correlated with the values that those properties will take in the other one of which it is entangled with. This can persist even with spatial and temporal separation.
Superposition	A mixed and indeterminant combination of finite states (e.g. 0 and 1) existing prior to some quantum measurements.
Non-locality	Used to describe correlated or entangled events which occur despite space-time separation.
Interference	Constructive or destructive interference of certain observables on others including itself.
Decoherence	The collapsing of a linear superposition (i.e. coherent) or potentiality states into any one of its possible states of actuality (e.g. when a coherent system interacts with or is disturbed by its environment such as during measurement).
Oracle	A 'black box' operation used as input to another algorithm.
Indeterminacy	The assertion that the state of a quantum system does not determine a unique collection of values for all its measurable properties at any one time.

2.1. Quantum mechanics

Classical mechanics is an approximate theory of nature (Banks 2019). The major difference between classical and quantum mechanics is a fundamental dissimilarity between the observed and unobserved states of an entity (e.g. an atom). In quantum mechanics, prior to observation (measurement), an entity is not constrained to existing in any precise position; but rather, exists in an indeterminate region of space. This may be within an area of greatest likelihood or expected likelihood, however, there is yet an underlying uncertainty and unpredictability in its exact positioning (Baaquie 2013). Heisenberg (1962) coined the terms potentiality and actuality to describe the indeterminate (unobserved) and definite (observed) condition of a quantum entity, respectively. Each measurement transitions a quantum entity from a potentiality state to one of its many possible and definite conditions.

One could quite reasonably question how quantum indeterminacy is different at all from classical randomness. Classical probability fails to explain quantum indeterminacy because a specific quantum state does not exist independent of any measurement. Without measurement, a quantum state exists in some superposition of all possible states and a probability is assigned only to the likelihood of possible outcomes of the measurement process itself (Baaquie 2013) rather than to some physically real, random variable as in classical probability.

Despite its complexity and often conceptually unfamiliar solutions, quantum mechanics has been widely successful and reliable in explaining many real-world phenomena (Englert 2013). For example, the transistor was developed and operates on quantum principles and became an enabling technology for a host of others including practically all modern and dated digital electronics and communication technologies (Kolawole 2021). Further, concepts and methods from quantum mechanics and probability have used to explain a growing list of complex human phenomenon such as human cognition and decision making (Ashtiani and Azgomi 2015; Busemeyer and Bruza 2012; Khrennikov 2015; Pothos and Busemeyer 2013), common sense (Noori and Spanagel 2013), consciousness (Atmanspacher 2004), and causal reasoning (Trueblood and Busemeyer 2012).

2.2. Quantum information

The physical nature of information implies that information abides by the laws of nature; in particular, those of quantum mechanics (Landauer 1996, 1999). This view makes possible new and powerful tools of transmission and information processing by leveraging the principles of quantum mechanics such as linearity, entanglement, superposition, non-locality, interference, and indeterminacy (Galindo and Martin-Delgado 2001). Classical information theory is concerned with information in binary (i.e. a state of zero or one), ternary (i.e. a state of zero, one or two, or when balanced negative one, zero or one), quaternary (i.e. a state of zero, one, two or three), and in general n-ary (i.e. a state of zero, one, two, three, ... $n-1$) forms wherein bits (classical bits or c-bits) carry information from source to destination over some noisy or noiseless channel (Shannon 1948). In quantum information theory, quantum bits (qubits) exist – prior to measurement – as a superposition of all possible states of the two classical states of zero and one (Schumacher 1995). Somewhat counterintuitively, the superposition of one qubit carries only as much information as a classical bit. However, with two or more qubits we start seeing more quantum gains, a concept known as quantum parallelism which, as discussed later in Section 2.4, is at the foundation of the unprecedented power of quantum computers (Galindo and Martin-Delgado 2001).

2.3. Quantum logic

In the same way that classical computers can perform sequences of one- and two-bit operations (e.g. AND, NOT, and OR logic gates), quantum computers can perform sequences of one- and two-qubit quantum operations (e.g. XOR logic gate) (Bennett and Shor 1998). Simply described, 'a quantum logic gate is an input-output device whose inputs and outputs are discrete quantum variables' (346). Any set of one- and two-qubit quantum logic gates can be used to construct a universal quantum computer and hence, perform any desired transformation on quantum variables (Lloyd 1995). In other words, generalisable quantum gates can be 'wired together' to produce quantum logic circuits that can simulate any quantum phenomena and perform any computations (Deutsch 1989) without the exponential slowdown which would, of course, be experienced by a classical computer (Feynman 1982).

2.4. Quantum computing

As early as the mid-1980s, Feynman (1982) suggested that certain quantum effects cannot be simulated efficiently on a classical computer. Indeed, there are also some important scientific problems for which quantum computers are suspected to be the only known means by which we can solve them practically (i.e. classical solutions may exist but are subject to either excessive time or memory constraints) (Resch and Karpuzcu 2019). Quantum computers can offer some reprieve for such problems and computations. Quantum superposition, as Moret-Bonillo (2018) explain, '(...) allows several operations to be performed simultaneously, depending on the number of qubits' (165) hence, enabling large input vectors to be subjected, simultaneously, to (reversible) quantum logic gates and operations. 'Computing classically in parallel means 'at the same time', while the quantum parallelism means 'using the same space', which also means there is no need in time synchronization (1)' (Ablayev and Vasiliev 2011). Hence, for classical systems, the amount of parallelism increases in direct proportion to system size whereas for quantum systems, it increases exponentially with size (Steane and Rieffel 2000). This is a key differentiator between classical and quantum computers as Moret-Bonillo (2018) explains in other words:

> The number of qubits indicates the number of bits there can be in superposition. With conventional bits, if we had a three-bit register there would be eight possible values, and the record could only take one of those values. On the other hand, if we have a vector of three qubits, the particle can take eight different values at the same time thanks to the quantum superposition. Thus, a vector of three qubits would allow a total of eight parallel operations. As expected, the number of operations is exponential with respect to the number of qubits (165–166)

As discussed, the power of quantum algorithms mostly derives from harnessing the benefits of quantum parallelism (Deutsch and Jozsa 1992) which is itself enabled by quantum concepts of superposition, entanglement (Rieffel and Polak 2000), and interference. Together, as Steane and Rieffel (2000) suggest, 'this massive parallelism, exponential in the number of particles used in the computation, (...) [enables quantum computers to] make any calculation on all values in roughly the same time an ordinary computer would take to make a calculation on a single value' (40). The potential for this sort of computation in the 'Big Data' age is immense and intuitively obvious. The properties of quantum entanglement have also enabled promising technological applications such as quantum teleportation (Bennett et al. 1993), quantum encryption (Barz et al. 2012), quantum internet (Kimble 2008), and quantum dense coding (Rieffel and Polak 2000). In general, as Orus, Mugel, and Lizaso (2019, 4) describes, a quantum algorithm is a sequence of five steps:

> ... 1. Encode the input data into the state of a set of qubits.
>
> 2. Bring the qubits into superposition over many states (i.e. use quantum superposition).
>
> 2. Apply an algorithm (or oracle) simultaneously to all the states (i.e. use quantum entanglement amongst the qubits); at the end of this step, one of these states holds the correct answer.
>
> 3. Amplify the probability of measuring the correct state (i.e. use quantum interference).
>
> 4. Measure one or more qubits.

It has been shown that for some computations (using the processes similar to that described above), quantum computers are capable of exponential speed-ups over classic computers with only a linear – as opposed to exponential in the case of classical computers – increase in physical space required to house such computational hardware (Deutsch and Jozsa 1992). Further, for some problems, Grover's algorithm can provide quadratic speedups not just over the naïve (brute force) classical algorithm but also over the more computationally efficient (less exhaustive) classical algorithms also. (Ambainis 2004). In other words, quantum computers hold promise even for the more general search problems and methods. This is a great outcome as 'even a small polynomial speed-up on average for these computationally difficult problems is of significant practical interest (323)'(Rieffel and Polak 2000) and hence, quantum computers and algorithms should at least be considered when performing certain complex computations for which quantum computers exhibit non-insignificant time or memory advantages. This can extend, for example, to hybrid quantum-classical systems. We direct the interested reader to Endo et al. (2020) for a well-covered review of hybrid quantum-classical computers, and Li et al. (2017) and Otterbach et al. (2017) for examples of practical applications – quantum optimal control and unsupervised machine learning, respectively.

One area of problem solving for which quantum computers can offer a unique advantage over classical computers is in search problems (Rieffel and Polak 2000). In particular, Grover's (1996) algorithm can utilise superposition to ask questions often posed by experts, such as: 'is one of the earlier records containing the desired information' (Sriboonchitta et al. 2019) and use amplitude amplification to derive the most probable and/or (with well-designed algorithms) desirable outcomes (Ambainis 2004). By doing so we can explore problem spaces which are too large or complex to be efficiently searched using a classical computer under reasonable time and memory constraints.

Other well-known quantum algorithms include Shor's (1994) algorithm for efficient prime factorisation (a fundamental complexity to many modern day cryptography technologies), quantum counting algorithm (Brassard, Hoyer, and Tapp 1998) for efficient counting of solutions for a given search problem, and the Harrow-Llyod algorithm (Harrow, Hassidim, and Lloyd 2009) for solving linear equations. Further, the 'true' randomness of quantum physics (Antonio and Lluis 2016) could be used to implement truly random number generators in Monte Carlo methods of simulation (Antonio and Lluis 2016) and provide quantum speedups as such (Montanaro 2015). These random number generators are also at the heart of key quantum technologies including Quantum Key Distribution and Cryptography (Krithika 2017). Artificial Intelligence (AI) algorithms – for example, see Dunjko and Briegel (2018), Zhaokai, Xiaomei, and Nanyang (2014), and Aerts and Czachor (2004) –

also benefit from the unique properties of quantum computing either by computational speedups, simplified search, or both.

Quantum potentiality states by their nature are unpredictable and highly susceptible to decoherence from both measurements and interactions (whether intended or unintended) with the environment. Further, these potentiality states must be maintained for some reasonable length of time to undertake the computation. Likewise, the ability to preserve and manipulate entangled states is at the source of both the power of quantum computers (and the computations they enable), and the difficulty experienced thus far in building them (Bennett and Shor 1998). Thus to enable the practical use of quantum computing (including their use in search problems), further development and technological advances (and research funding) are required to build robust quantum computers with a sufficiently high numbers of qubits (Resch and Karpuzcu 2019).

Novel and non-traditional programming techniques, such as quantum error correction coding, are expected overcome many outstanding issues with the fragility of maintaining potentiality states and the decoherence (collapsing) of these states following measurements (Rieffel and Polak 2000). Unfortunately, most methods of quantum error correction coding require access to computers with many qubits that are capable of maintaining useful decoherence times (Endo et al. 2020). As Rieffel and Polak (2000) explain, these developments are also crucial to our ability to empirically assess the efficacy of using quantum algorithms over their classical counterparts:

> (...) there is an exponential slowdown when simulating a quantum computer on a classical one, empirical testing of quantum algorithms is currently infeasible except in small cases. (...) Until sufficiently large quantum computers are built, or better techniques for analyzing such algorithms are found, the efficiency cannot be determined for sure (p.323).

As we gain access to more powerful, robust quantum machines and likewise, more sophisticated algorithms, the many promises of quantum computing will begin to be realised *and* verifiably so.

3. Is human expertise still alive or relevant?

Contrary to the AI pioneers such as Herb Simon or Allen Newell, a second generation of AI scholars around Edward Feigenbaum and Ray Reddy were less interested in modelling precisely how human intelligence works, and more interested in knowledge representation and devising ways to help humans achieve things (McCorduck 2019). Thanks to their work, knowledge representation became an important field of research, and expert systems, a promising application of technology.

The Dendral project – headed by Feigenbaum in collaboration with Lederberg – was one of the most prominent, successful, and long-standing AI research projects with more than one decade of continuously productive output (Lindsay et al. 1993). Owing to its success, in the following sections we trace through the history of Dendral-inspired knowledge engineering and expert systems theoretical and methodological developments. In Section 3.1 we introduce HEURISTIC DENDRAL – the first *inference machine* developed by the Dendral Project – and the 'knowledge is power' thesis of Dendral's followers. In Section 3.2 we introduce a later, but no less innovative Dendral produce – MYCIN, the first *inference engine* – and discuss its flexible approach to reasoning and its ability to handle uncertainty. In Section 3.3 we highlight some of the major progresses and setbacks / downfalls of expert systems. Finally, in Section 3.4 we propose some new hope for the furthering of knowledge engineering and expert systems in knowledge representation and how quantum computing can help.

3.1. HEURISTIC DENDRAL and the inference machine

In his book *The Emotion Machine*, Minsky (2006) regards conceptualisation as that which distinguishes us from other animals. Edward Feigenbaum was interested in creating models of thinking processes, and as a specific task environment, he selected the thinking process of scientists, 'especially the processes of empirical induction by which hypotheses and theories were inferred from data' (Shortliffe and Rindfleisch 2000). According to Feigenbaum, '[i]nduction is what we're doing almost every moment, almost all the time' (McCorduck 2019, 175). He identified the problem he was looking for after hearing Nobelists' Joshua Lederberg's talk about the problem of discerning the structure of a chemical compound from knowledge of its atomic constituents and from its mass spectrogram, using knowledge employed by skilled chemists when interpreting mass-spectral data (Nilsson 2009). Feigenbaum called it one of the most memorable scientific talks he ever attended (Feigenbaum 1968). Together with Lederberg he gathered a robust team, including the philosopher Bruce Buchanan and later Carl Djerassi – best known for contributing to the development of the oral contraceptive pills – for investigations into how scientists interpret the output of mass spectrometers (McCorduck 2019). The skilled chemists' knowledge was represented as rules, and the group named their first programme using this kind of knowledge the HEURISTIC DENDRAL; heuristics because it used knowledge from the chemists to control the search down process through the tree (Nilsson 2009). Heuristics included the specific chemical knowledge in the form of experience and intuition (McCorduck 2019). For example:

Rule 74 (Nilsson 2009, 199):

IF The spectrum for the molecule has two peaks

At masses X1 and X2 such that:

X1 + X2 = M + 28

and

X1 – 28 is a high peak

and

At least one of X1 or X2 is high

THEN The molecule contains a ketone group

Programmes developed by the Dendral project in the 1970s are still used by chemists today (Nilsson 2009). Feigenbaum was interested in moving away from a focus on reasoning – such as Allen Newell and Herb Simon's General Problem Solver – to knowledge as an important source of machine and human intelligence[3]:

> Knowledge can be refined, edited, and generalized to solve new problems, while the code to interpret and use the knowledge – the reasoning, the inference engine – remains the same. This is one reason why, in the last few years, AI has become noticeably smarter. The amount of knowledge on the Internet available to Watson, Google Brain, or language-understanding programs (or scores of start-ups) has grown dramatically (McCorduck 2019, 177–178).

He presented the importance of specific knowledge about the problem domain (i.e. the knowledge-is-power hypothesis) by calling it the knowledge principle (Nilsson 2009):

> We must hypothesize from our experience to date that the problem solving power exhibited in an intelligent agent's performance is primarily a consequence of the specialist's knowledge employed by the agent, and only very secondarily related to the generality and power of the inference method employed. Our agents must be knowledge-rich, even if they are methods-poor (200).

3.2. MYCIN and the inference engine

The team discovered that the more you train the system, the better it got, and Buchanan was eager for Dendral to go further and make its own discoveries (McCorduck 2019). The idea was to collaborate with additional scholars to build a computer programme that consults with physicians about bacterial infections and therapy, leading to a programme called MYCIN, a word coined by Edward

Shortliffe (Nilsson 2009). Shortliffe and Buchanan identified that physicians also appear to use IF–THEN reasoning: 'IF the symptoms are such-and-such, THEN the cause is likely to be so-and-so' (Nilsson 2009, 230). An important part in the construction of expert systems is therefore interviewing experts (McCorduck 2019; Nilsson 2009) and deriving a consulting system that interacts with the users (e.g. physicians) who supply information (e.g. specific patient) (Nilsson 2009). Shortliffe also decided to introduce certainty factors as the IF–THEN rules were hedged with uncertainty (Nilsson 2009). Here is an example (Nilsson 2009, 231):

RULE036

PREMISE: ($AND (SAME CNTXT GRAM GRAMEG)

(SAME CNTXTM MORPH ROD)

(SAME CNTXT AIR ANEAROBIC))

ACTION: (CONCLUDE CNTXT IDENTITY BACTEROIDES TALLY 0.6)

IF: 1) The gram stain of the organism is gramneg, and

2) The morphology of the organism is rod, and

3) The aerobicity of the organism is anaerobic

THEN: There is suggestive evidence (0.6) that the identity of the organism is bacteroides

Thus, the value 0.6 considers uncertainty, and thereby provides a degree of belief about the conclusions, incorporating some degree of 'expert intuition' rather than precise and certain knowledge. MYCIN also had the ability to explain its line of reasoning (McCorduck 2019). For example: 'Why did you ask whether the morphology of the organism is rod [?] … because I am trying to determine whether the identity of the organism is bacteroids' (Nilsson 2009, 231). A core innovation of MYCIN was the way in which the reasoning process (using a rule 'inference engine') remained separate from the medical knowledge (the rules themselves, 'knowledge base'). This provided flexibility in constructing new expert systems via changing the knowledge base but not the inference engine (Nilsson 2009). Future programmes encoded rules as partitioned semantic networks; rules could be linked together (inference networks); and inferences from rule premises to rule conclusions in the network were linked to Bayes' rule probabilities by giving numbers following principles of probability theory (Nilsson 2009).

3.3. The highs and lows of expert systems

Expert systems have been a very powerful tool for solving real-world problems (McCorduck 2019); thus, not surprisingly, many new companies have developed such systems (Nilsson 2009). The success of expert systems was due to their ability to solve narrowly- and well-defined problems (McCorduck 2019), yet they were deployed across many business functions such as manufacturing, sales, engineering, diagnostics/maintenance, and corporate knowledge management (Feigenbaum, McCorduck, and Nii 1989). The downfall of expert systems and knowledge engineering lies in the difficulty (cost, time and effort) of developing such systems (Turban 1988), their narrow scope of expertise and hence, fragility to novel problems (as opposed to more general knowledge systems which could contain hundreds of thousands or millions of linked concepts, facts, heuristics, relationships and symbolic models), their limited 'naturalness' of human-machine interactions, the demonstration (or lack thereof) of 'common sense' reasoning, and their limited capacity to learn by analogy (Feigenbaum, McCorduck, and Nii 1989). The knowledge transfer, acquisition, or elicitation process itself has also presented issues for designers of expert systems as people are not always able to give complete or accurate reports of their mental processes (Nisbett and Wilson 1977), nor are these reports purely objective descriptions of these processes (White 1988). Thus, the endeavour of expert systems engineering is often seen more as art than science (Feigenbaum 1977).

3.4. Knowledge representation and quantum computers – a new hope

Minsky's (2006) discussion on multiple ways of representing knowledge is instructive (see p. 280–297). An incident can be naturally represented with a story or script. Items named in a story or script can refer to more complex structures in a collection of symbols (i.e. semantic network), and such connecting links are very versatile as each connection-link can refer to another type of representation. Pairs of semantic networks can also represent the effects of actions and can co-evolve over time (in a similar sense to storied spaces) wherein agents respond, adapt, and contribute to their meaning over time and in different contexts (Baskin 2008). Minsky uses the term Trans-Frame (283) to name a pair of representations of the conditions before and after an action was conducted. Linking Trans-Frames allows the formation of a story or narrative and can also include information on common sense matters that provide answers to the following questions (284): Who performed the action, and why? Where and when did the action begin and end? Was it intentional or not? What purpose did it intend to serve? What kinds of methods or instruments were used? What obstacles were overcome? What were its other side effects? Which resources did it engage? What was expected to happen next? Default assumptions allow rapid access to common sense knowledge via activation of a frame. Minsky also derived the idea of a structure that can produce records of what you are doing at a certain moment – a so called K-line – which is a snapshot of a mental state that when later activated will put you into a similar state (see also Minsky 1988):

> You want to repair a bicycle. Before you start, smear your hands with red paint. Then every tool you need to use will end up with red marks on it. When you're done, just remember that red means 'good for fixing bicycles.' Next time you fix a bicycle, you can save time by taking out all the red-marked tools in advance. If you use different colors for different jobs, some tools will end up marked with several colors. That is, each agent can become attached to many different K-lines. Later, when there's a job to do, just activate the proper K-line for that kind of job, and all the tools used in the past for similar jobs will automatically become available' (suggestion by Kenneth Haase who was a student of Minsky, see Minsky 1988, p. 82).

Ultimately, it is a combination of these representations that could provide the most complete and flexible forms of knowledge representation and problem solving (Minsky 2006). In learning, humans often perform metaphorical extensions of new knowledge structures based on pre-existing knowledge (Carroll and Thomas 1982) by way of learning by analogy. Similarly, experts often draw upon case studies and examples in their approach to solving complex problems (Hinsley, Hayes, and Simon 1977) and later, in explaining their methods and reasoning. With this sort of flexibility and tolerance for the elaboration of existing concepts comes the ability to take into account new information, understand novel phenomena, and adapt knowledge (and hence, responses) in light of changing circumstances (McCarthy 1998).

A quantum computing approach could further bolster the flexibility of such an approach to knowledge representation and adaptation in situations where this is considerable uncertainty (Yukalov, Yukalova, and Sornette 2018), when order and context influence perception and decision making in non-insignificant ways, or when 'distinct' knowledge silos appear to exhibit some extreme dependencies (Pothos and Busemeyer 2013). In addition, a quantum computer's ability to search problem spaces of high dimensionality more efficiently than classical computers will enable the development of more general and far-reaching knowledge structures without having to compromise on the depth of specialist knowledge areas.

4. Examples of practical applications

Quantum computing allows us to rethink what we can learn from expert systems. It is no coincidence that quantum computing is regarded as a promising tool for making better products at lower costs in less time; for example, in the chemical industry, it allows modelling of molecules (e.g. molecules with heavy atoms), proteins, polymers, and – in particular – solids at a much higher level of precision and intensity, reducing time consuming feedback approaches such as trial-and-error experiments (Budde and Volz 2019). Quantum machine learning techniques have also improved classical machine learning algorithms by reducing the time required to train a machine, while providing a richer framework for deep learning (Wilson 2020). As Hickey (2016) points out, '[a]s computer hardware technology continues to improve (e.g. supercomputing, quantum computing) the trade-off between efficiency and thoroughness will move far toward thoroughness' (94).

An extended pre-print version of this paper (Bickley et al. 2021) highlights in detail three interesting areas for the more near-term application of quantum technologies in expert systems: scientific discovery and breakthrough thinking; the study of complex systems; and the future practice of professional (*and* amateur) sports. Quantum computing may help to provide multiple perspectives, particularly in those cases where the seeking and searching is less defined, or the problems are not well structured, and their problem-space is wide and complicated. Expert knowledge can guide the way information is collected whilst quantum computing can enable the simultaneous testing of novel combinations and recombinations of concepts, knowledge, and information, and likewise, the simulation or 'playing out' of many counterfactual worlds, situations, and outcomes (Torgler 2020). In particular, for problems and situations requiring an enormous amount of computational power which would be infeasibly time- and/or resource-intensive taking a classical approach (Resch and Karpuzcu 2019). Hence, a quantum approach can also help solve problems of information overload (Logesh et al. 2018).

5. Conclusions

In this contribution, we have highlighted the potential for quantum theories to reignite the art and science of expert systems and knowledge engineering. With their fundamental grounding in uncertainty, quantum concepts are able to expand theoretical and practical boundaries of research and exploration. We have demonstrated similarities between quantum concepts and expert knowledge, identified quantum advantages as well as limitations, and have shortly outlined three practical domains we regard as largely unexplored in popular accounts of quantum theory and contain highly fruitful applications of quantum technologies.

Notes

1. That part was also originally peer-reviewed by *Technology Analysis & Strategic Management* but we had to delete it in the final journal version to meet the journal's word limit.
2. Not all classical sciences are deterministic, many exhibit properties that are more probabilistic in nature and hence, also contain some element of uncertainty and unpredictability, despite their classical foundations.
3. McCorduck remembers Ed Feigenbaum's visit to Carnegie Mellon in the 1970s, and his teasing Al and Herb with the line 'Guys, you need to stop fooling around with toy problems' (McCorduck 2019, 181).

Acknowledgements

This paper and the conceptual thinking behind it would not have been possible without the exceptional support of all three of my PhD thesis supervisors; Professor Benno Torgler, Dr Stephen Whyte, and Dr Ho Fai (Ben) Chan. Their enthusiasm, knowledge and consistently interdisciplinary approach to the study of human behaviour and economic phenomenon have been an ongoing source of inspiration and variety that have led down paths of research and exploration I would've never foreseen at the beginning of my PhD thesis. I am also grateful for the insightful comments offered by the anonymous peer reviewers at Technology Analysis & Strategic Management. Their generous review, constructive feedback, and expertise have improved this paper in innumerable ways and saved me from many errors and inconsistencies. Finally, it is with true pleasure that I acknowledge the contributions of my amazing partner, Alana Morrissy, who has given up many hours over the past few months to read and comment on the many revisions this paper has seen.

Disclosure statement

No potential conflict of interest was reported by the author(s).

ORCID

Steve J. Bickley http://orcid.org/0000-0002-9579-4231
Ho Fai Chan http://orcid.org/0000-0002-7281-5212
Sascha L. Schmidt http://orcid.org/0000-0002-8794-3604
Benno Torgler http://orcid.org/0000-0002-9809-963X

References

Ablayev, F., and A. Vasiliev. 2011. "Classical and Quantum Parallelism in the Quantum Fingerprinting Method." International Conference on Parallel Computing Technologies.

Aerts, D., and M. Czachor. 2004. "Quantum Aspects of Semantic Analysis and Symbolic Artificial Intelligence." *Journal of Physics A: Mathematical and General* 37 (12): L123.

Ambainis, A. 2004. "Quantum Search Algorithms." *ACM SIGACT News* 35 (2): 22–35.

Antonio, A., and M. Lluis. 2016. "Certified Randomness in Quantum Physics." *Nature* 540 (7632): 213. doi:10.1038/nature20119.

Ashtiani, M., and M. A. Azgomi. 2015. "A Survey of Quantum-Like Approaches to Decision Making and Cognition." *Mathematical Social Sciences* 75: 49–80. doi:10.1016/j.mathsocsci.2015.02.004.

Atmanspacher, H. 2004. Quantum approaches to consciousness.

Baaquie, B. E. 2013. *The Theoretical Foundations of Quantum Mechanics*. New York: Springer Science & Business Media.

Banks, T. 2019. Quantum mechanics: an introduction. http://search.ebscohost.com/login.aspx?direct=true&scope=site&db=nlebk&db=nlabk&AN=1897033.

Barz, S., E. Kashefi, A. Broadbent, J. F. Fitzsimons, A. Zeilinger, and P. Walther. 2012. "Demonstration of Blind Quantum Computing." *Science* 335 (6066): 303–308.

Baskin, K. 2008. "Storied Spaces: The Human Equivalent of Complex Adaptive Systems." *Emergence: Complexity and Organization* 10 (2): 1–12.

Bennett, C. H., G. Brassard, C. Crépeau, R. Jozsa, A. Peres, and W. K. Wootters. 1993. "Teleporting an Unknown Quantum State via Dual Classical and Einstein-Podolsky-Rosen Channels." *Physical Review Letters* 70 (13): 1895.

Bennett, C. H., and P. W. Shor. 1998. "Quantum Information Theory." *IEEE Transactions on Information Theory* 44 (6): 2724–2742.

Bickley, S. J., H. F. Chan, S. L. Schmidt, and B. Torgler. 2021. "Quantum-Sapiens: The Quantum Bases for Human Expertise, Knowledge, and Problem-Solving (Extended Version with Applications)." CREMA Working Paper No. 2021–14, Zürich, Switzerland.

Born, M. 1926. "Quantenmechanik der Stoßvorgänge." *Zeitschrift für Physik* 38 (11–12): 803–827.

Brassard, G., P. Hoyer, and A. Tapp. 1998. Quantum Counting. arXiv.org. doi:10.1007/BFb0055105.

Budde, F., and D. Volz. 2019. The Next Big Thing? Quantum Computing's Potential Impact on Chemicals.

Busemeyer, J. R., and P. D. Bruza. 2012. "Quantum Models of Cognition and Decision." In *The Oxford Handbook of Computational and Mathematical Psychology*. New York: Oxford University Press.

Carroll, J. M., and J. C. Thomas. 1982. "Metaphor and the Cognitive Representation of Computing Systems." *IEEE Transactions on Systems, Man, and Cybernetics* 12 (2): 107–116.

Deutsch, D. 1989. "Quantum Computational Networks." *Proceedings of the Royal Society of London. Series A, Mathematical and Physical Sciences* 425 (1868): 73–90.

Deutsch, D., and R. Jozsa. 1992. "Rapid Solution of Problems by Quantum Computation." *Proceedings of the Royal Society of London. Series A: Mathematical and Physical Sciences* 439 (1907): 553–558.

Dunjko, V., and H. J. Briegel. 2018. "Machine Learning & Artificial Intelligence in the Quantum Domain: a Review of Recent Progress." *Reports on Progress in Physics* 81 (7): 074001.

Endo, S., Z. Cai, S. C. Benjamin, and X. Yuan. 2020. Hybrid Quantum-classical Algorithms and Quantum Error Mitigation. arXiv preprint arXiv:2011.01382.

Englert, B.-G. 2013. "On Quantum Theory." *The European Physical Journal D* 67 (11): 1–16. doi:10.1140/epjd/e2013-40486-5.

Feigenbaum, E. A. 1968. Artificial Intelligence: Themes in the Second Decade.

Feigenbaum, E. A. 1977. The Art of Artificial Intelligence. 1. Themes and Case Studies of Knowledge Engineering.

Feigenbaum, E. A., P. McCorduck, and H. P. Nii. 1989. *The Rise of the Expert Company; How Visionary Companies Are Using Artificial Intelligence to*. New York: Crown Publishing Group.

Feynman, R. P. 1982. "Simulating Physics with Computers." *Int. J. Theor. Phys* 21 (6/7): 467–488.

Galindo, A., and M. Martin-Delgado. 2001. "Information and Computation: Classical and Quantum Aspects." *arXiv.org* 74 (2), doi:10.1103/RevModPhys.74.347.

Grover, L. K. 1996. A Fast Quantum Mechanical Algorithm for Database Search.

Haag, R. 2013. "On the Sharpness of Localization of Individual Events in Space and Time." *Foundations of Physics* 43 (11): 1295–1313.

Harrow, A., A. Hassidim, and S. Lloyd. 2009. "Quantum Algorithm for Solving Linear Systems of Equations." *arXiv.org* 103 (15). doi:10.1103/PhysRevLett.103.150502.

Heisenberg, W. 1962. *Physics and Philosophy. The Revolution in Modern Science, 1958*. New York: Harper & Row Publishers.

Hickey, T. J. 2016. Twentieth-Century Philosophy of Science: A History. Thomas J. Hickey. https://books.google.com.au/books?id=L_y-CwAAQBAJ.

Hinsley, D. A., J. R. Hayes, and H. A. Simon. 1977. "From Words to Equations: Meaning and Representation in Algebra Word Problems." In *Cognitive Processes in Comprehension*. New Jersey: Lawrence Erlbaum Associates.

Khrennikov, A. 2015. "Quantum-like Modeling of Cognition." *Frontiers in Physics* 3: 77.

Kimble, H. J. 2008. "The Quantum Internet." *Nature* 453 (7198): 1023–1030.

Kolawole, M. O. 2021. *Electronics: From Classical to Quantum*. 1st ed. Boca Raton: CRC Press.

Krithika, S. 2017. "Quantum Key Distribution (QKD): A Review on Technology, Recent Developments and Future Prospects." *Research Journal of Engineering and Technology* 8 (3): 291–294. doi:10.5958/2321-581X.2017.00049.6.

Landauer, R. 1996. "The Physical Nature of Information." *Physics Letters A* 217 (4): 188–193. doi:10.1016/0375-9601(96)00453-7.

Landauer, R. 1999. "Information is a Physical Entity." *Physica A: Statistical Mechanics and its Applications* 263 (1–4): 63–67. doi:10.1016/S0378-4371(98)00513-5.

Li, J., X. Yang, X. Peng, and C.-P. Sun. 2017. "Hybrid Quantum-Classical Approach to Quantum Optimal Control." *Physical Review Letters* 118 (15): 150503.

Lindsay, R. K., B. G. Buchanan, E. A. Feigenbaum, and J. Lederberg. 1993. "DENDRAL: a Case Study of the First Expert System for Scientific Hypothesis Formation." *Artificial Intelligence* 61 (2): 209–261.

Lloyd, S. 1995. "Almost any Quantum Logic Gate is Universal." *Physical Review Letters* 75 (2): 346.

Logesh, R., V. Subramaniyaswamy, V. Vijayakumar, X.-Z. Gao, and V. Indragandhi. 2018. "A Hybrid Quantum-Induced Swarm Intelligence Clustering for the Urban Trip Recommendation in Smart City." *Future Generation Computer Systems* 83: 653–673.

McCarthy, J. 1998. Elaboration Tolerance. Common Sense.

McCorduck, P. 2019. *This Could be Important: My Life and Times with the Artificial Intelligentsia*. Morrisville: Lulu Press.

Minsky, M. 1988. *The Society of Mind*. Simon and Schuster.

Minsky, M. 2006. *The Emotion Machine: Commensense Thinking, Artificial Intelligence, and the Future of the Human Mind*. New York: Simon & Schuster.

Mirowski, P. 1990. "From Mandelbrot to Chaos in Economic Theory." *Southern Economic Journal* 57 (2): 289–307. doi:10.2307/1060611.

Montanaro, A. 2015. "Quantum Speedup of Monte Carlo Methods." *Proceedings of the Royal Society A: Mathematical, Physical and Engineering Sciences* 471 (2181): 20150301.

Moret-Bonillo, V. 2018. "Emerging Technologies in Artificial Intelligence: Quantum Rule-Based Systems." *Progress in Artificial Intelligence* 7 (2): 155–166.

Nilsson, N. J. 2009. *The Quest for Artificial Intelligence*. New York: Cambridge University Press.

Nisbett, R. E., and T. D. Wilson. 1977. "Telling More Than we Can Know: Verbal Reports on Mental Processes." *Psychological Review* 84 (3): 231.

Noori, H., and R. Spanagel. 2013. "Quantum Modeling of Common Sense." *Behavioral and Brain Sciences* 36 (3): 302. doi:10.1017/S0140525X1200307X.

Orus, R., S. Mugel, and E. Lizaso. 2019. "Quantum Computing for Finance: Overview and Prospects." *Reviews in Physics* 4: 100028.

Otterbach, J., R. Manenti, N. Alidoust, A. Bestwick, M. Block, B. Bloom, S. Caldwell, N. Didier, E. S. Fried, and S. Hong. 2017. "Unsupervised Machine Learning on a Hybrid Quantum Computer." arXiv preprint arXiv:1712.05771.

Peres, A. 2002. *Quantum Theory: Concepts and Methods*. 1st ed. Springer Netherlands. doi:10.1007/0-306-47120-5.

Pothos, E. M., and J. R. Busemeyer. 2013. "Can Quantum Probability Provide a new Direction for Cognitive Modeling?" *The Behavioral and Brain Sciences* 36 (3): 255. doi:10.1017/S0140525X12001525.

Resch, S., and U. R. Karpuzcu. 2019. "Quantum Computing: An Overview across the System Stack." arXiv preprint arXiv:1905.07240.

Rieffel, E., and W. Polak. 2000. "An Introduction to Quantum Computing for non-Physicists." *ACM Computing Surveys (CSUR)* 32 (3): 300–335.

Schumacher. 1995. "Quantum Coding. Physical Review. A." *Atomic, Molecular, and Optical Physics* 51 (4): 2738. doi:10.1103/PhysRevA.51.2738.

Shannon, C. E. 1948. "A Mathematical Theory of Communication." *The Bell System Technical Journal* 27 (3): 379–423.

Shor, P. W. 1994. "Algorithms for Quantum Computation: Discrete Logarithms and Factoring." 124–134. doi:10.1109/SFCS.1994.365700.

Shortliffe, E. H., and T. C. Rindfleisch. 2000. "Presentation of the Morris F. Collen Award to Joshua Lederberg, PhD." *Journal of the American Medical Informatics Association* 7 (3): 326–332.

Siler, W. 2005. "Fuzzy Expert Systems and Fuzzy Reasoning." Wiley-Interscience. doi:10.1002/0471698504.

Sriboonchitta, S., H. T. Nguyen, O. Kosheleva, V. Kreinovich, and T. N. Nguyen. 2019. "Quantum Approach Explains the Need for Expert Knowledge: On the Example of Econometrics." International Conference of the Thailand Econometrics Society.

Steane, A. M., and E. G. Rieffel. 2000. "Beyond Bits: The Future of Quantum Information Processing." *Computer* 33 (1): 38–45.

Stehr, N. 2011. *Experts: the Knowledge and Power of Expertise*. New York: Routledge.

Torgler, B. 2020. "Big Data, Artificial Intelligence, and Quantum Computing in Sports." In *21st Century Sports*, edited by S. Schmidt, 153–173. Switzerland: Springer.

Trueblood, J. S., and J. R. Busemeyer. 2012. "A Quantum Probability Model of Causal Reasoning." *Frontiers in Psychology* 3: 138–138. doi:10.3389/fpsyg.2012.00138.

Turban, E. 1988. "Review of Expert Systems Technology." *IEEE Transactions on Engineering Management* 35 (2): 71–81. doi:10.1109/17.6007.

Tversky, A., and D. Kahneman. 1983. "Extensional Versus Intuitive Reasoning: The Conjunction Fallacy in Probability Judgment." *Psychological Review* 90 (4): 293.

White, I. 1988. "W (h) Ither Expert Systems?—A View from Outside." *AI & SOCIETY* 2 (2): 161–171.

Wilson, D. S. 2020. *This View of Life: Completing the Darwinian Revolution*. New York: Pantheon Books.

Yukalov, V. I., E. P. Yukalova, and D. Sornette. 2018. "Information Processing by Networks of Quantum Decision Makers." *Physica A: Statistical Mechanics and its Applications* 492: 747–766.

Zhaokai, L., L. Xiaomei, and X. Nanyang. 2014. Experimental Realization of Quantum Artificial Intelligence. arXiv preprint arXiv:1410.1054.

OPEN ACCESS

Temporal work by consultants in nascent market categories: constructing a market for knowledge in quantum computing

Oona Hilkamo, Anne-Sophie Barbe, Nina Granqvist and Amber Geurts

ABSTRACT

The literatures on market categories and temporal work pay limited attention to the agentic role of intermediaries in nascent market categories. Through an inductive analysis of quantum computing, we explore how management consultancies perform temporal work in such settings. We find that management consultancies construct a market for knowledge by engaging in three types of temporal work. First, they bring the future market category into present existence and thus make it an object for action. Second, they construct ultimate uncertainty and ambiguity and therefore a need for external knowledge. Third, they create a sense of urgency for immediate market engagement. Our findings shed light on the active intermediating role of management consultancies in nascent market categories, allowing them to capitalise on novel markets very early on.

Introduction

Market categories are shared socio-cultural sets of meanings that guide assessments of the similarity of firms and products belonging to a category or attempting to enter it (Kennedy and Fiss 2013; Khaire and Wadhwani 2010). While established markets have relatively clear boundaries and member identities, emerging categories are characterised by a lack of prototypes and categorical structures and unclear actor roles and identities (Durand and Khaire 2017; Granqvist, Grodal, and Woolley 2013). Unknown user needs and a lack of standards lead to a high degree of divergence in the available technical solutions and evoke sensemaking processes. In such settings, multiple possible technologies compete for dominance through community-level meaning-making and contestation (Grodal, Gotsopoulos, and Suarez 2015).

Emerging settings are thus characterised by open-endedness, which implies both ambiguity and uncertainty. Ambiguity refers to the simultaneous existence of multiple meanings regarding the boundaries of a category with respect to the kinds of products and services it encompasses, as well as the potential range of valid identities for category members (Granqvist, Grodal, and Woolley 2013; Santos and Eisenhardt 2009). Uncertainty is a temporal construct referring to multiple possible future developments – it is very difficult, for instance, to determine how a new market category is developing and to identify the right timing for engagement. Due to such ambiguity and uncertainty, market category emergence is characterised by individual and collective processes in which category participants – customarily defined as producers, intermediaries and audiences –

construct the category boundaries and expectations. In so doing, they are influenced by their perceptions, interests, and prior knowledge (Durand and Paolella 2013; Granqvist and Ritvala 2016).

Temporal work, in particular, is central to market category emergence. The concept refers to how market participants both make sense of temporal structures and also produce them (Granqvist and Gustafsson 2016; Kaplan and Orlikowski 2013). Studies have looked at expectations regarding future market category developments (Garud, Schildt, and Lant 2014; Granqvist, Grodal, and Woolley 2013), how actors construct understandings about the right timing for market entry (Granqvist and Gustafsson 2016), and how the experiences of actors 'over the temporal horizons of the past, present, and future (..) endow them with uniquely crafted identities and action repertoires, as well as dreams and visions for the future' (Pontikes and Rindova 2020, 150). Importantly, temporal work is impacted by the particular community-specific temporal frames held by actors (Barley 1988). Early actors negotiate and invest in what they *expect* will be relevant in a potential, future industry – with the very real risk that this market may never emerge (Helfat and Lieberman 2002; Moeen and Mitchell 2020).

While previous studies have looked at the role of audiences and producers during market category emergence, the role of intermediaries has received less attention. This is a major shortcoming because intermediaries often join the nascent category early on (Granqvist, Grodal, and Woolley 2013; Grodal 2018) and play an important role in the process of market-making (Brès and Gond 2014). Management consultants, in particular, have a major role in nascent markets as they act as key brokers of knowledge and networks in the early stages (Granqvist, Grodal, and Woolley 2013; Grodal 2018). They also have a long-standing interest in developing business opportunities and tradable services around new issues or knowledge (Brès and Gond 2014). The focus of this study is to explore how management consultancies, as key intermediaries, construct a nascent market category, and particularly, how they engage in temporal work.

Based on an inductive study of the role of management consultants in quantum computing, we identify three forms of temporal work in which consultants engage during market category emergence: bringing the future market category into present existence, which makes it a relevant object for action; constructing ultimate unpredictability, thereby creating a need for audiences to obtain external knowledge; and creating a sense of urgency regarding market engagement in order to immediately engage audiences with the new market. Drawing on these findings, we discuss how consultants constitute new markets through temporal work.

Management consultancies as key intermediaries during market category emergence

Previous studies on market categories have focused on agency in categorisation, with an emphasis on producers and audiences, rather than on intermediaries. Market intermediaries are defined as all the 'third parties' that attempt 'to facilitate market exchanges between producers (i.e. sources of supply) and clients (i.e. sources of demand)' (Boulongne, Cudennec, and Durand 2019, 68). These middlemen (Biglaiser 1993), who intervene at the interface between the producers and consumers of a market, encompass a variety of actors, such as critics at the interface between wine producers and wine consumers (Hsu, Roberts, and Swaminathan 2012), ranking providers situated between schools and students (Espeland and Sauder 2007), and employment agencies acting between labour supply and labour demand (Stigler 1962). Market intermediaries are acknowledged to play key roles in market categories; they enforce existing categories by providing sanctions or rewards to producers according to their category positioning (Zuckerman 1999) or participate in the (re)categorisation of existing market producers (Durand and Khaire 2017), for instance through development of new labels (Curchod, Patriotta, and Neysen 2014) or new classifications (Ruef and Patterson 2009).

However, market category emergence is characterised by ambiguity and uncertainty (Suarez, Grodal, and Gotsopoulos 2015). In such contexts, which lack a shared understanding of what constitutes market supply and demand, the role of market intermediaries within established market structures appears problematic. Thus, despite growing recognition that 'most extant research on market intermediaries has been conducted in the context of established markets' (Lee, Hiatt, and Lounsbury 2017, 3) and that 'future work should continue to explore how intermediaries create and shape boundaries of nascent market categories' (Zhao et al. 2018, 607), there is a lack of research on market category emergence that addresses the role of market intermediaries. Although some recent studies have started to address this gap, they focus on contexts where products are already traded even if 'weakly entrenched' (Zhao et al. 2018, 1) or lacking standards (Lee, Hiatt, and Lounsbury 2017). In this paper, we thus explore the role of market intermediaries in the very early phases of category emergence, with a particular focus on management consultancies.

The focus on management consultancies is warranted as they often join the nascent category early on (Granqvist, Grodal, and Woolley 2013; Grodal 2018). Indeed, there is growing recognition that management consultants have a 'visible hand' (Brès and Gond 2014, 1347) in the process of market-making. Thus, a burgeoning literature explains how management consultants have an interest in 'translating' new issues or knowledge into tangible business opportunities (Brès and Gond 2014). Management consulting firms also engage in construction of social-symbolic meanings (Pontikes and Rindova 2020) and in forms of temporal work whose influence on the agency of category members has not yet been captured by either market category research or research on management consultancies.

In the early stages of market category emergence, management consultancies engage in such activities in two ways. First, they develop and sell reports and analyses (Bloomfield and Vurdubakis 1994) about the nascent category. Although the consultants may not have first-hand knowledge of the science and technology involved, especially when they are complex in nature, this may provide them with a learning opportunity. Also, consultants are well-known for their skill in translating knowledge between different parties (Bres and Gond 2014), producing compelling narratives about the growth of the markets (Granqvist, Grodal, and Woolley 2013), and by such means foregrounding demand for knowledge. Thus, the reports often have a prospective, future-oriented tone. This has a major impact on market formation especially when consultants portray the market as fast-growing and ground-breaking.

Second, during the early emergence of a category, there is also a demand for networking – getting to know others who are active in the market. In this vein, consultancies help shape emerging categories by organising events. This provides another early business opportunity as it allows them to position themselves in an emerging market while also being among the first to generate income. Events are trans-organisational structures with the potential to configure and reconfigure a market category by bringing together potential participants around common interests and issues (Anand and Jones 2008). For example, events such as conferences and trade shows can act as venues for participants to signal membership in the field (Granqvist, Grodal, and Woolley 2013) and as forums for interaction and contestation (Lampel and Meyer 2008). Events thus provide temporal discursive spaces that are not normally available, thereby facilitating multiple and conflicting discourses that may lead to new narratives about the field (Garud 2008). For emerging market categories conferences are particularly important, as these are occasions for members to 'define and redefine the field in dynamic ways' (Garud 2008, 1085). For example, in his study on the emergence of cochlear implants, Garud (2008) found that conferences provided stakeholders with a venue for enactment of competing technologies, collective sensemaking, and consensus building.

In sum, although management consultancies may be somewhat peripheral in the emerging category with respect to their knowledge and development activities, they are active participants in category construction; they shape its social and symbolic boundaries by authoring reports and organising events (Grodal 2018). Due to their future-orientated narratives and growth forecasts, they play a major role in shaping the expectations and understandings of category members regarding the right timing for engagement. Nevertheless, the literature remains unclear on the role of management consultancies in construction of temporal structures during the emergence of a market category. Hence we set out to answer the following question: *How do consultants engage in temporal work during market category emergence*?

Methodology

Our investigation aimed to enhance knowledge on the role of consultants in an emerging market category. For this purpose, we studied quantum computing as an emerging domain of science and technology (Rotolo, Hicks, and Martin 2015) that provides a research context with ample material on consultants' activity. We used a data-driven, inductive approach (Langley 1999) to investigate what consultants do during market category emergence when quantum futures are brought into present existence.

Empirical setting

Quantum computing is a young discipline at the interface between computer science and quantum physics (Paraoanu 2011). The field focuses on development of universal *quantum computers,* i.e.computing devices that instead of classical bits use quantum bits, or qubits, to store and process information. Although current quantum computers still underperform classical computers, they promise major increases in processing capacity that would enable solutions to problems deemed unsolvable with classical computers within any reasonable time frame (Vermaas 2017). Decades of laboratory work and the growing ability to manipulate quantum effects are now paving the way towards the first, near-market-ready quantum computer (Mohseni et al. 2017). Quantum computing is expected to create a new paradigm in computing and have a real, game-changing practical impact for science, business, and society in ways we cannot yet foresee. As a result, several players have announced their interest in the emerging market of quantum computing, among them big tech companies such as IBM and Google, smaller startups such as Rigetti and IonQ, and consulting firms such as McKinsey, Deloitte, and Accenture. The speed of industrial activity has surprised scientists (Preskill 2018) and many recognise that quantum computing is at present surrounded by hype, especially since a prototypical design and use cases are yet to emerge. Hence this setting, characterised by extreme ambiguity and uncertainty, provides an excellent context for studying the dynamics of market category emergence.

Data sources and analysis

Our exploration of the role of consultants in the emerging market category of quantum computing is part of a larger, long-term project. The data for this project encompass interviews with industry players, substantive archival material consisting of news stories and reports, and observations of numerous events and conferences. Using insights from this larger project, we observed that the role of management consultants during early market formation comprised two main activities: producing industry reports and organising networking events.

Accordingly, our primary data for this paper are reports and events. We systematically collected all the published *consultancy reports* on quantum technologies in general and quantum computing in particular. These reports numbered 24 and comprised 464 pages of material for analysis. Additionally, we collected data from eight *quantum computing events* organised or sponsored by consulting firms. We collected publicly available event materials, including presentation slides, agendas, and press releases, as well as presentations of speakers when available and took observation notes during the events. A summary of our data is provided in Table 1.

We began our analyses by writing a historical narrative about the key scientific and industry advancements in quantum technologies and quantum computing. For this, we used secondary sources from our project, including archival data and interviews. The narrative developed continuously as we integrated new information emerging from the on-going data collection.

Table 1. Summary of data.

Reports published by management consultancy firms					
N	Authoring firm		Year	Pages	Title
1	Accenture		2017	16	Innovating with Quantum Computing
2			2017	20	Think beyond ones and zeros. Quantum computing. Now
3			2020	18	In Quantum we trust
4	BCG		2018	19	The Coming Quantum Leap in Computing
5			2018	30	The Next Decade in Quantum Computing and How to Play
6			2019	19	Where Will Quantum Computers Create Value and When?
7			2019	6	Will Quantum Computing transform Biopharma R&D?
8	CB Insights		2019	31	What Is Quantum Computing?
9	Deloitte		2017	10	From fantasy to reality: Quantum computing is coming to the marketplace
10			2019	20	Quantum computers: The next supercomputers, but not the next laptops
11			2020	20	The realist's guide to quantum technology and national security
12	Inside Quantum Technology		2019	7	Quantum Computing Strategies: 2019
13	KPMG		2019	2	Quantum Computing 101
14	McKinsey		2016	3	The growing potential of quantum computing
15			2019	7	The next big thing? Quantum computing's potential impact on chemicals
16			2020	8	The next tech revolution: quantum computing
17			2020	9	A game plan for quantum computing
18	Patinformatics		2017	65	Practical Quantum Computing: A Patent Landscape Report
19	PwC		2017	6	Information Security in the Age of Quantum Technologies
20			2019	44	Advancing a strategy for quantum computing that will inspire, support and safeguard economic growth in the Middle East
21			2019	22	Quantum Computing: A technology of the future already present
22	The Hutch report		2018	44	Quantum Computers: The game changers?
23	Wavestone		2019	23	Quantum Computing: Ready for the Huge Leap?
24	Yole Development		2020	22	Quantum Technologies
			Total	*464*	
Events materials					
N	*Name of the event*	*Related consultancy firm*	*Year (s)*	*Place*	*Data details*
1	The Quantum Countdown	Z/Yen	2018	Webinar	Materials publicly provided
2	Quantum Computing Business Conference	McKinsey	2019	Paris, France	Materials publicly provided
3	Inside Quantum Technology Europe	Inside Quantum Technology	2019	The Hague, the Netherlands	Event attended
4	Inside Quantum Technology New York Online	Inside Quantum Technology	2020	Online	Event attended
5	BCI Summit Quantum	Social Venture Circle	2019	New York, USA	Materials publicly provided
6	Getting Ahead in the Quantum Economy: A Deep Dive into the Hardware	e2i	2019	Singapore, Singapore	Materials publicly provided
7	Quantum Tech Congress	Several	2019	London	Materials publicly provided
8	Quantum Computing Summit	KPMG	2020	London, Silicon Valley	Materials publicly provided

Following inductive, data-driven analyses of our primary data, we started the analysis with a close reading of the data, with each of the authors independently analysing part of the material (Glaser and Strauss 1967). We then discussed and compared our initial findings and decided on more focused themes for deeper analysis. Our second round of analysis focused on three broad themes that emerged as the key actions taken by the consultants: *bringing the future into present existence, constructing unpredictability, and creating a sense of urgency.* We analysed our data to uncover how meaning is constructed around these complex topics. At the final stage, we focused our analysis on the motivations and claims of the consultants regarding the emerging market of quantum computing.

Temporal work by consultants to create a market for knowledge

In this section, we present our findings. First, we show how the consultants bring 'a quantum future' into present existence. Second, we show how they sketch a path between present and possible futures, thereby constructing ultimate unpredictability, and third, we show how they create a sense of urgency for market engagement. Taken together, our findings shed light on the role of the consultants during market category emergence by creating a 'market for knowledge'.

Bringing an emerging market category into present existence

By authoring reports and organising events around quantum computing, consultants bring this novel market category into present existence. First, they engage in temporal and technological demarcation by presenting quantum computers as a profoundly different, disruptive technology that will lead society into a new era. Second, they depict the future existence of quantum computers as inevitable by providing estimates of the future market.

Temporal and technological demarcation

The consultants present quantum computers as a new market category that differs profoundly from earlier computing technologies; the emergence of quantum computers creates a boundary between what is now and what will be in the future. The technology behind the devices is described as 'fantastical' (Schatsky and Puliakodil 2017, 2) and quantum computing is envisioned to have 'the potential to be both transformative and disruptive.' (Hazan et al. 2020, 3). Quantum computers are presented as paradigm-breaking and revolutionary: 'The very nature of quantum physics creates opportunities to completely disrupt existing technologies, and break the paradigms of classical computation' (Ward et al. 2020, 4) and '[i]ts disruptive potential exceeds that of the internet, smartphones and cloud computing combined' (Vernacchia 2019, 9). The emergence of quantum computing demarcates the beginning of a new era: '[w]e're at the dawn of the quantum-computing age' (Brownell and Chui 2016, 1). This temporal demarcation suggests that there will be a post-quantum world with new opportunities and threats. Even though the timeline for this future is uncertain, consultants propose that executives 'begin to prepare their enterprises for *the era of quantum computing*' (Schatsky and Puliakodil 2017, 5, emphasis added).

To demarcate the new technology, quantum computers are described as offering 'an entirely new model of computing' that is as far from classical computing as light bulbs are from candles (Carriere et al. 2019, 10). In a more modest discourse, quantum computing is portrayed as a continuation of the computing paradigm, enabling 'the fifth generation of computers' (Carrel-Billiard, Garrison, and Dukatz 2017, 5). Quantum computers are differentiated from classical computers by explaining that their abilities extend beyond those of classical computers. Quantum computers 'will be able to perform certain kinds of calculations exponentially faster than the fastest computers currently known' (Schatsky and Puliakodil 2017, 2) and solve 'certain problems far faster than conventional machines' (Quantum Business Conf. Paris programme leaflet, 2019). As a general-purpose quantum computer is yet to be built, there is uncertainty about what such a device could do: 'In fact, researchers don't yet know all the types of problems at which quantum computing could excel' (Schatsky and Puliakodil 2017, 3). However, despite such a high level of uncertainty, the consultants contend that quantum computing will have a bright future: 'In the long term, such machines will very likely shape new computing and business paradigms by solving computational problems that are currently out of reach' (Gerbert and Ruess 2018, 3).

Narrating the future existence of quantum computers

Though current quantum computers are early prototypes, the consultants portray the future presence of a universal quantum computer as certain. It is not a matter of if, but rather of when, in fact they maintain that the 'quantum countdown' (Z/Yen, 2018, event brochure) has already started. The only future available to actors is the one in which the emergence of quantum computers leads to more disruptive change than that instigated by previous technologies. Indeed, consultants state that 'we believe that this technology is within our reach and will be available in the next coming years' (Haddad and Chinasi-Halet 2019, 19).

This future existence or even imminent reality of quantum computing are portrayed in the titles of reports produced by consultants: for example 'A technology of the future already present' (Haddad and Chinasi-Halet 2019) and 'From Fantasy to Reality: Quantum Computing is coming to the marketplace' (Schatsky and Puliakodil 2017). Even though their much-vaunted superiority over classical computers has not yet been verified, the consultants state that 'such a demonstration is deemed imminent' (Gerbert and Ruess 2018, 9). Ambiguity around the emergence of the novel market category is dispelled by evoking images of other successful technologies: 'Remember that deep learning, which today dominates the fast-growing field of AI, was also once a purely experimental success' (Gerbert and Ruess 2018, 19).

Consultants also categorise market participants and make forecasts about the future size of the market. The technology is deemed developed enough 'for an ecosystem of hardware and software architects and developers, contributors, investors, potential users, and collateral players to take shape' (Gerbert and Ruess 2018, 6). Moreover, some consultants provide estimates on the potential value of the market; Hazan et al. (2020, 4) estimate a '+$1 trillion value potential by the mid-2030s in 5 industries' and Lee et al. (2019, 5) a future market 'about the size of today's supercomputer market – around US$50 billion'.

Constructing ultimate unpredictability

To create demand for their 'knowledge services', consultants frame the path from the present to the inevitable quantum future as extremely open-ended and difficult to foresee. In essence, they construct ultimate unpredictability. Our data show that the consultants devise a complex narrative of *uncertainty* about future developments and *ambiguity* about the forms of quantum computers to describe how the market will evolve and create demand for their knowledge services.

Uncertainty in the timeline

The consultants portray a timeline that separates the present (in which quantum computers are not available) from the future. They infuse the latter with uncertainty by emphasising that the nature of this technology is still unknown, especially because it is evolving at an unpredictable pace. They make fuzzy claims such as 'it isn't far away' (Vernacchia 2019, 12), predict 'upcoming real-world applications' (Quantum Computing Business Conference, 2019), or on the contrary argue that 'none of this will happen overnight' (Ménard et al. 2020, 1). The overall tone of the consultants' reports is one of uncertainty – 'there is no exact timeline for commercial availability of a general-purpose universal quantum computer' (Buchholz et al. 2020, 7). While some reports provide a '*likely* timetable for development' (Russo, Thaker, and Adam 2018, 4, emphasis added), others emphasise that 'experts are divided on the timing of quantum computing's impact' (Langione et al. 2019b, 13).

As the consultants portrayed the pace at which the timeline is developing as unpredictable, the ultimate horizon appears even more uncertain; indeed 'the progress in recent years is hard to overstate' (Gerbert and Ruess 2018, 3) given that such technologies 'can emerge at unpredictable speed' (Ménard et al. 2020, 9). Thus, if some consultants highlight the surprising speed of its development – outlining for instance that 'quantum computer development is progressing at a faster pace than expected' (PwC and Russian Quantum Center 2017, 2) – others warn of its probable slowness – 'since the technology is nascent, progress *might* be slow' (Hazan et al. 2020, 6, emphasis added). The latter group explains that the technologies underlying development of quantum computers – such as those enabling operation in a 'vacuum environment or at cryogenic temperatures' (Gerbert and Ruess 2018, 3) eventually reaching known physical limits such as 'the lowest temperature that's physically possible in the universe' (Brownell and Chui 2016, 2) – are 'technical hurdles that quantum computing faces' (Gerbert and Ruess 2018, 3). Thus, the consultants contend that 'maturity in quantum computing will not follow a smooth, continuous curve. Instead, a *precipitous breakthrough* that may come at any time' (Langione et al. 2019b, 2, emphasis added), with the 'ultimate pace and roadmap [being] still uncertain' (Gerbert and Ruess 2018, 24).

Ambiguity about the potential technological designs and market structures

The consultants not only portray an uncertain timeline separating the present (in which quantum computers are not available) from the future, but also connect this present to several possible futures (in which some quantum computers will be available). To do so, they envisage a multiplicity of possible technological designs for quantum computers and provide blurred categorisations of eventual market providers, thereby giving rise to ambiguity.

Several technological designs coexist in the emerging market category. The consultants depict the different existing designs for qubits and their related technological challenges and acknowledge that there are currently 'several approaches to building quantum computers' (Carrel-Billiard, Garrison, and Dukatz 2017, 8), that 'there is no consensus to date on how to physically create qubits' (Carriere et al. 2019, 22), and that 'nobody knows what will be the right technology, that's gonna work' (Quantum Computing Business Conference (2019) roundtable moderator). The consultants also acknowledge the uncertainty regarding the future forms of qubits: 'who knows, new types of qubits might ease [one] constraint in the future' (Carriere et al. 2019, 22). Since there are a number of potential technological designs, the ultimate form of the underlying architecture remains unclear (Gerbert and Ruess 2018). With respect to technological design, the final computers could be hybrids (Gerbert and Ruess 2018).

Furthermore, the consultants suggest a multiplicity of possible futures by providing blurred categorisations of eventual quantum computer providers, by for instance distinguishing between 'end-to-end providers', 'hardware players', 'services players' and 'specialists' (Gerbert and Ruess 2018, 7) or 'worldwide tech giants' and 'start-ups' (Vernacchia 2019, 11) or even 'components', 'software' and 'hardware' providers (Carriere et al. 2019, 32). However, they also note that 'the lines between layers [are] easily blurred or crossed, in particular by maturing hardware players extending into the higher-level application, or even service layers' (Gerbert and Ruess 2018, 8).

Thus, while the consultants envision the inevitability of the new market category, they also build fundamental uncertainty and ambiguity into their narratives about the timeline and nature of the market category's emergence to convince participants that they need new knowledge and networks.

Creating a sense of urgency for market engagement

Finally, the consultants argue strongly for immediate market engagement with quantum computing as a condition for future market success and highlight the steps that others have already taken. This is exemplified in a rhetorical question we found on the website of the Quantum Computing Summit,

'Quantum is a thing of the future, right? No, you can take advantage of this right now!' Hence the consultants contend that there is a current need for their services in the area.

Framing early engagement as a condition for keeping up with the competition

The consultants frame present or near-future market engagement as a condition for future success. They describe early engagement with quantum computing as essential efforts by businesses to achieve top performance in their market categories. As exemplified in a report published by BCG (Langione et al. 2019a, 5) for the category of biopharma, the consultants state that 'a quantum-advantaged world will probably witness *a race* to find and patent the best molecules for a given target' and that biopharma firms 'should take the necessary steps *now* to prepare for quantum computing's role in R&D' (emphasis added). For almost every existing market category, the consultants assert that 'early movers will almost certainly gain advantages that followers will have a tough time matching' (Langione et al. 2019a, 1). Overall, the consultants urge their readers to 'act now' (Budde and Volz 2019, 1) because it will soon 'be too late to develop a strategic position and investment plan' (Vernacchia 2019, 12) given that 'the time to look at options for a quantum-safe architecture is at a minimum 10 years ahead of the expected need date' (Ward et al. 2020, 17).

Highlighting steps already taken by possible competitors

Another way to urge actors to take part in constructing the market is to highlight how other actors already have a quantum strategy and are taking the action needed to become industry leaders in the new market. For example, in the financial industry, where quantum computing will supposedly bring early benefits, the consultants emphasise that 'major banking actors are already involved in this initiative' (Haddad and Chinasi-Halet 2019, 13). In another report, they call for investments in talent management, as 'companies such as Airbus already offer quantum training programmes to prepare their engineers for the future' (Langione et al., 2019a, 5). The consultants also point to the consequences of not preparing for the coming quantum age: 'In an extreme scenario, biopharma companies risk being relegated to focusing mainly on clinical development, medical affairs, and sales' (Langione et al., 2019a, 5). By showing what others have done, the consultants establish that actions have already been taken and thereby create potential benchmarks.

Temporal work by consultants to build a market for knowledge during category emergence

According to our analyses, the consultants perform three types of temporal work during category emergence: (1) they bring the future market category into present existence, thereby making it subject to actions taken by their audiences; (2) they construct ultimate unpredictability, which implies that audiences need external knowledge to engage with the future; and (3) they create a sense of urgency around market engagement, which implies that the audiences need to take action now.

Through this temporal work, the consultants construct a 'market for knowledge' as displayed in Figure 1. This market designates a space where they portray a knowledge shortage on the demand side and then then urge their audiences to engage immediately with the future technology. The forms of temporal work we have identified are all necessary yet independently non-sufficient. By bringing the future into present existence, the consultants enable their audiences to envisage the necessary action. Only by portraying such action as urgent and complex can they convince their audiences of the existence of a 'knowledge shortage' and the need for concrete steps to address it.

The supply side of this market for knowledge is partly fuelled by the consultant firms themselves; in the emerging industry of quantum computing, consultants are keen to 'help [the audience] move forward' (Haddad and Chinasi-Halet 2019, 17) or to propose working 'with clients to conduct quantum business experiments' to assist them in gaining 'unique insights into how quantum computing can be applied to their enterprises' (Carrel-Billiard, Garrison,

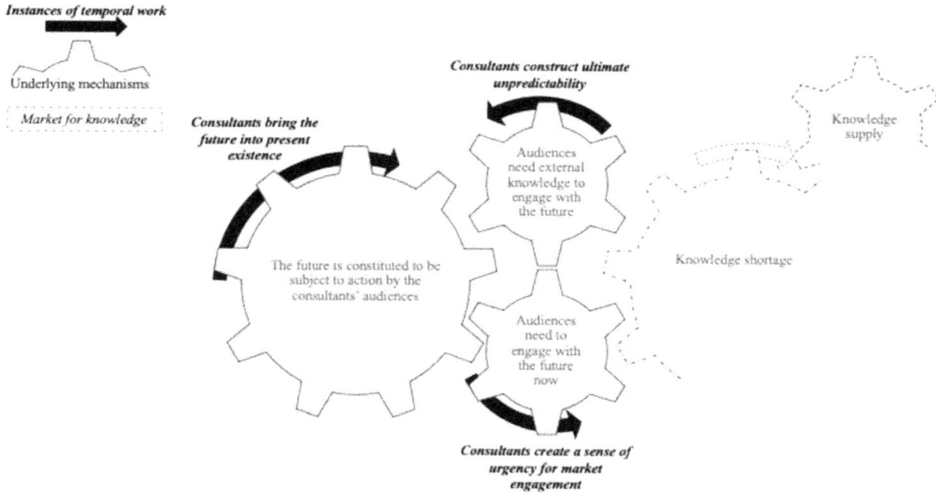

Figure 1. Temporal work and the creation of a market for knowledge.

and Dukatz 2017, 14). However, they also incentivise their audiences to manage 'partnerships, or patent acquisition opportunities' (Patinformatics, 2017, 3) especially with start-ups or even to envision a 'one-off partnership with a quantum community player (a manufacturer, publisher, university, start-up, VC firm, consulting firm, etc.) – to define or prototype a use case specific to the business's needs' (Carriere et al. 2019, 37). In sum, the consultants construct a market for their services in the nascent market category through these forms of temporal work.

Discussion and conclusions

Our findings contribute to the literature on market category emergence by showing how consultants acting as market intermediaries actively shape emerging market categories. While positioning themselves in an emerging market through temporal work, they shape the emerging category and thus increase their possibilities to gain a central intermediating position within that market.

Temporal work by management consultants during category emergence

The literature on temporal work refers to how market participants are embedded in and develop new temporal structures that then guide behaviours in markets (Granqvist and Gustafsson 2016; Kaplan and Orlikowski 2013; Pontikes and Rindova 2020). While previous studies have looked at how market actors construct expectations and understandings about the timing for market entry (Garud, Schildt, and Lant 2014), there is still little understanding of how such activities constitute novel markets. Our study on the activities of management consultants during the emergence of the quantum computing market category casts light on this issue. First, we find that consultants bring the future market category into present existence, thereby making the category *ontologically real*. By stating that the category will inevitably emerge, they make it a relevant object for action. Second, consultants construct extreme open-endedness, which implies that their audiences may need *external knowledge and networking* to proceed to such actions. The third aspect is that they create *a sense of urgency* to engage with the market category in the present. We show that the inherent combination of extreme open-endedness and the need to engage with the category to keep up with the competition support formation of a market for knowledge where consultants enable their clients to alleviate the 'knowledge shortage' between the present market and its potential future manifestations. Our study thereby provides important insights into the role of management consultancies as key knowledge intermediaries in nascent market categories.

Practical implications and suggestions for future research

Our study also raises relevant practical implications for the role of management consultants in constructing a market for knowledge, thereby foreshadowing a future industry. It shows that while narratives can be used as a tool to translate emerging markets into present action, they also produce equivocality. By narrating markets in this way, management consultants create a sense of urgency that persuades market players to consider undertaking present action towards an inevitable, yet uncertain, future market. Our study also shows that management consultants create a market for knowledge by actively constructing a knowledge shortage, for which they propose to supply their consulting services. While few other organisations can generate revenue in a nascent market category, management consultants can and thus sustain their activities by continuously producing a knowledge shortage and partially supplying the missing knowledge. Policymakers planning interventions to support an emerging market should thus keep in mind that their market-specific insights might be influenced by the stories of market intermediaries who are interested in sustaining a market for knowledge over prolonged periods. While previous research has pointed to this (Granqvist, Grodal, and Woolley 2013), our study identifies the specific types of temporal work that may instigate outcomes such as prolonged hypes.

For future research, our findings direct attention to the novel and interesting insights that can be gained by exploring nascent market categories. Specifically, our findings indicate the need to engage in *real-time empirical research* to explore how emerging technologies and market categories advance – free from the posthoc rationalisation of knowing the future end state of that technology, market, or category. In this paper, such a perspective enabled identification of a market for knowledge in a nascent market category. Future research could extend these findings to include the insights of other market intermediaries to give a more complete picture of the variety of activities and strategies employed by market intermediaries when working on nascent market categories. Moreover, our findings point to the role of management consultants in the construction of temporal structures in the very early phases of market category emergence. In particular, our empirical study emphasises the role of these consultants in convincing end-users of the urgency of engagement in the nascent market. Future studies on the role of management consultants in the emergence of new market categories could focus on cases in which management consultants construct other forms of temporal structures (such as 'non-urgent'). It could also examine how the temporal work of consultants succeeds (or fails) to enhance engagement by end-users or explore the underlying reasons leading management consultants to undertake such temporal work.

Our study sheds light on how market intermediaries can shape emerging market categories through temporal work. We show how management consultants as market intermediaries construct a market for knowledge that foreshadows the future industry. This market for knowledge allows intermediaries to capitalise on the emerging market early on, before more central actors in the field are able to reap profits.

Disclosure statement

No potential conflict of interest was reported by the author(s).

Funding

This work was supported by Academy of Finland: [Grant Number 323119].

ORCID

Oona Hilkamo http://orcid.org/0000-0002-0459-8172
Anne-Sophie Barbe http://orcid.org/0000-0002-7127-8064
Nina Granqvist http://orcid.org/0000-0001-8603-2908
Amber Geurts http://orcid.org/0000-0003-0478-0713

References

Anand, N., and B. C. Jones. 2008. "Tournament Rituals, Category Dynamics, and Field Configuration: The Case of the Booker Prize." *Journal of Management Studies* 45: 1036–1060.

Barley, S. R. 1988. "On Technology, Time, and Social Order: Technologically Induced Change in the Temporal Organization of Radiological Work." In *Making Time: Ethnographies of High-Technology Organizations*, edited by F. A. Dubinskas, 123–169. Philadelphia: Temple University.

Biglaiser, G. 1993. "Middlemen as Experts." *Rand Journal of Economics* 24 (2): 212–223.

Bloomfield, B. P., and T. Vurdubakis. 1994. "Re-presenting Technology: IT Consultancy Reports as Textual Reality Constructions." *Sociology* 28: 455–477.

Boulongne, R., A. Cudennec, and R. Durand. 2019. "When do Market Intermediaries Sanction Categorical Deviation? The Role of Expertise, Identity, and Competition." In *Microfoundations of Institutions*, edited by P. Haack, J. Sieweke, and L. Wessel, 67–83. Emerald: Bingley.

Brès, L., and J.-P. Gond. 2014. "The Visible Hand of Consultants in the Construction of the Markets for Virtue: Translating Issues, Negotiating Boundaries and Enacting Responsive Regulations." *Human Relations* 67: 1347–1382.

Brownell, W., and M. Chui. 2016. *The Growing Potential of Quantum Computing*. McKinsey and Company.

Buchholz, S., J. Mariani, A. Routh, A. Keyal, and P. Kishnani. 2020. *The Realist's Guide to Quantum Technology and National Security*. The Deloitte Center for Government Insights.

Budde, F., and D. Volz. 2019. *The Next Big Thing? Quantum Computing's Potential Impact on Chemicals*. McKinsey and Company.

Carrel-Billiard, M., D. Garrison, and C. Dukatz. 2017. *Think Beyond Ones and Zeros*. Accenture Labs.

Carriere, F., R. Gayrard, A. Rabayrol, and M. Tordeux. 2019. *Quantum Computing: Ready for the Huge Leap*. France Digitale and Wavestone.

Curchod, C., G. Patriotta, and N. Neysen. 2014. "Categorization and Identification: The Identity Work of 'Business Sellers' on EBay." *Human Relations* 67: 1293–1320.

Durand, R., and M. Khaire. 2017. "Where do Market Categories Come from and how? Distinguishing Category Creation from Category Emergence." *Journal of Management* 43: 87–110.

Durand, R., and L. Paolella. 2013. "Category Stretching: Reorienting Research on Categories in Strategy, Entrepreneurship, and Organization Theory." *Journal of Management Studies* 50: 1100–1123.

Espeland, W. N., and M. Sauder. 2007. "Rankings and Reactivity: How Public Measures Recreate Social Worlds." *American Journal of Sociology* 113: 1–40.

Garud, R. 2008. "Conferences as Venues for the Configuration of Emerging Organizational Fields: The Case of Cochlear Implants." *Journal of Management Studies* 45: 1061–1088.

Garud, R., H. A. Schildt, and T. K. Lant. 2014. "Entrepreneurial Storytelling, Future Expectations, and the Paradox of Legitimacy." *Organization Science* 25: 1479–1492.

Gerbert, P., and F. Ruess. 2018. *The Next Decade in Quantum Computing-and How to Play*. Boston Consulting Group.

Glaser, B. G., and A. L. Strauss. 1967. *The Discovery of Grounded Theory: Strategies for Qualitative Research*. Piscataway, NJ: Transaction publishers.

Granqvist, N., S. Grodal, and J. L. Woolley. 2013. "Hedging Your Bets: Explaining Executives' Market Labeling Strategies in Nanotechnology." *Organization Science* 24: 395–413.

Granqvist, N., and R. Gustafsson. 2016. "Temporal Institutional Work." *Academy of Management Journal* 59: 1009–1035.

Granqvist, N., and T. Ritvala. 2016. "Beyond Prototypes: Drivers of Market Categorization in Functional Foods and Nanotechnology." *Journal of Management Studies* 53: 210–237.

Grodal, S. 2018. "Field Expansion and Contraction: How Communities Shape Social and Symbolic Boundaries." *Administrative Science Quarterly* 63: 783–818.

Grodal, S., A. Gotsopoulos, and F. F. Suarez. 2015. "The Coevolution of Technologies and Categories During Industry Emergence." *Academy of Management Review* 40: 423–445.

Haddad, M., and G. Chinasi-Halet. 2019. *Quantum Computing, a Technology of the Future Already Present*. PwC.

Hazan, E., A. Ménard, I. Ostojic, and M. Patel. 2020. *The Next Tech Revolution: Quantum Computing*. McKinsey and Company.

Helfat, C. E., and M. B. Lieberman. 2002. "The Birth of Capabilities: Market Entry and the Importance of pre-History." *Industrial and Corporate Change* 11: 725–760.

Hsu, G., P. W. Roberts, and A. Swaminathan. 2012. "Evaluative Schemas and the Mediating Role of Critics." *Organization Science* 23: 83–97.

Kaplan, S., and W. J. Orlikowski. 2013. "Temporal Work in Strategy Making." *Organization Science* 24: 965–995.

Kennedy, M. T., and P. C. Fiss. 2013. "An Ontological Turn in Categories Research." *Journal of Management Studies* 50: 1138–1154.

Khaire, M., and R. D. Wadhwani. 2010. "Changing Landscapes: The Construction of Meaning and Value in a new Market Category—Modern Indian art." *Academy of Management Journal* 53: 1281–1304.

Lampel, J., and A. D. Meyer. 2008. "Field-configuring Events as Structuring Mechanisms: how Conferences, Ceremonies, and Trade Shows Constitute new Technologies, Industries, and Market." *Journal of Management Studies* 45: 1025–1035.

Langione, M., J.-F. Bobier, C. Meier, S. Hasenfuss, and U. Schulze. 2019a. *Will Quantum Computing Transform Biopharma R and D*. Boston Consulting Group.

Langione, M., C. Tillemann-Dick, A. Kumar, and V. Taneja. 2019b. *Where Will Quantum Computers Create Value— and When?*. Boston Consulting Group.

Langley, A. 1999. "Strategies for Theorizing from Process Data." *Academy of Management Review* 24: 691–710.

Lee, B. H., S. R. Hiatt, and M. Lounsbury. 2017. "Market Mediators and the Trade-Offs of Legitimacy-Seeking Behaviors in a Nascent Category." *Organization Science* 28: 1–18.

Lee, P., S. Stewart, J. Loucks, and C. Arkenberg. 2019. *Technology, Media, and Telecommunications Predictions*. Deloitte.

Ménard, A., I. Ostojic, M. Patel, and D. Volz. 2020, February. "A Game Plan for Quantum Computing." *McKinsey Quarterly*.

Moeen, M., and W. Mitchell. 2020. "How do pre-Entrants to the Industry Incubation Stage Choose Between Alliances and Acquisitions for Technical Capabilities and Specialized Complementary Assets?" *Strategic Management Journal* 41: 1450–1489.

Mohseni, M., Read, P., Neven, H., Boixo, S., Denchev, V., Babbush, R., Fowler A. Smelyanskiy, V., & Martinis, J. (2017). Commercialize Quantum Technologies in Five Years. *Nature*, 543, 171-174.

Paraoanu, G. S. 2011. "Quantum Computing: Theoretical Versus Practical Possibility." *Physics in Perspective* 13: 359–372.

Pontikes, E., and V. Rindova. 2020. "Shaping Markets Through Temporal, Constructive, and Interactive Agency." *Strategy Science* 5: 149–159.

Preskill, J. 2018. "Quantum Computing in the NISQ era and Beyond." *Quantum* 2: 79.

Pwc, and Russian Quantum. 2017. *Information Security in the Age of Quantum Technology*. PwC.

Rotolo, D., D. Hicks, and B. R. Martin. 2015. "What is an Emerging Technology?" *Research Policy* 44: 1827–1843.

Ruef, M., and K. Patterson. 2009. "Credit and Classification: The Impact of Industry Boundaries in Nineteenth Century America." *Administrative Science Quarterly* 54: 486–520.

Russo, M., A. Thaker, and S. Adam. 2018. *The Coming Quantum Leap in Computing*. The Boston Consulting Group and BCG Henderson Institute.

Santos, F. M., and K. M. Eisenhardt. 2009. "Constructing Markets and Shaping Boundaries: Entrepreneurial Power in Nascent Fields." *Academy of Management Journal* 52: 643–671.

Schatsky, D., and R. K. Puliyakodil. 2017. *From Fantasy to Reality: Quantum Computing is Coming to the Marketplace*. Deloitte University Press.

Stigler, G. J. 1962. "Information in the Labor Market." *Journal of Political Economy* 70: 49–73.

Suarez, F. F., S. Grodal, and A. Gotsopoulos. 2015. "Perfect Timing? Dominant Category, Dominant Design, And The Window Of Opportunity For Firm Entry." *Strategic Management Journal* 36: 437–448.

Vermaas, P. E. 2017. "The Societal Impact of the Emerging Quantum Technologies: a Renewed Urgency to Make Quantum Theory Understandable." *Ethics & Information Technology* 19: 241–246.

Vernacchia, S. 2019. *Quantum Leap: Advancing a Strategy for Quantum Computing that Will Inspire, Support and Safeguard Economic Growth in the Middle East*. World Government Summit 2019 & PwC.

Ward, C., Y. Lu, C. Y. Lam, and A. Lamas-Linares. 2020. *In Quantum We Trust*. Accenture Pte Ltd and SpeQtral Pte Ltd.

Zhao, E. Y., M. Ishihara, P. D. Jennings, and M. Lounsbury. 2018. "Optimal Distinctiveness in the Console Video Game Industry: An Exemplar-Based Model of Proto-Category Evolution." *Organization Science* 29: 588–611.

Zuckerman, E. W. 1999. "The Categorical Imperative: Securities Analysts and the Illegitimacy Discount." *American Journal of Sociology* 104: 1398–1438.

Exploring landscapes of quantum technology with Patent Network Analysis

Syuan-Yi Jiang and Shin-Liang Chen

ABSTRACT
While the new chapter of quantum technologies is bringing transformative changes to our society, a quantum ecosystem, which synergises the supportive activities from both social and scientific & technological sides, is acknowledged as a critical force to push the movements. Despite the importance of a quantum ecosystem, current articles barely illustrated its interconnected relations, essential elements and the long-term attributes of developing technologies. We apply the innovation ecosystem and social-technical system theories to bridge such research gaps by realising the patent network analysis. The analytical contents include focal actors, main technological clusters and technological trajectory, and most of them correspond to relevant reports. Particularly, quantum computation is an eye-catching subfield due to its high and intensive knowledge engagements in the past years. Last, we conclude the analytical results and provide two discussions in the discussion & conclusion section as the main contributions. One is to illustrate the long-term attributes and backgrounds of the analytical contents through the lens of the multi-level perspective framework. The other illustrates a path toward a focal actor.

1. Introduction

1.1. Quantum technology

The *quantum* of an object is the smallest unit (if there exists) composing it. Normally, a quantum is so small, say, smaller than 1 nanometer, that we cannot manipulate it or predict its motion by Newton's laws. *Quantum theory* is currently the only theory that can explain and predict the behaviour of such a tiny object. Since we human beings live in a large-scale world, there are many phenomena in quantum theory, dubbed as *quantum phenomena*, that are counterintuitive to our daily life. The famous 'Schrödinger's cat' is one of the instances (Schrödinger 1935). If some of these counterintuitive quantum phenomena have applications in our technological advancement, we call such integrations between quantum theory and technology as *quantum technology*.

The revolution of quantum technology can be divided into two stages (Jaeger 2018). Starting from the early of 1900, the first revolution of quantum technology appeared most in semiconductor materials, as they are stable and easier to manipulate and manufacture. Today, we benefit from many applications in the first revolution, such as laser (The Nobel Prize in Physics 1964), the photoelectric effect (The Nobel Prize in Physics 1921) and electrical signals. Also, nuclear magnetic resonance (The Nobel Prize in Physics 1952) enables us to create medical devices such as magnetic resonance imaging. The display devices based on quantum dots can produce pure monochromatic colour (Wood and Bulović 2010).

The second revolution is based on the unusual quantum phenomena (Jaeger 2018), such as *quantum entanglement* (Horodecki et al. 2009), *quantum coherence* (Streltsov et al. 2017), *superposition* (Nielsen et al. 2010), *and these* phenomena are hard to observe in semiconductor materials with the usual environment (e.g. the temperature or pressure). The applications of the second revolution are still under exploration and development in different fields of quantum technologies. The main categories of the quantum technologies include 'quantum computation', 'quantum communication', 'quantum simulation', 'quantum sensing', and 'quantum theory' (Acín et al. 2018).

Note that the physical principles behind the quantum phenomena of the two quantum revolution are different. Therefore, companies or institutions with advantages in the first quantum revolution do not necessarily imply they also have advantages in the second revolution.

Quantum technologies are bringing fundamental changes to our society. In commerce, the quantum annealing algorithm is used to solve budget pricing in auctions, phylogenetics, satellite scheduling, etc., problems (McGeoch et al. 2019). Quantum cryptography is used in some high-security need institutions, such as banks, governments (Riedel et al. 2017). Post-quantum cryptography standardisation brings the security and interoperability on communications protocols between classic and quantum computers (Beullens et al. 2021; Moody et al. 2020). Due to the advantages of calculating particle dynamics, quantum simulation and quantum computing are expected to accelerate the development of new drugs (Popkin 2019). Generally, quantum technologies are changing the infrastructural settings gradually in different aspects and thus lead to systematic transition in the following decades.

Despite the optimism of quantum applications, the developing process is facing several challenges on both scientific & technological and social sides. On the scientific & technological side, scalability, controllability and applicability are the issues. In labs, scientists could control quantum machines under 20 qubits (Acín et al. 2018). However, the key milestone toward a commercial quantum computer is a machine that can successfully operate around 100 logic qubits simultaneously (Acín et al. 2018). Also, although a superconducting circuit has advantages of integrating the wide types of qubit-based devices, the circuit is limited to its fabrication production and device parameter adjustment. The 'quantum supremacy' only exists if there are killer applications that operate better than classic computers, such as simulating molecular dynamics (Shen and Yang 2018). Solutions from various disciplines, such as engineers, data scientists, etc., matter to these challenges.

On the social side, talents and networking activities are critical to build the quantum ecosystem (Kagermann et al. 2020). Currently, numerous projects are to enhance these critical elements, such as Quantum Flagship[1] of European Commission (Mlynek 2021), a national quantum initiative[2] (Monroe et al. 2019) of the USA, the 13th five-year plan of China (People's Republic of China 2016–2020) or the Global University Programs[3] from global companies. Generally, these projects aim to create a quantum ecosystem, which increases resource engagement in science and technologies (Zhang et al. 2019), the encouragement to the industry involvement (Knight and Walmsley 2019), and cultivation of talents and the curiosity culture (National Science and Technology Council (U.S.) 2018).

In summary, the success of quantum technologies relies on the contributions between social and scientific & technological sides, and the quantum ecosystem is critical to push the movement of quantum technologies.

2. Research gap

Some research gaps remain in current studies. While policymakers acknowledge the importance of a quantum ecosystem, articles seldom presented its contents, such as the interconnectedness relations between sub-fields and elements simultaneously. Also, since the progress of quantum technologies is a long-term race, understanding the aggregations in the past time is important to resource allocations and blueprint making.

Thus, our research questions conclude as follows: How does the quantum ecosystem look like? Specifically, how the subfields of quantum technologies and the elements interconnect? Last, what elements in the ecosystem we should notice for long-term plans?

3. Theoretical background

3.1. Innovation ecosystem and multi-level perspective

We apply the theories of the innovation ecosystem and the social-technical system & multi-level perspective framework to answer the research questions. While the innovation ecosystem describes the necessary elements for the innovation activities (Granstrand and Holgersson 2020), the social-technical system emphasizes the long-term co-evolutionary progress between technological and social sides in a multi-level perspective framework (Geels 2004; Markard and Truffer 2008). Generally, the innovation ecosystem tells us the basic components to create similar innovative activities continually. The social-technical system tells us how those innovative activities are becoming popular and then change our society transformatively. In practice, we can find numerous cases, such as the Internet, computers, to be illustrated by the two theories. Thus, we believe it is appropriate to apply the two theories to the quantum technology case.

The common thread of the social-technical system and innovation ecosystem relies on similar elements, including the actor (such as university or company), the artefact (such as technology), and interconnectedness (such as the institution or co-created value activities). The artefact, especially the technology, could act as a driving force to the innovation activities and the linkages to connect various actors in the ecosystem (Amitrano et al. 2018).

In some studies, an innovation ecosystem also refers to the social-technical system (Nykänen 2017) or relevant to the social-technical system design (Pasmore et al. 2019; Baxter and Sommerville 2011). The actor acts as a receiver of social awareness in the environment. In the meanwhile, the actor also acts as the moderator in the production side to respond the messages from the enviornment (Walrave et al. 2018). Since an actor acts as the information channel between the social and production sides, the actor is at the front line to feel the transition activities in society. The actor is also the essential unit to participate in the evolutionary events in the ecosystem (Granstrand and Holgersson 2020).

Scholars had broadly used the social-technical system theory to analyze the profound transition activities in the society in a multi-level perspective framework (Geels 2005; Müller and Blanquart 2018). From top to bottom, the multi-level perspective framework is a three-layer analytical framework, including social-technical landscape, social-technical regime and technological niche level. The social-technical landscape stands for exogenous contents in the environment, such as the public awareness of quantum supremacy. The social-technical regime represents groups of opinion leaders in the society, who usually have a decisive influence on the rule-making activities, such as government, scientist, industrial experts. The technological group in the social-technical regime level represents the actors who dominate the mainstream technologies. Technologies in the technological niche level represent those under exploring or not well-accepted by current society. At the technological niche level, a technological trajectory converges from relative technological paradigms with continual improvements from technical regimes, such as the engineers in similar industries (Dosi 1982). A technological trajectory represents a knowledge accumulation path with updated advancements from engineers in the long run. The technologies in the technological niche level may level up to be the mainstream technology in the social-technical regime level for many possibilities, such as the rising of unexpected infectious diseases in the landscape level, a breakthrough technology in the niche level, policy (lobbying) in the regime level (Müller and Blanquart 2018; Edmondson, Kern, and Rogge 2019).

Despite the similarities between the social-technical system and innovation ecosystems, one major notion is that the social-technical system emphasizes long-term and sustainable properties (Geels 2019). The second major difference is that the key driving forces of innovations. While the innovation ecosystem emphasizes the strength of elements, especially actors, technologies and their interconnectedness, the social-technical system emphasizes the forces in multi-levels and their mutual effects to change the society transformatively. The personal hygiene case described such complex relations and mutual effects (Geels 2005).

These differences lead to preferred methods and relavant critics. While social-technical system studies usually used multiple cases in a wide range of period to interpret such long-lasting transition, innovation ecosystem studies usually adopted empirical analysis and figures in a relatively short term. The former studies heavily rely on the insights of experienced scholars, and thus it has been requested to add more empirical analysis for a long time (Geels 2019). Although the latter studies provide objective figures, sometimes the analytical results did not fit the understandings from the practical side. For instance, China has many patents of the 5G technologies, but it does not guarantee that China is the leader in the international infrastructural setting activities (Noble, Mutimear, and Vary 2019).

In short, both theories provide insights into the innovation activities, and we may learn a better and complete story of innovation activities if we take advantages of both theories.

4. Research method

We apply network analysis on patent data from the United States Patent and Trademark Office (USPTO) to answer research questions. We utilise granted patents in the USPTO to investigate quantum technologies due to several reasons. First, the patent is a common source of innovation studies in academia. Second, a granted patent is a technical document and an instrument to protect the potential markets in the future. The United States is a competitive market and a main driving force of quantum technology. Third, since applying a patent requires much cost, the continual patent publications reflect strong commitments and expectation on values to the future. Fourth, it is less complicated to construct a well-linked patent network structure as an ecosystem in a nation scope.

In views of the social-technical system, we propose that the granted patents reflect the entire system for two reasons. First, the motivations to apply for patents are complicated and highly affected by the environment. The motivations may include market protection, policy encouragement, creating standard-like architecture, technological progress, catch-up strategy, etc., and these motivations seldom exist independently (Blind, Pohlisch, and Zi 2018). Second, a granted patent is like a qualified product that wins recognitions from representative actors, such as engineers from the technical side, examinators from the government, and assignees (companies) from the market side, etc. These attributes allow the granted patent to be one representative data to reflect the social-technical system.

We focus on the network analysis method instead of quantity indicators, such as the number of citations, number of inventors, or number of forward citations,etc. The network analysis has its advantage on the feature investigation in many nodes with complex connections (De Nooy, Mrvar, and Batagelj 2018). We rely on positions and connections in the network structure to find significant patents or interested actors, such as the alliance-like structure in the network. The network method has been used to investigate various ecosystems, such as knowledge and business ecosystems (Clarysse et al. 2014), food, pharmacy ecosystem, etc. (Ashton 2008). In this study, we rely on patent citation relations to construct the quantum ecosystem.

To obtain the initial and most general patents of quantum technologies, we queried 'quantum' in the Google BigQuery database[4] from 2000 to June 2020. As a result, we searched 1,531 patents which top terms include 'quantum' in its patent description. Then, we expanded relevant patents by their forward and backward citations in the PatentsView database (Baker 2019). Finally, a weakly connected citation network with 8,343 patents is created and mapped by the VOSviewer[5] (van Eck and Waltman 2010).

We focus on the two analytical units, technology and actors, in the innovation ecosystem (Granstrand and Holgersson 2020). Then, we investigate the technological trajectory and focal actors as the outcome of the long-term co-evolutionary process of quantum technologies.

In the technology element, we first reveal 35 innovation topics of the quantum innovation via the community detection algorithm - Louvain Method (Multi-level coarsening + Multi-level refinement), which is based on the measurement of the link density in a subnetwork in the Pajek software[6] (De Nooy, Mrvar, and Batagelj 2018). Then, we rely on the modularity score to measure the fitness of cluster detection. The score ranges from 0 to 1. Usually, it would be a good clustering result if the modularity score is above 0.3 (Clauset, Newman, and Moore 2004). In this paper, we finalise the result of the cluster detection by relative high modularity scores, and the modularity score of cluster detection is 0.90.

We identified the technological trajectory by the main path analysis (Lu, Hsieh, and Liu 2016), a link connectivity measurement in the network. The identified trajectory is based on the maximum summation of knowledge flow in the entire network (Verspagen 2005). Thus, patents on the trajectory are the milestones to a field, and it is hard to skip them as developing technologies.

In the focal actor element, we define the focal actor as a player whose technologies are widely adopted or continually improved by third parties. We rely on the clique algorithm to find the focal actors. A clique is a complete subgraph that a pair of nodes that has at least one link, such as a triangle, which is the smallest clique. In other studies, the clique has been utilising to investigate innovative productivity (Gomez Solorzano, Tortoriello, and Soda 2019), social behaviours, such as bully behaviours (Lodder et al. 2016), social cohesion (Moody and White 2003). In our case, we first transform the technology citation network into a weighted assignee network. Then, we investigate the assignees in the largest clique by the R igraph package (Csardi and Nepusz 2006) as the focal actors in clusters.

5. Results

We arrange general, technological cluster, focal actor and technological trajectory analysis to reflect the framework of the multi-level perspective from top to bottom. The boundaries between levels are ambiguous due to the dynamic progress and mutual influence (Geels 2004; Geels 2005). Thus, we focus on the analytical contents and their backgrounds instead of classifying the analytical results in which levels specifically. This operation allows us to observe the social-technical system flexibly and effectively, which also fits the understanding of the prior studies. Further illustrations between empirical analysis and the social-technical system are presented in the conclusion & discussion section.

5.1. General analysis

Figure 1 presents the number of granted years of itsrelevant assignee type. The grey dash line shows the total number of the granted patents every year. The bar chart shows the assignees type. For instance, 82 patents of the 194 granted patents in 2019 belong to foreign companies.

As Figure 1 presents, the attention of quantum technologies is getting popular in recent three years. Most of the time, foreign companies withhold more granted patents than US companies, such as in 2018, 2017, 2014. However, the granted patents surge and the US company surpass the foreign company largely in recent years. Probably, these phenomena correspond to the relevant policies in the EU (Acín et al. 2018) and the United States (National Science and Technology Council (U.S.) 2018) in recent years.

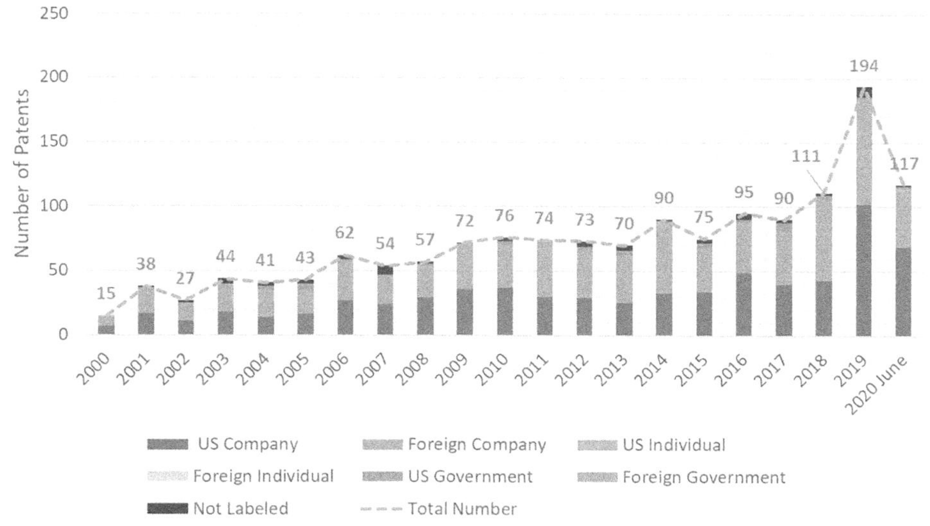

Figure 1. The number of granted patents in each year. The vertical axis represents the number of granted patents, while the horizontal axis is the year between 2000–2020. We also divide the total number of patents into the numbers claimed by the US companies, the US government, the non-US (foreigner) companies, and the foreign governments.

5.1.1. Technological Clusters

We classified the 8,343 patents into 35 clusters, as shown in Figure 2. Clusters whose number of patents are over 100 are identified as major nodes in the network. We label each cluster a

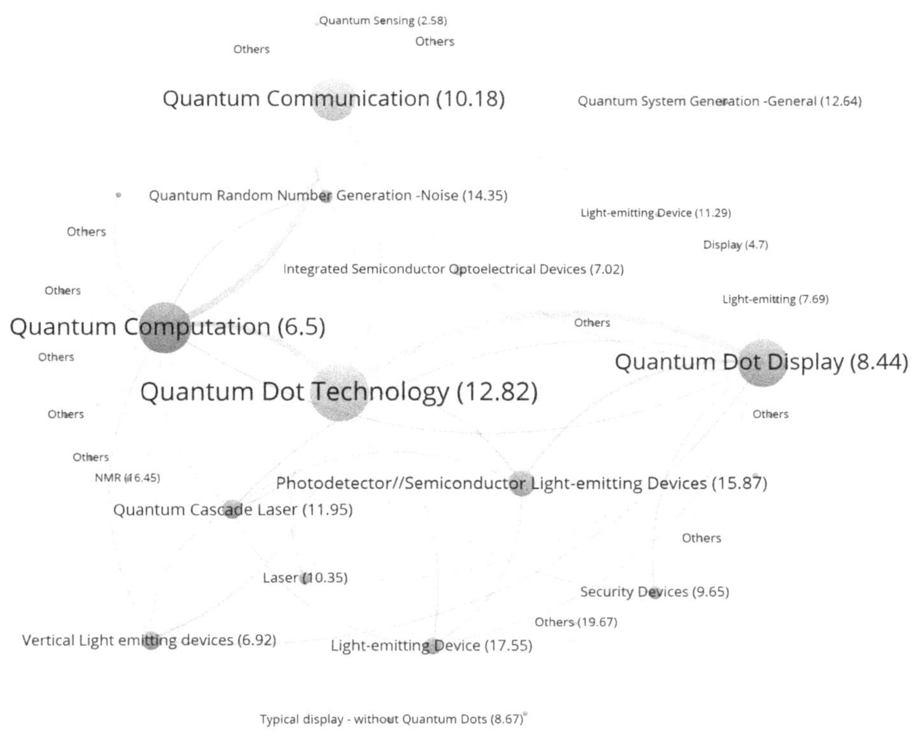

Figure 2. The patent network composed of patents related to quantum technology. Each cluster is the set of patents with the same category of quantum technology, while the link between two clusters describes their simplified citation relations.

Table 1. Keywords in the top 5 Technological Clusters. We obtain these keywords by reading the titles of the patents in the clusters and classify each cluster a proper category.

Rank	Configuration	Count	Accumulation	Keywords
1	Quantum Dot Display	1,775	21.28%	Quantum dots, light-emitting, LCD, LED, opsistor, optoelectronic devices, colloidal nanocrystals, electro-optical devices, lighting apparatus, Illumination system, nanocrystal, nanoparticle
2	Quantum Computation	1,377	37.78%	Quantum computing, quantum gate, quantum processor, quantum computer, quantum circuit, grover's algorithm, factoring numbers, adiabatic quantum computer, Josephson junctions, Deutsch-Jozsa's quantum algorithm, superconducting circuit, SQUID
3	Quantum Communication	990	49.65%	Quantum key generation, quantum cryptography, quantum repeater, quantum random number generator, quantum teleportation, key bank systems, watch dog detector
4	Quantum Dot Technology	850	59.83%	Quantum dot, light-emitting device, semiconductor device, optoelectronic, photovoltaic, superlattice
5	Photodetector & Semiconductor Light-emitting Devices	582	66.81%	Metalorganic chemical vapor deposition (MOCVD), light emitting, quantum well, photodetector, radiation detector, electromagnetic wave detector, superlattices

category by reading the titles and abstracts of patents. For instance, in the first rank of the cluster, most of the patents' titles contain 'quantum dots', 'electro-optical devices', 'LED', etc.; therefore, we label it as 'quantum dot display'. The keywords of the rest of the clusters can be found in Table 1.

The network composed of the clusters is summarised in Figure 2. The node's size represents the number of patents of the cluster, while the thickness of the link indicates the number of citations between two clusters. The number in the brackets is the median age of patents in a cluster. The median age of all clusters is 9.85. The age of a cluster implies whether the following technologies contribute to the relevant topics. Generally, quantum technologies are quite innovative and fresh because most of them are developed within 10 years. The older a cluster is, the progress of the technologies in that cluster is more steady or more mature. Considering that the patent protection period is 20 years, the older age of a patent implies losing much market value as time pass by. On the other hand, the younger age of a patent may indicate that it is still in an early stage of a technology or a market, and the value of a patent is barely significant. Thus, a better inference of the clusters should consider the number of patents and the cluster age.

Considering the technology significance and market application, we conclude four main clusters: quantum communication, quantum computation, quantum dot technology, and quantum dot display. Note that quantum sensing technology may be the next promising cluster after the four main clusters due to the popularity in recent three years.

As shown in Figure 2, quantum dot technology is essential to the quantum ecosystem, influencing other quantum technologies, such as quantum communication, quantum computation and quantum dot display. Quantum dot technology originates from the first quantum revolution. Since quantum dots emit monochromatic light, the most famous application is that they can improve the efficiency of light-emitting diodes (LED), or even more, they can be directly manufactured as displays (e.g. television display). Quantum dots also have quantum effects such as coherence and entanglement, so they have applications in the second quantum revolution, such as quantum computation (Loss and DiVincenzo 1998). The age of the quantum dot display cluster is 8.44, which is much younger than the age of the photodetector & semiconductor light-emitting devices cluster, which implies that the quantum dot technologies provide another life cycle of the display market. The quantum computation cluster should be the most eye-catching one due to its youngest age and relatively high number of patents among the four main clusters. That is, quantum computation won most public awareness and grew rapidly in recent years.

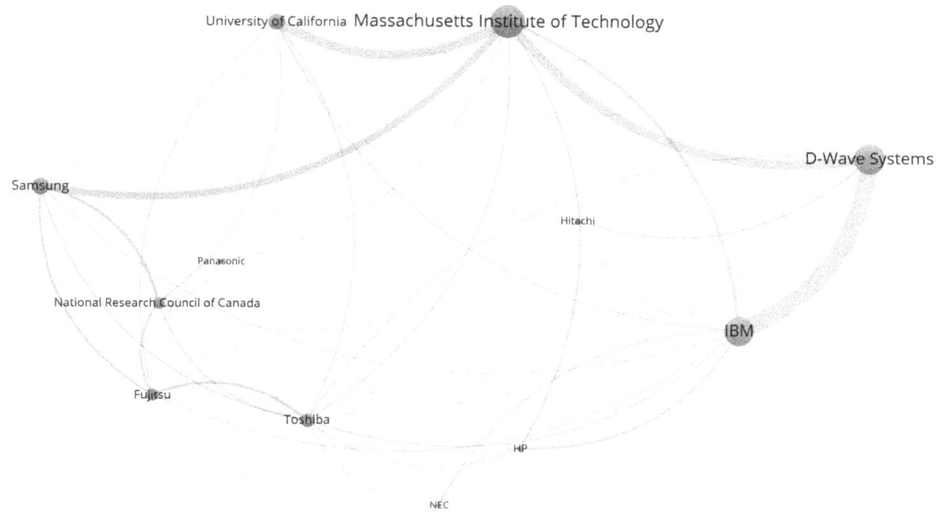

Figure 3. Focal actors of the global network. Each node is a set of patents of an assignee. The connection is the citation relation, which describes as the interactions between assignees.

5.2. Focal actors

Figure 3 shows the focal actors in the entire technology network. Although these focal actors connect each other, the weight of the links distinguishes the focal actors in groups. The assignees in the same colour group imply that they have more interactions within similar fields. On the other hand, the assignees connected between groups implies interactions and knowledge flows from different fields.

Academia institute, such as the University of California and Massachusetts Institute of Technology, plays one major role in the quantum ecosystem. The two academic actors have strong connections (frequent citations) with the other two assignees in different groups, such as Samsung in the red and D-Wave Systems in the green group. Since assignees in the green and red group seldom connected relatively, we infer that academic institutes are important knowledge mediators or provider to the ecosystem. The further analysis in the following section discloses that the red group is related to quantum dot display and photodetector & semiconductor light-emitting devices technologies, and the green group is related to quantum computation and quantum communication technologies.

Geographical location also affects the citation of the patents. For instance, most of the focal actors in the red group are from the Asia area, such as Samsung (Korea), Panasonic (Japan), Toshiba (Japan). Most of the focal actors in the green group are from North American area, such as D-wave systems (Canada) and IBM (US).

5.2.1. Focal actors of clusters

As shown in Figure 4, we see that the focal assignees are quite different in two revolutions of quantum technologies. For instance, most of the assignees from North America area, such as IBM, Magiq Technologies, and D-Wave Systems, dominate the second revolution of the quantum technologies, such as in the clusters of quantum computation and quantum communication. However, most of the assignees from Asia area, such as Samsung and Toshiba, Fujitsu, have more influences on the first revolution, such as quantum dot display clusters, quantum dot technology.

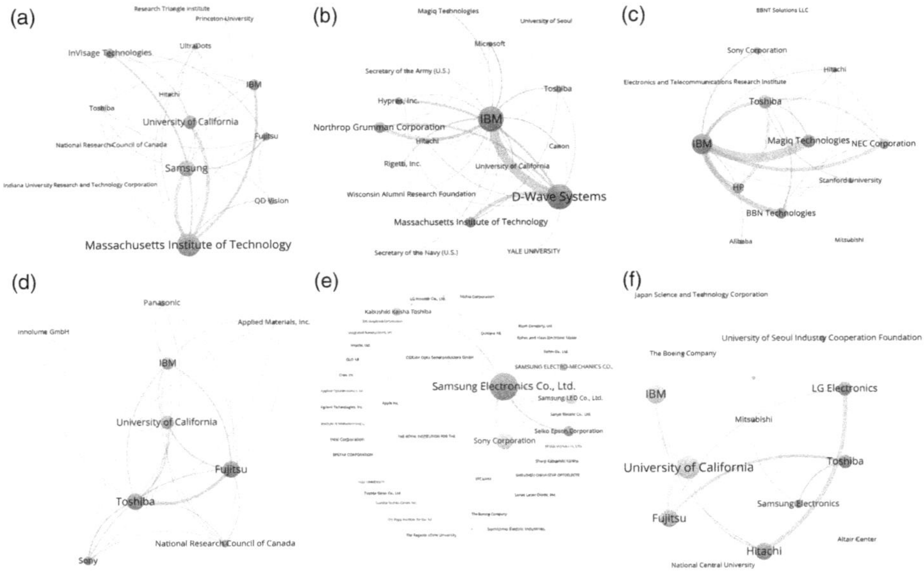

Figure 4. Focal actors of important quantum technologies. With the clique algorithm, we show the focal companies and institutions of the major quantum technologies. (a) Quantum dot display. (b) Quantum computation. (c) Quantum communication. (d) Quantum dot technology. (e) Photodetector and semiconductor light-emitting devices. (f) Vertical light-emitting devices.

Most of the assignees are specialised in certain technological topics. For instance, Samsung is an active and key players in quantum dot display and quantum dot display clusters. Thus, it is reasonable to infer that Samsung has more capabilities in manufacturing quantum dot display devices.

Although IBM is active in different clusters and plays a key role, we can see that IBM still focuses on certain clusters, such as quantum computation and quantum communication cluster, compared with other clusters. D-Wave Systems is the only focal assignee which only focuses on the field of quantum computation. Among the top clusters, quantum computation is the most special one

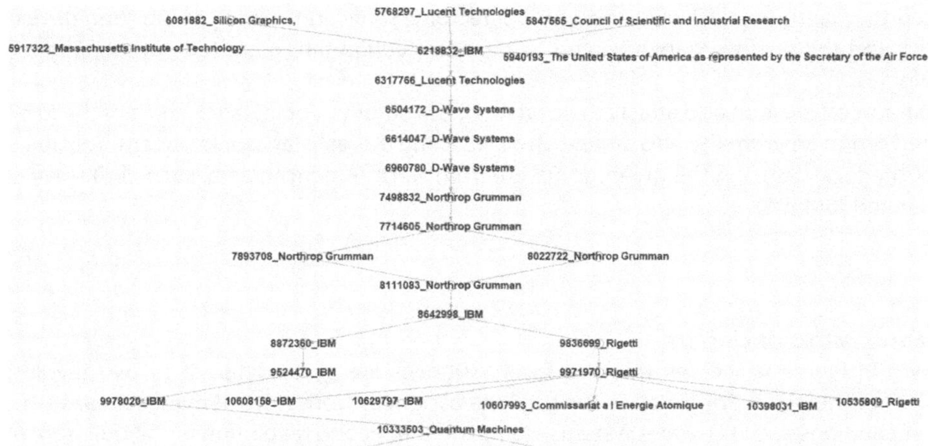

Figure 5. The evolution of the patents of quantum technology. We search for the 'main branches' from the patent network, which are with the most patents summing from the source patents to the sink patents.

due to its focal assignees from governments, including the Secretary of the Army, Secretary of the Navy. Figure 4 presents other focal assignees in the clusters.

5.3. Technological trajectory

Figure 5 shows the technological trajectory in the entire technological network. Relevant patent number and assignee are labelled on each node. The patents on the trajectory happen to be the members in the quantum computation cluster, which implies that technologies of quantum computation have much higher knowledge density and continual refinement from prior arts. Patents on the trajectory are milestones to a specific field.

At first, IBM integrated the technologies (patent number: 6218832) from multiple sources, such as Secretary of the Army, Massachusetts Institute of Technology, Lucent technologies, etc. Then, technologies from D-Wave Systems are as the backbone until Northrop Grumman took over it. Northrop Grumman developed two paths and then integrated the routes on the trajectory. After the patent of IBM (patent number: 8642998), the applications of the technologies are divided into two paths. Rigetti Computing Inc dominates one, and IBM dominates the other. Note that IBM also had granted patents, such as patent 10398031, patent 10629797, which referenced the patents of Rigetti Computing Inc.

Based on the collection positions on the trajectory and counts of patents, we infer that IBM is relatively critical to quantum computation and the standardisation activities in the future. Because technologies of IBM had referenced most of the other assignees, such as D-Wave Systems, Northrop Grumman, Rigetti Computing Inc., the computation system of IBM should be the most compatible (interoperable) to different system designs.

6. Conclusion & discussion

Aside from presenting the innovation ecosystem of quantum technologies, there are other two contributions in this study. We promote using the patent data to reflect the phenomena in the social-technical system (Geels 2019). Also, we try to make our empirical analysis close to the understandings of practitioners (Noble, Mutimear, and Vary 2019), especially in the early stage of technological development—relevant illustrations presented as following.

6.1. Summary of the quantum ecosystem

We present the main subfields of quantum technologies and relevant actors interconnectedly in a quantum ecosystem. Generally, academic institutes are important knowledge providers. Technologies in the first revolution include quantum dot display and quantum dot technology, and the technologies in the second revolution include quantum computation, quantum communication and quantum sensing. While most of the focal assignees in the first revolution are from the Asian area, focal assignees in the second revolution are from the North American area. Quantum computation is the most competitive field due to its high knowledge density and continual refinement of the prior arts. Note that the different physical principles behind the revolutions lead to the discontinuity to the competitive advantages, and thus it may be the new opportunities for some new economies.

6.2. Insights from social-technical system

From the lens of the social-technical system, the analytical contents in Figure 1, Figure 2, and Figure 3 somehow reflect the phenomena at the social-technical landscape level. That is, quantum technologies obtain attention increasingly in the recent three years. The main categories of quantum technologies include quantum communication, quantum computation, quantum dot technology, quantum dot display, and quantum sensing technology, which corresponds to the official reports (Acín et al. 2018; National Science and Technology Council (U.S.) 2018). Thus, it is straightforward to accept that actors in Figure 3, such as IBM, D-Wave systems, Samsung, etc., are focal to quantum technologies in general.

The focal actors could be at the regime level and niche level at the same time. For instance, IBM is one focal actor in the current regime level, which dominates some technologies in the classic computer field or the quantum dot technology, as shown in Figure 4. Meanwhile, IBM is also one focal actor in quantum computation trajectory, as shown in Figure 5, which should be at the technological niche level in the current background.

A focal actor stays at different level in different field. For instance, Samsung is decisive in the quantum dot display field but do not have many involvements in the quantum communication field. If the quantum dot display technology becomes the mainstream technology on the display devices in the future, then Samsung should be one focal actor at the social-technical regime level, which is likely to be the provider of standard-like specifications in the industry. However, if the case is the quantum computation, Samsung is less likely to be the focal actors in the social-technical regime level. In short, the level and the importance of an actor depend on the analytical contents and its background.

Last, we demonstrate a technological trajectory of quantum computation as the instance in the technological niche level. Our analysis supports that quantum computation is likely to transform the world massively due to its high and intensive resource engagement in recent years. Those actors who are interested in quantum computation should not avoid the knowledge on the trajectory and possible litigation issues in the future. At the same time, those actors who are not involved in quantum computation should also notice the progress due to its spill-over effects on other technologies.

6.3. A path to be a focal actor

The acknowledgement of quantum supremacy increases the coopetition in the international world. Due to the data limitation, we do not mention the situation in other countries, especially China. China has invested many resources in quantum science, especially in quantum communication. In 2017, China launched a satellite, Mozi, for quantum experiments, and then Chinese scientists published an article on Nature, which is about the design and test on large scale information transmission (Gibney 2016). An official publication from the European Union also showed that China applied for patents aggressively than most countries in subfields of quantum information, including quantum key distribution, entanglement, cold-atom interferometry (Travagnin 2019). China is undoubtedly an ambitious player in quantum information. However, readers may wonder why our analytical results only reveal focal actors from the US, Canada and Japan, etc., without actors from China.[7]

Here we provide possible explanations on the missing of China as a focal country. First, our patent data is limited to a single country scope, and we only select granted patents instead of application patents. In our dataset, China ranks the 10th place of 1,531 granted patents with top quantum keywords, which is less than 100 patents. Generally, the United States focus on quantum computation. However, China puts more emphasis on quantum communication. These reasons may explain why we have fewer granted patents from China in the data pool.

Second, China is still a young player in (quantum) science, and it needs time and continual investment to be the focal actors in the ecosystem. Our study defines the focal actors as the players whose technologies are widely adopted or continually improved by third parties. In other words, it is not enough to apply for patents aggressively, and it also needs time to win recognition, such as granted patents, increasing forward citation from other players. Simultaneously, quantum applications are still in the exploring stage, which means that it is not clear to find out the best practice currently, and players are flexible to search or make better solutions. These reasons lead to the value uncertainty of patents from China, and it needs time to verify the role of China and its patent values.

Last, although technology is the prime importance in the multi-level perspective framework (Müller and Blanquart 2018), patent data as a presentation of the technology element is still a part of the entire social-technical system. Since there is no comprehensive data, which record all the events in the social-technical system (Geels 2019), we suggest that it may be more accessible to use several representative data, such as patents and others, simultaneously to investigate the transition in society.

Notes

1. Quantum Flagship website: https://qt.eu/about-quantum-flagship/
2. National Quantum Initiative website: https://www.quantum.gov/
3. IBM Global University Programs website: https://www.research.ibm.com/university/
4. See the webpage for more details: https://cloud.google.com/blog/products/data-analytics/expanding-your-patent-set-with-ml-and-bigquery
5. SNA Software – VOSviewer: https://www.vosviewer.com/
6. SNA Software - Pajek: http://mrvar.fdv.uni-lj.si/pajek/
7. We find the supporting materials on our focal actor analysis on a publication of European Union, "Patent analysis of selected quantum technologies", in 2019. Both articles indicated that IBM, D-wave, Northrop Grumann, Mass. Inst Tech and Toshiba, etc. are players in the quantum computation area. However, the publication denoted the significant patent applications from China and its importance in recent years, which is inconsistent to our analytical results.

Acknowledgement

We appreciate anonymous reviewers for improving the readability and enriching the contents. SYJ acknowledges the support of Ministry of Education Taiwan (Government Scholarship to Study Abroad / GSSA). SLC acknowledges the support of the Ministry of Science and Technology Taiwan (MOST Grants No. 108-2811-M-006-515).

Disclosure statement

No potential conflict of interest was reported by the author(s).

Funding

This work was supported by Ministry of Education Taiwan; Ministry of Science and Technology Taiwan.

Data availability statement

The data that support the findings of this study are openly available in the United States Patent and Trademark Office (USPTO) at [https://www.uspto.gov/], from the year of 2000 to June 2020.

ORCID

Syuan-Yi Jiang http://orcid.org/0000-0002-3952-5336
Shin-Liang Chen http://orcid.org/0000-0002-3453-4794

References

"The Nobel Prize in Physics 1921." *NobelPrize.org*. Accessed Sep. 30, 2020. https://www.nobelprize.org/prizes/physics/1921/summary/.

"The Nobel Prize in Physics 1952." *NobelPrize.org*. Accessed Sep. 30, 2020. https://www.nobelprize.org/prizes/physics/1952/summary/.

"The Nobel Prize in Physics 1964." *NobelPrize.org*. Accessed Sep. 30, 2020. https://www.nobelprize.org/prizes/physics/1964/summary/.

Acín, Antonio, Immanuel Bloch, Harry Buhrman, Tommaso Calarco, Christopher Eichler, Jens Eisert, Daniel Esteve, et al. 2018. "The Quantum Technologies Roadmap: a European Community View." *New Journal of Physics* 20 (8): 080201. doi:10.1088/1367-2630/aad1ea.

Amitrano, C. C., M. Tregua, T. R. Spena, and F. Bifulco. 2018. "On Technology in Innovation Systems and Innovation-Ecosystem Perspectives: A Cross-Linking Analysis." *Sustainability* 10 (10): 3744–3715.

Ashton, W. 2008. "Understanding the Organization of Industrial Ecosystems." *Journal of Industrial Ecology* 12 (1): 34–51. doi:10.1111/j.1530-9290.2008.00002.x.

Baker, C. *patentsview: An R Client to the "PatentsView" API*. 2019.

Baxter, G., and I. Sommerville. 2011. "Socio-technical Systems: From Design Methods to Systems Engineering." *Interacting with Computers* 23 (1): 4–17. doi:10.1016/j.intcom.2010.07.003.

Beullens, Ward, Jan-Pieter D'Anvers, Andreas Hülsing, Tanja Lange, Lorenz Panny, Cyprien de Saint Guilhem, and Nigel P. Smart. 2021. "Post-Quantum Cryptography: Current state and quantum mitigation." *European Union Agency for Cybersecurity (ENISA)*. doi: 10.2824/92307.

Blind, K., J. Pohlisch, and A. Zi. 2018. "Publishing, Patenting, and Standardization: Motives and Barriers of Scientists." *Research Policy* 47 (7): 1185–1197. doi:10.1016/j.respol.2018.03.011.

Clarysse, B., M. Wright, J. Bruneel, and A. Mahajan. 2014. "Creating Value in Ecosystems: Crossing the Chasm Between Knowledge and Business Ecosystems." *Research Policy* 43 (7): 1164–1176. doi:10.1016/j.respol.2014.04.014.

Clauset, A., M. E. J. Newman, and C. Moore. 2004. "Finding Community Structure in Very Large Networks." *Physical Review E* 70 (6): 066111. doi:10.1103/PhysRevE.70.066111.

Compilation and Translation Bureau, Central Committee of the Communist Party of China. 2016–2020. "13th Five-Year Plan For Economic and Social Development of the People's Republic of China (2016-2020)". China: National Development and Reform Commission (NDRC). Accessed Jan. 19, 2021. https://policy.asiapacificenergy.org/node/2509.

Csardi, Gabor, and Tamas Nepusz. 2006. "The Igraph Software Package for Complex Network Research." *InterJournal, Complex Systems* 1695 (5): 1–9

De Nooy, W. , A. Mrvar, and V. Batagelj. 2018. *Exploratory Social Network Analysis with Pajek: Revised and Expanded Edition for Updated Software (3rd ed.)*. Cambridge: Cambridge University Press.http://doi.org/10.1017/9781108565691

Dosi, G.. 1982. "Technological Paradigms and Technological Trajectories: A Suggested Interpretation of the Determinants and Directions of Technical Change." *Research Policy* 11 (3): 147–162. doi: 10.1016/0048-7333(82)90016-6.

Edmondson, D. L., F. Kern, and K. S. Rogge. 2019. "The co-Evolution of Policy Mixes and Socio-Technical Systems: Towards a Conceptual Framework of Policy mix Feedback in Sustainability Transitions." *Research Policy* 48 (10): 103555. doi:10.1016/j.respol.2018.03.010.

Geels, F. W. 2004. "From Sectoral Systems of Innovation to Socio-Technical Systems: Insights About Dynamics and Change from Sociology and Institutional Theory." *Research Policy* 33 (6): 897–920. doi:10.1016/j.respol.2004.01.015.

Geels, F. 2005. "Co-evolution of Technology and Society: The Transition in Water Supply and Personal Hygiene in the Netherlands (1850–1930)—a Case Study in Multi-Level Perspective." *Technology in Society* 27 (3): 363–397. doi:10.1016/j.techsoc.2005.04.008.

Geels, F. W. 2019. "Socio-technical Transitions to Sustainability: a Review of Criticisms and Elaborations of the Multi-Level Perspective." *Current Opinion in Environmental Sustainability* 39: 187–201. doi:10.1016/j.cosust.2019.06.009.

Gibney, E. 2016. "Chinese Satellite is one Giant Step for the Quantum Internet." *Nature* 535 (7613): 478–479. doi:10.1038/535478a.

Gomez Solorzano, M., M. Tortoriello, and G. Soda. "Instrumental and Affective Ties within the Lab: The Impact of Informal Cliques on Innovative Productivity." Social Science Research Network, Rochester, NY, SSRN Scholarly Paper ID 3396413, Apr. 2019. doi: 10.2139/ssrn.3396413.

Granstrand, O., and M. Holgersson. 2020. "Innovation Ecosystems: A Conceptual Review and a new Definition." *Technovation* 90-91: 102098. doi:10.1016/j.technovation.2019.102098.

Horodecki, Ryszard, Paweł Horodecki, Michał Horodecki, and Karol Horodecki. 2009. "Quantum Entanglement." *Reviews of Modern Physics* 81 (2): 865–942. http://dx.doi.org/10.1103/RevModPhys.81.865.

Jaeger, Lars. 2018. *The Second Quantum Revolution - From Entanglement to Quantum Computing and Other Super-Technologies*. Cham: Springer

Kagermann, Henning, Florian Süssenguth, Jorg Körner, and Annka Liepold. 2020. The Innovation Potential of Second-generation Quantum Technologies." National Academy of Science and Engineering (acatech) Germany.https://en.acatech.de/publication/the-innovation-potential-of-second-generation-quantum-technologies/

Knight, P., and I. Walmsley. 2019. "UK National Quantum Technology Programme." *Quantum Science and Technology* 4 (4): 040502. doi:10.1088/2058-9565/ab4346.

Lodder, G. M. A., R. H. J. Scholte, A. H. N. Cillessen, and M. Giletta. 2016. "Bully Victimization: Selection and Influence Within Adolescent Friendship Networks and Cliques." *Journal of Youth and Adolescence* 45: 132–144. doi:10.1007/s10964-015-0343-8.

Loss, D., and D. P. DiVincenzo. 1998. "Quantum Computation with Quantum Dots." *Physical Review A* 57 (1): 120–126. doi:10.1103/PhysRevA.57.120.

Lu, L. Y. Y., C.-H. Hsieh, and J. S. Liu. 2016. "Development Trajectory and Research Themes of Foresight." *Technological Forecasting and Social Change* 112: 347–356. doi:10.1016/j.techfore.2016.07.040.

Markard, J., and B. Truffer. 2008. "Technological Innovation Systems and the Multi-Level Perspective: Towards an Integrated Framework." *Research Policy* 37 (4): 596–615. doi:10.1016/j.respol.2008.01.004.

McGeoch, C. C., R. Harris, S. P. Reinhardt, and P. I. Bunyk. 2019. "Practical Annealing-Based Quantum Computing." *Computer* 52 (6): 38–46. doi:10.1109/MC.2019.2908836.

Mlynek, Jürgen. January 2021. "The European Quantum Flagship: First Results and Future Perspectives.." Fundamental Research 1 (1): 3–4. doi:10.1016/j.fmre.2021.01.003..

Monroe, Christopher, Michael G Raymer, and Jacob Taylor. 2019. "The U.S. National Quantum Initiative: From Act to action." *Science* 364 (6439): 440–442. http://dx.doi.org/10.1126/science.aax0578.

Moody, Dustin, Dustin Alagic, Daniel C Apon, David A Cooper, Quynh H Dang, John M Kelsey, Yi-Kai Liu, and et al. 2020. "Status Report on the Second Round of the NIST Post-Quantum Cryptography Standardization Process." *NIST*. doi:10.6028/nist.ir.8309.

Moody, J., and D. R. White. 2003. "Structural Cohesion and Embeddedness: A Hierarchical Concept of Social Groups." *American Sociological Review* 68 (1): 103–127. doi:10.2307/3088904.

Müller, S., and C. Blanquart. 2018. "The Inventor's Perspective on Conditions for Radical Innovations in Freight Transportation: Case Studies from France and Germany." *Journal of Innovation Economics & Management* 25 (1): 211–238.

Nielsen, Michael A, and Isaac L. Chuang. 2010. *Quantum Computation and Quantum Information*. 10th Anniversary Edition. Cambridge: Cambridge University Press. http://doi.org/10.1017/CBO9780511976667.

Noble, Matthew, J. Mutimear, and R. Vary. "Determining which companies are leading the 5G race." Wireless Technology, IAM-Media., Aug. 2019. Accessed: Apr. 28, 2021. [Online]. https://www.iam-media.com/frandseps/determining-which-companies-are-leading-5g-race.

Nykänen, P. 2017. "Chapter 7 - Implementation and Evaluation of E-Health Ecosystems in Two-Sided Markets." In *E-Health Two-Sided Markets*, edited by V. Vimarlund, 125–141. Academic Press.

Pasmore, W., S. Winby, S. A. Mohrman, and R. Vanasse. 2019. "Reflections: Sociotechnical Systems Design and Organization Change." *Journal of Change Management* 19 (2): 67–85. doi:10.1080/14697017.2018.1553761.

Popkin, G. 2019. "Waiting for the Quantum Simulation Revolution." *Physics* 12: 112–112. https://physics.aps.org/articles/v12/112.

Riedel, M. F., D. Binosi, R. Thew, and T. Calarco. 2017. "The European Quantum Technologies Flagship Programme." *Quantum Science and Technology* 2: 030501. doi:10.1088/2058-9565/aa6aca.

Schrödinger, E. 1935. "Die Gegenwärtige Situation in der Quantenmechanik." *Die Naturwissenschaften* 23 (48): 807–812. doi:10.1007/BF01491891.

Shen, L., and W. Yang. 2018. "Molecular Dynamics Simulations with Quantum Mechanics/Molecular Mechanics and Adaptive Neural Networks." *Journal of Chemical Theory and Computation* 14 (3): 1442–1455. doi:10.1021/acs.jctc.7b01195.

Streltsov, Alexander, Gerardo Adesso, and Martin B Plenio. 2017. "*Colloquium* : Quantum Coherence as a Resource." *Reviews of Modern Physics* 89 (4). http://dx.doi.org/10.1103/RevModPhys.89.041003.

Subcommittee on QIS; Committee on Science; National Science & Technology Council (U.S.). 2018. "National Strategic Overview for Quantum Information Science." https://www.hsdl.org/?view&did=816367.

Travagnin, M.. 2019. *Patent Analysis of Selected Quantum Technologies*. EUR 29614 EN. Luxembourg: Publications Office of the European Union. https://publications.jrc.ec.europa.eu/repository/handle/JRC115251.

van Eck, N. J., and L. Waltman. 2010. "Software Survey: VOSviewer, a Computer Program for Bibliometric Mapping." *Scientometrics* 84 (2): 523–538. doi:10.1007/s11192-009-0146-3.

Verspagen, B. "Mapping Technological Trajectories as Patent Citation Networks. A Study on the History of Fuel Cell Research." Maastricht University, Maastricht Economic Research Institute on Innovation and Technology (MERIT), 019, 2005. Accessed: Apr. 30, 2018. [Online]. https://ideas.repec.org/p/unm/umamer/2005019.html.

Walrave, B., M. Talmar, K. S. Podoynitsyna, A. G. L. Romme, and G. P. J. Verbong. 2018. "A Multi-Level Perspective on Innovation Ecosystems for Path-Breaking Innovation." *Technological Forecasting and Social Change* 136: 103–113. doi:10.1016/j.techfore.2017.04.011.

Wood, V., and V. Bulović. 2010. "Colloidal Quantum dot Light-Emitting Devices." *Nano Reviews* 1 (1): 5202. doi:10.3402/nano.v1i0.5202.

Zhang, Q., F. Xu, L. Li, N.-L. Liu, and J.-W. Pan. 2019. "Quantum Information Research in China." *Quantum Science and Technology* 4 (4): 040503. doi:10.1088/2058-9565/ab4bea.

The centrality and innovation performance of the quantum high-level innovation team: the moderating effect of structural holes

Yue Yang, Yi She, Jin Hong and QingQiu Gan

ABSTRACT

As a frontier area with a high threshold, quantum science research is often undertaken by high-level innovation teams. Previous work has rarely studied the impact of structured positions found in the network of high-level innovation teams on innovation. This area represents an important gap in our understanding given whether the central position in the network of high-level innovation teams is conducive to innovation and whether there are interactions between structural characteristics in the network. This article attempts to study the network characteristics of quantum innovation teams and their impacts on innovation performance. In this study, three quantum high-level innovation teams (Jianwei Pan, Guangcan Guo and Jiangfeng Du) of the University of Science and Technology of China were selected as research objects, and panel data for 143 researchers for 2010 to 2019 were constructed. We draw the following interesting conclusions. The degree centrality, closeness centrality and between centrality of the quantum high-level innovation team network have a positive impact on a team's innovation performance. Structural holes have no direct effect on innovation but actively moderate the positive impact of the three centralities on innovation performance.

1. Introduction

As one of the theoretical supports of modern physics, quantum science has become a breakthrough means to advance the development of science and technology, triggering a technological revolution with a wide-ranging and far-reaching impact. Quantum science represents the emergence of the 'second quantum revolution', and it has precipitated profound breakthroughs in the industrial economy, in social development, in national security and in other fields. Facing the increasing competition in the 'quantum battle', developed economies such as Europe and the United States took the lead in exploring the field of quantum sciences in as early as the 1960s. As shown in Table 1, governments have issued a series of policies and invested in every aspect of production, education and research. As a result, quantum science construction in Europe and the United States has achieved international status and great developments.

The level of quantum innovation team directly reflects the level of national quantum technology, so there is no doubt about the importance of quantum high-level innovation team research. Existing quantum-related research conducted in the current social sciences and humanities mainly refers to the qualitative description of the development of quantum science (Kumar, Altepeter, and Hall 2010;

Table 1. Development policies and plans of quantum science adopted in the United States/European Union/China.

	2007: DARPA includes quantum technology as a core technology foundation in its strategic plan.
	2009: NSF established and released the 'Quantum Information Science Interdisciplinary Research Program'.
	2009: NSTC published the Federal Vision for Quantum Information Science.
	2014: UMD and NIST established the Joint Center for Quantum Information and Computer Science (QuICS).
	2015: Quantum physics is listed as a strategic investment project by DARPA.
	2016: NSTC released the report 'Advancing the Development of Quantum Information Science: Challenges and Opportunities in the United States'.
	2016: NSF selected 'Advancing Communication Quantum Information Research in Engineering' as an emerging frontier research and innovation area.
	2016: DOE released the report 'Quantum Sensors Intersecting with Basic Science, Quantum Information Science and Computing'.
	2018: OSTP released the report 'National Strategic Overview for Quantum Information Science'.
European Union	2008: EU releases 'Quantum Information Processing and Communication Strategy Report'.
	2008: EU released a business white paper on quantum cryptography.
	2014: The UK has formulated a five-year quantum technology plan.
	2014: The Netherlands has formulated a 10-year quantum computing development plan.
	2016: The EU promulgated the 'Quantum Declaration'.
	2016: The UK has formulated a quantum technology labour training programme.
	2016: Germany announced the QUTEGA plan.
	2018: The EU launched the 'Quantum Technology Flagship Program'.
China	2006: 'The Eleventh Five-Year Plan' Launches Modern Metrology Benchmark Research Based on Quantum Physics.
	2011: Achieved 100-kilometer free space quantum teleportation and two-way entanglement distribution.
	2012: The Ministry of Science and Technology issued the 'Twelfth Five-Year Special Plan for the National Major Scientific Research Plan for Quantum Control Research'.
	2015: 'Thirteenth Five-Year Plan' deploy quantum communication technology project.
	2016: National Strategy of Innovation-Driven puts forward the development Quantum information technology.
	2017: Quantum secure communication 'Beijing-Shanghai trunk line' completed.
	2019: Catalogue for the Guidance of Industrial Restructuring Encourage R&D and Application of Quantum Communication Equipment.

Arun and Mishra 2014; Raymer and Monroe 2019), and there is very little research on quantum innovation teams. This article attempts to expose the network characteristics of quantum innovation teams through a study of Chinese quantum research teams. Previous studies on the social networks of enterprises and teams have focused on collaboration networks based on alliance partnerships (Gilsing et al. 2008; Vanhaverbeke, Gilsing, and Duysters 2012; Durmuşoğlu 2013; Gilsing, Vanhaverbeke, and Pieters 2014). However, the collaboration network is different from the knowledge network because the former is actually based on relations rather than knowledge (Dong and Yang 2016). We believe that the quantum innovation team network has two features, that is, it is a network based on relations and knowledge (Oh, Choi, and Kim 2005; Badar, Hite, and Ashraf 2015). Network centrality denotes the degree to which actors are at the centre of the network and is one of the most important structural attributes explored in network research (Freeman 1977; Dong and Yang 2016). Different centrality measures are used in network research, including degree, closeness and between centrality (Freeman 1978). Previous work has rarely studied the impact of structured positions found in high-level innovation team networks on innovation. This limitation forms an important gap in our understanding because if central positioning in the network of high-level innovation teams is conducive to innovation, the most helpful central location is not clear to researchers and actors (Dong and Yang 2016). Past research has largely discussed the direct impact of centrality and structural holes on innovation, but these may involve certain interactions that are also reflective of network characteristics.

Since the 1990s, Chinese universities and research institutions headed by the University of Science and Technology of China (USTC) have been actively following up on the latest developments in international quantum science research. In August 2016, the launch of the world's first quantum communication satellite 'Mozi' led by the USTC meant that China had reached the forefront in the industrialisation of quantum communications, which involves national information security. At present, quantum high-level innovation teams represented by Guangcan Guo, Jianwei Pan, Jiangfeng Du and others have formed. According to 'Quantum Technology 2.0 from the Global Patent Map'(2019) issued by the Center for Research and Development Strategy (CRDS) under the Japan Agency for the Promotion of Science and Technology, China owns 1,387 of the 4,088 quantum-related patents produced, ranking first in the world, while the United States ranks second with 921 patents. Therefore, the rise of quantum technology in China provides a suitable background for our research on quantum innovation teams. This paper takes Guo, Pan, and Du from the USTC as research objects to analyse the network characteristics of a quantum innovation team and their impact on innovation performance.

2. Literature review and theoretical hypotheses

2.1. High-level innovation teams

Katzenbach and Smith (1993) believe that a team is a group composed of two or more actors who have complementary abilities, follow the same rules, aim to achieve a shared vision, and assume common responsibilities. Based on the theory of organisational knowledge, Madsen and Desai (2010) put forward the following view: an organisation harbours a collection of knowledge and experience, and knowledge within the organisation will change as actors learn from experience and update their knowledge frequently. Due to mutual trust and communication among team actors, cooperation and shared responsibilities are ensured so that team performance far exceeds the total performance of individual actors. Based on the above theories and viewpoints, this study believes that the high-level innovation team is a team led by high-level researchers, aiming to achieve scientific research and major innovations in frontier fields, and team participants collaborate with each other and share responsibilities. These high-level innovation teams have two main characteristics: first, the team has high-level research and innovation capabilities; second, the research field is the frontier of global high-tech, such as nanomaterials, artificial intelligence and robots.

2.2. Social networks

Social network research has drawn the attention of many scholars as a new field of social science since it first emerged in the 1990s. The field has become a new research paradigm related to social capital research (Walker, Kogut, and Shan 1997; Burt 2000), knowledge diffusion (Cowan and Jonard 2004; Bell and Zaheer 2007), innovation research (Asheim and Isaksen 2002; Graf 2011), strategic research (Gilsing, Lemmens, and Duysters 2007; Hu et al. 2011) and organisational behaviour research (Landis 2016). Social networks refer to the collection of relationships between network actors, and relational data are generally used as research objects. As there are network connections between actors of high-level innovation teams, we can study the characteristics of high-level innovation teams from the perspective of social networks.

The combination of social network methods with bibliometrics is often used to study coauthor networks and innovation networks (Otte and Rousseau 2002). Actors act as nodes in a network, and connections and networks between them are formed when they work together (Newman 2004). It is precisely due to the intellectual characteristics of this social relationship that knowledge can flow within this network (Badar, Hite, and Ashraf 2015). Therefore, even when the coauthor and innovation network are collaboration network, they can also be called a knowledge network (Oh, Choi, and Kim 2005). Authors embedded in these knowledge networks can benefit from the flow of knowledge within the network through structural advantages (Badar, Hite, and Badir 2014) to produce beneficial results, including enhanced innovation performance (Badar, Hite, and Ashraf 2015).

2.3. Network centrality

In the social network literature, network centrality can be used to measure the structural advantages of actors in social networks. Network centrality can be defined as the degree to which actors are at the centre of the network, which reflects the nature and level of connections between network actors (Freeman 1978; Wasserman and Faust 1994; Houston et al. 2004; Wang et al. 2014). The term can be regarded as the difference in network connections between each actor (Sparrowe et al. 2001), reflecting the concentration of interactions among a few actors rather than even distribution among all actors (Tang and Ye 2015). Core actors within a cooperative network can benefit from knowledge flowing within the network, thereby achieving enhanced research results (Abbasi, Altmann, and Hossain 2011; Lee et al. 2012; Badar, Hite, and Ashraf 2015). Obtaining more network information can improve actors' awareness of available information, and differences in network locations can partially explain differences in the profitability of actors in the network (Stuart and Sorenson 2005; Ferriani, Cattani, and Baden-Fuller 2009). Freeman (1978) was the first to propose the presence of centrality in social networks, and the term has developed into degree, closeness and between centrality. These centralities are conceptualized and measured from different perspectives, which can characterise differences in the network relationships of actors (Valente et al. 2008; Dong and Yang 2016). Actors occupy different positions in each dimension of centrality, and the benefits of these positions may also differ (Badar, Hite, and Badir 2014; Badar, Hite, and Ashraf 2015). However, due to the costs, conflicts, pressures and random drifts associated with these positions, the benefits of structural centre positions may be reduced (Podolny and Baron 1997; Ahuja and Katila 2004; McFadyen and Cannella 2004; Rotolo and Messeni Petruzzelli 2013; Badar, Hite, and Ashraf 2015).

2.3.1. Degree centrality and innovation performance

As the most frequently used tool in the analysis of social network relationship centrality, degree centrality is measured from the number of direct connections between a node and other nodes in the network, reflecting the direct influence of the actor (Freeman 1978). Since degree centrality does not consider indirectly connected nodes, it is also called 'local centrality' (Badar, Hite, and Badir 2014). It is generally believed that if a node has a higher degree centrality than other nodes, it is located at the centre of the network, making it easier to facilitate information exchange and to secure more 'rights' (Badar, Hite, and Ashraf 2015). Actors with more collaborators in the network will show a high degree of concentration, providing these central authors with more shared knowledge, which they can use to improve their innovation performance (Badar, Hite, and Badir 2013; Badar, Hite, and Ashraf 2015). Dong and Yang (2016) use a panel dataset from the U.S. pharmaceutical industry to find that degree centrality in the corporate network is positively associated with subsequent new product development performance.

However, some scholars believe that establishing a coauthor relationship takes more time, attention and energy, including startup costs (Badar, Hite, and Ashraf 2015). Therefore, from the perspective of degree centrality, there is a limit to the number of collaborators that actors in the collaboration network can maintain, and there is no guarantee that collaborators will improve innovation performance (Zucker et al. 1995). Therefore, the presence of too many direct partners (that is, a high degree of concentration) may prevent actors from pursuing greater innovation performance (Badar, Hite, and Ashraf 2015). Wang et al. (2014) used patent data from a leading U.S. microprocessor manufacturer and found degree centrality in the collaboration network to have a negative effect. Some scholars believe that degree centrality may have both positive and negative effects on innovation performance: high levels of degree centrality can help increase mutual trust between subjects and provide convenient conditions for obtaining innovative resources, but degree centrality may create much redundant information when its levels are too high (Wang et al. 2014; Badar, Hite, and Ashraf 2015; Dong and Yang 2016).

When studying the networks of quantum high-level innovation teams, we recognise that actors with high levels of degree centrality have more direct contact with other actors and greater influence in the team. It is helpful to develop knowledge and technologies of quantum science between teams, and the diffusion and integration of knowledge are of great benefit for promoting innovation output. However, actors with lower levels of degree centrality are generally at the edge of the network and have less direct contact with other actors. These actors divorce themselves from others, which is not conducive to the sharing of knowledge and negatively affects innovation. Based on the above analysis, we propose the following hypothesis:

H1: The degree centrality of the quantum high-level innovation team network has a positive impact on teams' innovation performance.

2.3.2. Closeness centrality

Closeness centrality can be defined as the distance between actors in the network (Newman 2004). High centrality among actors indicates that they can access most knowledge flowing within the network (Perry-Smith and Shalley 2003). Therefore, more closeness centrality will cause knowledge to spread to actors faster and earlier (Badar, Hite, and Ashraf 2015) and improve an actor's innovation efficiency and performance. Although many actors in the network may create pressure and conflict due to them being positioned too close (Podolny and Baron 1997), lower levels of pressure and conflict that are easy to control may improve innovation performance (Badar, Hite, and Ashraf 2015). Frontier innovation teams such as quantum are more focused on more specific know-how, and are less susceptible to the negative effect of pressure and information noise (Yan and Guan 2018). Based on the above analysis, we propose the following hypothesis:

H2: The closeness centrality of the quantum high-level innovation team network has a positive impact on teams' innovation performance.

2.3.3. Between centrality

Between centrality can be defined as the degree to which an actor is positioned between other actors (Burt 2005; Badar, Hite, and Ashraf 2015), and it can also be interpreted as the frequency with which actors are located on the shortest path between other nodes in the network (Freeman 1978). Between centrality between actors involves the ability of actors to obtain and transmit relevant information to effectively solve problems (Mehra, Kilduff, and Brass 2001), so it reflects the degree to which each actor is structurally advantageous. The higher the between centrality of an actor is, the greater the actor's capacity to serve as a structural channel connecting other actors of the network becomes and thus the greater the variation in the degree to which actors dominate network knowledge transfer becomes (Tang and Ye 2015). Actors with connections across social gaps may acquire and use a large amount of non-redundant and diverse knowledge that can be used to enhance innovation performance (Badar, Hite, and Badir 2013).

However, some scholars argue that accessing different or non-redundant knowledge consumes time and resources (Gilsing et al. 2008). At the same time, non-redundant relationships may also spur random drift, causing the author's knowledge base to change in different and unrelated directions and making it difficult to absorb and integrate the various forms of knowledge acquired (Ahuja and Katila 2004; Badar, Hite, and Ashraf 2015). However, other studies conclude that the diversified knowledge of team actors contributes to team creativity (Jehn, Northcraft, and Neale 1999; Rodan and Galunic 2004; Tang and Ye 2015). Therefore, based on the above discussion, we propose the following hypothesis:

H3: The centrality of the quantum high-level innovation team network has a positive impact on teams' innovation performance.

2.4. Structural holes and innovation performance

Burt (1992), who first proposed the theory of structural holes, defined a structural hole as a 'non-redundant connection between two actors'. Because not all nodes have direct connections, structural holes are common in the network. Burt (2005) believes that a structural hole in a competitive advantage serves as a kind of social capital. Structural holes can generate social capital from two advantages: the first are information advantages, that is, structural holes can separate non-redundant information, so resources are enhanced rather than overlapped; the second are control or third-party advantages, which enable them to obtain benefits from their position as an intermediary (Tortoriello 2015). In simple terms, structural holes are gaps between unrelated individuals/groups in social networks, and the actors who occupy these gaps are 'bridgers'. The greater the difference in the span that can connect groups, the more difficult it is to replace the position of the structural hole. It is worth noting that the structural hole does not emphasise the ability of 'bridgers' to transmit and master information but to raise the information advantage to a control advantage and ultimately enhance personal influence in the network.

Past research is still inconclusive on the impact of structural holes on innovation. Wu et al. (2020) discovered a positive impact of structural holes on innovation performance in an artificial intelligence environment. However, Ahuja and Katila (2004) showed that an increase in structural holes in inter-firm collaboration networks has a negative impact on innovation. Guan and Wei (2015) compared the National Center for Nano Science and Technology of China and the California Institute of Nano-systems and found no significant relationship between structural holes and innovation. Structural holes in the network provide a supplementary resource exchange channel for the relatively dispersed network. When a node is located in a structural hole, it can obtain social capital gains from the position of the 'bridge' and obtain a competitive advantage through information and control advantages (Tortoriello 2015). Therefore, based on the above discussion, we propose the following hypothesis:

H4: The structural holes of the quantum high-level innovation team network have a positive impact on teams' innovation performance.

Past research has largely discussed the direct impacts of centrality and structural holes on innovation, but they may involve certain interactions that are also reflective of network characteristics. Degree centrality reflects the direct influence of actors (Freeman 1978). Actors with a more degree centrality can obtain direct information and knowledge from other actors. When an actor is positioned in structural hole, he can gain benefits from acting as an intermediary, which can raise the information advantage to a control advantage and ultimately enhance his personal influence in the network. When nodes are located in more structural holes, they can obtain more competitive advantages through information and control advantages (Tortoriello 2015). The control of speed and time allows the node to obtain more information from directly related nodes (Yan and Guan 2018), and the control and integration of information can improve innovation performance. Thus, we propose:

H4.1: The structural hole in the quantum high-level innovation team network positively moderates the effect of degree centrality on innovation performance.

Closeness centrality can be expressed as the distance between actors in the network (Newman 2004). Therefore, higher closeness centrality will cause knowledge to spread to an actor faster and earlier (Badar, Hite, and Ashraf 2015). When an actor is positioned in a structural hole, he can distinguish non-redundant information, identify increased but not overlapping resources, and promote efficient knowledge transfer. Therefore, when actors are located in more structural holes, more effective knowledge can be identified and transferred from closeness centrality to improve innovation performance. Thus, we propose:

H4.2: The structural hole in the quantum high-level innovation team network positively moderates the effect of closeness centrality on innovation performance.

Between centrality can be defined as the degree to which an actor is located between other actors (Burt 2005). Between centrality indicates the degree to which an actor serves as a structural pipeline

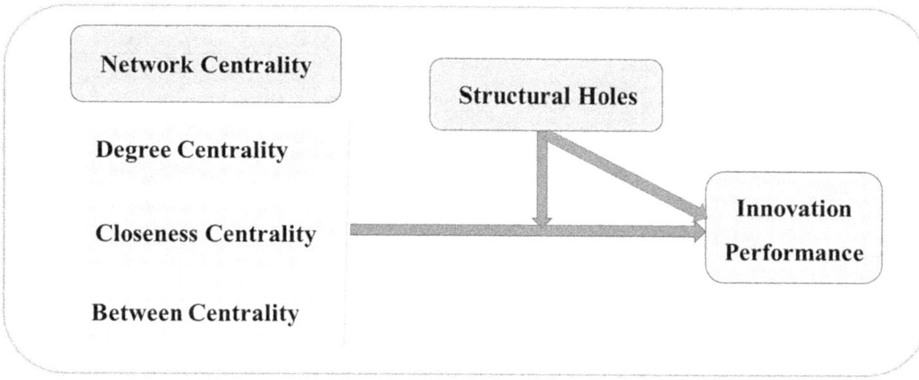

Figure 1. Structural model.

connecting other actors of the network. It is worth noting that the structural hole does not emphasise the ability for 'bridgers' to transmit and master information but to raise the information advantage to a control advantage and ultimately enhance personal influence in the network. It can be understood that the former pays more attention to the 'quantity' of the intermediary, while the latter pays more attention to its 'quality'. Therefore, we believe that mutual promotion should occur between the two. When actors are located in more structural holes, 'bridgers' will transmit and master richer and more important information from between centrality. Thus, we propose:

H4.3: The structural hole in the quantum high-level innovation team network positively moderates the effect of between centrality on innovation performance.

In summary, the hypothetical model is shown in Figure 1.

3. Methodology

3.1. Data collection

This study investigates the quantum high-level innovation teams represented by Guo Guangcan, Pan Jianwei, and Du Jiangfeng at the USTC. These teams are similar in size, and their leaders are academicians of the Chinese Academy of Sciences (CAS). The teams have won many honours and considerable funding support and have contributed a wealth of innovation performance. The teams are China's top quantum innovation teams with more interactions and connections. Therefore, the three teams are representative and selected as study objects.

We conducted interviews and surveys with three quantum innovation teams. Taking into account the main contributors of innovation performance, the research objects are identified as the professor and associate professor and postdoctoral of each team. We searched for articles published by each team from 2010 to 2019 on the Web of Science and drew a matrix diagram reflecting the relationships between actors according to the authors of the papers. Finally, we formed panel data on three teams of 143 actors. Table 2 lists descriptive statistics for the main variables.

3.2. Dependent variables

For innovation teams such as quantum high-level innovation teams, the publication status of papers can intuitively characterize their innovation performance. Generally, papers of higher quality are more likely to be published in journals with high impact factors (Levin and Stephan 1991). Therefore, we believe that compared to the number of papers published, the impact factor can better reflect

Table 2. Descriptive statistics for the variables.

Variables	*N*	Mean	S.D.	Min	Max
Gender	984	1.036	0.188	1	2
Age	984	34.842	8.100	20	77
Size	984	7.409	6.909	9	59
Relationship Strength	984	50.444	84.062	0	660
Network Density	984	72.342	32.315	0	100
The Amount of Cliques	984	3.052	5.218	0	59
Degree Centrality	984	17.647	25.218	0	233
Closeness Centrality	984	31.941	15.860	0	100
Between Centrality	984	2.617	10.103	0	81.56
Structural Holes Restriction	984	0.682	0.356	0	1.849
Innovation performance	984	35.936	50.891	1.355	526.51

the true level of innovation. We use a five-year comprehensive impact factor to avoid fluctuations in journal impact factors and provide a more objective evaluation (Della Sala and Grafman 2009). Therefore, the calculation formula is as follows:

$$Innovation\ performance = \sum_{i=1}^{n} F_{it} \tag{1}$$

where *Fit* represents the five-year comprehensive impact factor of the *i*-th paper for year *t*. Based on interviews and surveys with three quantum innovation teams, we found that the average publication time of papers is approximately two years. Therefore, we decided to lag the dependent variable by two years.

3.3. Independent variables

The degree centrality of a node is defined the number of other nodes directly connected to it (Freeman 1978). The formula for degree centrality is as follows:

$$C_D(n_{it}) = \sum_{jt} d_{ijt} \tag{2}$$

where d_{ijt} is 0 or 1 depending on whether nodes *i* and *j* are connected in year *t*.

Closeness centrality is used to measure the degree to which a node is located at the shortest distance between other nodes in the network (Freeman 1978). The formula for closeness centrality is as follows:

$$C_c = \left[\sum_{j=1}^{n} c_{ijt}\right]^{-1} \tag{3}$$

where c_{ijt} represents the shortest paths between nodes *i* and nodes *j* in year *t*.

Betweenness centrality is measured by the sum of distances between a node and other connected nodes in the network (Freeman 1978). The formula is as follows:

$$C_B = \sum_{j<k} b_{jkt}(i)/b_{jkt} \tag{4}$$

where b_{jkt} represents the number of lines with the shortest distance between nodes *i* and *j* in year *t*, $b_{jkt}(i)$ represents the number of shortcuts through the third nodes *i* that exist between *j* and *k* in year *t*. Collaborator network diagrams of the three quantum high-level innovation teams of the USTC are shown in Figure 2.

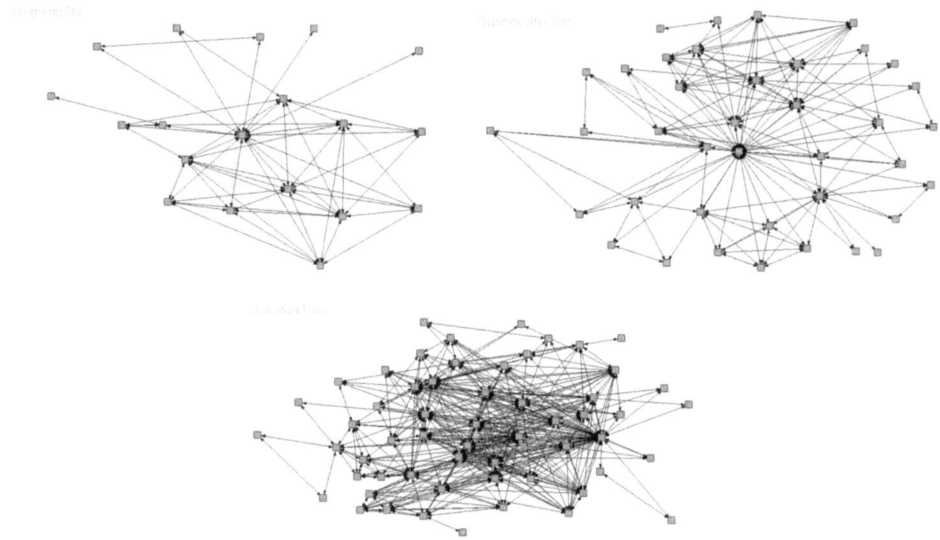

Figure 2. Network diagram of collaborators of Guangcan Guo, Jiangfeng Du, and Jianwei Pan for 2019.

3.4. Moderating variables

The structural hole index proposed by Burt (2009) generally considers four indicators: effective size, efficiency, constraint and hierarchy. Many studies conclude that constraints are the most important effective indicator and can effectively measure a lack of structural holes (Koka and Prescott 2008). The stronger the structural hole constraint of a network actor is, the fewer structural holes he has. The formula is as follows:

$$H_{ijt} = (P_{ijt} + \sum_{qt} P_{iqt}P_{jqt})^2 \tag{5}$$

where j represents all nodes connected to node i, q represents third-party nodes other than i and j, and P_{iqt} and P_{jqt} represent the degree of redundancy between i and j in year t, respectively. The lower constraints of the actors mean that the more 'bridges' they occupy, the stronger their ability to obtain information and knowledge becomes (Burt 1992).

3.5. Control variables

Given the influence of individual and network characteristics of the innovation team, we select six control variables. First, we select gender and age as individual control variables. Second, we use team size, the strength of relationships between actors, the density of the individual network and the number of cliques as network control variables.

Network size denotes the number of nodes in the network. A larger network can provide diversified resources and promote innovation performance (Landry, Amara, and Lamari 2002). Relationship strength refers to the total number of relationships between network actors that exclude the relationship between each actor and the 'self'. Network density represents the strength of links between actors in the network. Lower network density will create information asymmetry among actors, resulting in a decrease in mutual trust and hindering the diffusion of network knowledge (Schilling and Phelps 2007). The calculation formula is:

$$Network\ Denisty = Relationship\ strength/Pairs \tag{6}$$

Pairs refers to 'the sum of all relationships' of actors in the network. The calculation formula is:

$$Pairs = (number\ of\ network\ sizes) \times (number\ of\ network\ sizes - 1) \tag{7}$$

In graph theory, clique refers to the largest complete subgraph with at least three nodes. 'Quick' connections within and between cliques can promote network knowledge spillover, sharing and absorption (Lovejoy and Sinha 2010). The formula is:

$$N = \sum_t f(n_{it}) \tag{8}$$

where n_{it} represents all subgraphs of the cooperative network in year t, and n_{it} is the largest complete subgraph containing at least three nodes, $f(n_{it}) = 1$; otherwise, $f(n_{it}) = 0$.

4. Results and analysis

4.1. Regression analysis

We performed an *F*-test and *Hausman*-test to determine that the fixed effects model should be used. Our main regression results are shown in Table 3.

First, from the regression analysis of Model 1, the results indicate that degree centrality has a significantly positive impact on teams' innovation performance (*Coef* = 0.4226, $p < 0.01$***) and has significantly positive effects in Models 2, 3 and 6. Therefore, the results show that degree centrality promotes innovation performance, corroborating some previous studies (Badar, Hite, and Ashraf 2015; Dong and Yang 2016). Thus, hypothesis H1 is supported. Closeness centrality has a significantly positive impact on teams' innovation performance (*Coef* = 0.0742, $p < 0.1$*); thus, hypothesis H2 is supported. Between centrality has a significantly positive impact on teams' innovation performance (*Coef* = 0.6715, $p < 0.1$*); thus, hypothesis H3 is supported. These results illustrate that core actors with high levels of centrality in the cooperative network can benefit from knowledge flowing in the network, thereby achieving enhanced innovation efficiency and performance (Abbasi, Altmann, and Hossain 2011; Lee et al. 2012; Badar, Hite, and Ashraf 2015). In Model 2, structural holes have a positive but insignificant effect on innovation performance (*Coef* = −3.9627, $p > 0.1$),

Table 3. Regression analysis results.

Variable	Model 1	Model 2	Model 3	Model 4	Model 5	Model 6
Innovation (*T+2*)	FE	FE	FE	FE	FE	FE
Gender	−1.0873*	−4.6085*	−4.0646	−5.8267	−6.2459***	−6.9607***
Age	0.0101***	0.0103**	0.0109**	0.1122**	0.0109***	0.0139***
Size	−0.9575*	−1.1840*	−0.6891	−1.8904**	−1.6710*	−1.6236*
Relationship Strength	−0.3688***	−0.3649***	−0.4371***	−0.2931***	−0.3509***	−0.3709***
Network Density	0.0845***	0.1486**	0.0739*	0.1598***	0.1149*	0.1437**
The Amount of Cliques	7.2383***	7.3258***	6.8724***	7.2821***	7.4071***	6.7348***
Degree Centrality	0.4226***	0.4231***	0.9711***	0.2857**	0.4258***	0.8694***
Closeness Centrality	0.0742*	0.0771*	−0.0921	0.7485***	0.1367	0.6705***
Between Centrality	0.6715*	0.6900*	0.5838	0.4571	2.7052***	2.0017***
Structural Holes Restriction		−3.9627	−5.3938	2.1411*	−6.9827	16.1878
Degree Centrality * Structural Holes Restriction			−1.7242***			−1.4709***
Closeness Centrality * Structural Holes Restriction				−1.1030***		−1.0051***
Between Centrality * Structural Holes Restriction					−7.3573***	−6.6792***
Constant	7.8907	10.6912	13.9181	1.2803	16.2921	11.8653
Year	Y	Y	Y	Y	Y	Y
Observations	984	984	984	984	984	984
F-statistic	21.48	20.13	20.21	20.08	20.14	19.08

Note: (*T+2*) represents two periods of lag, $p < 0.01$***, $p < 0.05$**, $p < 0.1$*.

so hypothesis H4 is not supported. In short, the centrality of the quantum high-level innovation team has a significantly positive effect, but the structural hole has no direct effect.

Second, we added the interaction terms of three centrality and structural holes to Models 3, 4, and 5. The regression results show that structural holes have a positive moderating effect between centrality and innovation performance (*Coef* = −1.7242, −1.1030 and −7.3573, $p < 0.01$***), and they also have significant positive effects in Model 6. Therefore, hypotheses H4.1, H4.2 and H4.3 are supported. When the node is located in a structural hole, it can obtain social capital gains as a middleman and can obtain a competitive advantage through information and control advantages (Tortoriello 2015). Therefore, structural holes in the quantum high-level innovation team network positively moderate the effect of centrality on innovation performance.

According to the above regression results, the individual control variables of gender (*Coef* = −1.0873, $p < 0.1$*) have a significantly negative impact on innovation performance, indicating that women exhibit weaker performance than men. However, age (*Coef* = 0.0101, $p < 0.01$***) has a significant effect in promoting innovation performance, indicating that older actors achieve greater innovation performance. Among the network control variables, size (*Coef* = −0.9575, $p < 0.1$*) and relationship strength (*Coef* = −0.3688, $p < 0.01$***) have significantly negative effects. This result shows that the larger the team is and the stronger relationships between actors are, the less conducive conditions become to innovation. However, the number of cliques (*Coef* = 7.2383, $p < 0.01$***) and network density (*Coef* = 0.0845, $p < 0.01$***) have significantly positive effects. Cohesive subgroups usually exhibit high levels of knowledge overlap and transferability and can transfer knowledge and benefits smoothly to improve innovation (Snijders et al. 2006). Higher levels of network density will reduce information asymmetry between actors and promote mutual trust and network knowledge transfer (Schilling and Phelps 2007).

4.2. Robustness test

Finally, we conduct some robustness tests. We conduct an empirical analysis using the number of papers published as the dependent variable, and added past performance as a control variable. The regression results (Tables 3 and 4) are roughly the same as those given in Table 3. Therefore, the model used in this article is robust.

Table 4. Robustness test (papers published as the dependent variable).

Variable	Model 7	Model 8	Model 9	Model 10	Model 11
Innovation (*T*+2)	FE	FE	FE	FE	FE
Past Performance (*T*+1)	0.2834**	0.2142**	0.2456**	0.2104**	0.2200**
Gender	−51.3669	−63.1521	−49.2692	−32.3339	93.0947
Age	0.0160**	0.0091*	0.0122*	0.0219**	0.0220***
Size	−2.7064*	−2.156**	−3.3216**	−2.6351*	−3.4135***
Relationship Strength	−0.1646***	−0.2021***	−0.1987***	−0.1156*	−0.2160*
Network Density	−0.2458*	−0.2812**	−0.2413**	−0.1898*	0.2197***
The Amount of Cliques	4.7931***	4.7931***	4.7931***	4.7931***	4.6622***
Degree Centrality	0.6817***	0.4891***	0.7211***	0.6172*	1.1965***
Closeness Centrality	0.2815**	0.3516**	0.6151*	0.3215*	0.8501***
Between Centrality	1.0517**	1.8951**	1.2165**	1.5013*	3.6644***
Structural Holes Restriction	−0.1021	−0.1021	−0.1021	−0.1021	9.2153
Degree Centrality * Structural Holes Restriction		−1.2015***			−1.3787***
Closeness Centrality * Structural Holes Restriction			−0.1332***		−0.3268
Between Centrality * Structural Holes Restriction				−6.3122*	−12.6250***
Constant	46.3523***	62. 2213***	56.2103***	46.2214***	−92.2829***
Year	Y	Y	Y	Y	Y
Observations	984	984	984	984	984
F-statistic	32.15	33.65	29.07	32.16	39.45

Note: (*T*+2), (*T*+1) represents two and one periods of lag, $p < 0.01$***, $p < 0.05$**, $p < 0.1$*.

5. Conclusion

5.1. Conclusion and implications

Previous work has rarely studied the impact of structured positions in the network of high-level innovation teams on innovation. This area represents an important gap in our understanding in terms of whether central positioning in the network of high-level innovation teams is conducive to innovation and whether there are interactions between structural characteristics in the network. This article explores the network characteristics of quantum innovation teams and their impacts on innovation performance. First, three quantum high-level innovation teams of the USTC were selected as research objects, and papers published by these teams from 2010 to 2019 were used as samples to construct a team network matrix. Then, we calculated team network characteristics and investigated the impact of three network centralities (degree, closeness and between centrality) on team innovation performance and the moderating role of structural holes. We draw the following interesting conclusions. The degree, closeness and between centrality of a quantum high-level innovation team network have a positive impact on the team's innovation performance. Structural holes have no direct effect on innovation but actively moderate the positive impact of the three centralities on innovation performance.

This paper enriches the literature on innovation and team networks in three ways. First, when studying the impact of network centrality on team innovation performance, we believe that high-level innovation teams such as quantum research teams form both cooperative and knowledge networks (Oh, Choi, and Kim 2005; Badar, Hite, and Ashraf 2015). Many previous studies on enterprise or alliance networks generally conclude that cooperative and knowledge networks are decoupled (Dong and Yang 2016). We found that special frontier research teams have unique network characteristics, and their structural positioning in the network plays an important role in their innovation activities. Second, our research compares the effects of different measures of team network centrality on innovation performance. By distinguishing the three centrality measures and their impacts on innovation, we deepen our understanding of the centrality of an innovation team's network. Some previous studies have found that network centrality may be a double-edged sword and have negative effects on innovation (Ahuja and Katila 2004; McFadyen and Cannella 2004; Rotolo and Messeni Petruzzelli 2013; Dong and Yang 2016). However, our findings differ from those of previous studies; the centrality of the team network has a positive effect on innovation performance to varying degrees. Finally, past studies largely discuss the direct impacts of centrality and structural holes on innovation, but they ignore the interactions of network characteristics. The present article fills this gap in research by showing that the combination of network centrality (quantity) and structural holes (quality) in a network position significantly improves the innovation performance of team actors.

The conclusions of this study also have certain practical implications for quantum high-level innovation teams. First, close and direct connections between actors of a quantum high-level team will reduce the transmission of redundant information, promoting cooperation efficiency and innovation performance. Shorter distances between network actors cause knowledge to spread to actors faster and earlier (Badar, Hite, and Ashraf 2015) and to improve their innovation efficiency and performance. Actors who act as 'bridges' between other network actors may gain nonredundant and diverse knowledge that can be used to improve innovation performance. Therefore, team managers need to take measures to strengthen direct and indirect connections, shorten distances between team network actors and improve the effective transfer of network knowledge, which is critical to a team's innovation performance. Second, we found that excessively large teams and excessively high levels of network strength hinder a team's innovation performance. At the same time, the development of cliques in a team will significantly promote innovation performance. Thus, team managers should consider dividing large teams into several subgroups. More subgroups within a team can enable the diversification of knowledge and resources and promote the team's innovation performance.

5.2. Limitations and future research

Our study has limitations that provide directions for future research. First, in addition to the three teams of the USTC, there are also many well-known quantum innovation teams. To further understanding of quantum high-level innovation teams, future research should consider more quantum innovation teams both in China and abroad and compare differences in network characteristics between them. Second, this study does not consider dynamics of the team network. Future research may thus be further subdivided and processed into phases and years.

Disclosure statement

No potential conflict of interest was reported by the author(s).

Funding

This work was supported by National Natural Science Foundation of China: [Grant Number 71572188].

ORCID

QingQiu Gan http://orcid.org/0000-0002-1731-2866

References

Abbasi, A., J. Altmann, and L. Hossain. 2011. "Identifying the Effects of co-Authorship Networks on the Performance of Scholars: A Correlation and Regression Analysis of Performance Measures and Social Network Analysis Measures." *Journal of Informetrics* 5 (4): 594–607.

Ahuja, G., and R. Katila. 2004. "Where do Resources Come from? The Role of Idiosyncratic Situations." *Strategic Management Journal* 25 (8/9): 887–907.

Arun, G., and V. Mishra. 2014. "2014 2nd International Conference on Emerging Technology Trends in Electronics, Communication and Networking, IEEE, 1–5." A review on quantum computing and communication.

Asheim, B., and A. Isaksen. 2002. "Regional Innovation Systems: the Integration of Local Sticky and Global Ubiquitous Knowledge." *The Journal of Technology Transfer* 27 (1): 77–86.

Badar, K., J. M. Hite, and N. Ashraf. 2015. "Knowledge Network Centrality, Formal Rank and Research Performance: Evidence for Curvilinear and Interaction Effects." *Scientometrics* 105 (3): 1553–1576.

Badar, K., J. M. Hite, and Y. F. Badir. 2013. "Examining the Relationship of co-Authorship Network Centrality and Gender on Academic Research Performance: the Case of Chemistry Researchers in Pakistan." *Scientometrics* 94 (2): 755–775.

Badar, K., J. M. Hite, and Y. F. Badir. 2014. "The Moderating Role of Academic age and Institutional Sector on the Relationship Between co-Authorship Network Centrality and Academic Research Performance." *Aslib Journal of Information Management* 66 (1): 38–53.

Bell, G. G., and A. Zaheer. 2007. "Geography, Networks, and Knowledge Flow." *Organization Science* 18 (6): 955–972.

Burt, R. S. 1992. *Structural Holes: the Social Structure of Competition*. Cambridge, MA: Harvard University Press.

Burt, R. S. 2000. "The Network Structure of Social Capital." *Research in Organizational Behavior* 22: 345–423.

Burt, R. S. 2005. *Brokerage and Closure: The Social Capital of Structural Holes*. Oxford: Oxford University Press.

Burt, R. S. 2009. *Structural Holes: The Social Structure of Competition*. Cambridge, MA: Harvard university press.

Cowan, R., and N. Jonard. 2004. "Network Structure and the Diffusion of Knowledge." *Journal of Economic Dynamics and Control* 28 (8): 1557–1575.

Della Sala, S., and J. Grafman. 2009. "Five-year Impact Factor." *Cortex* 45 (8): 911.

Dong, J. Q., and C. H. Yang. 2016. "Being Central is a Double-Edged Sword: Knowledge Network Centrality and new Product Development in US Pharmaceutical Industry." *Technological Forecasting and Social Change* 113: 379–385.

Durmuşoğlu, S. S. 2013. "Merits of Task Advice During new Product Development: Network Centrality Antecedents and new Product Outcomes of Knowledge Richness and Knowledge Quality." *Journal of Product Innovation Management* 30 (3): 487–499.

Ferriani, S., G. Cattani, and C. Baden-Fuller. 2009. "The Relational Antecedents of Project-Entrepreneurship: Network Centrality, Team Composition and Project Performance." *Research Policy* 38 (10): 1545–1558.

Freeman, L. C. 1977. "A set of Measures of Centrality Based on Betweenness." *Sociometry*, 40 (1): 35–41.

Freeman, L. C. 1978. "Centrality in Social Networks Conceptual Clarification." *Social Networks* 1 (3): 215–239.

Gilsing, V. A., C. E. Lemmens, and G. Duysters. 2007. "Strategic Alliance Networks and Innovation: a Deterministic and Voluntaristic View Combined." *Technology Analysis & Strategic Management* 19 (2): 227–249.

Gilsing, V., B. Nooteboom, W. Vanhaverbeke, G. Duysters, and A. Van Den Oord. 2008. "Network Embeddedness and the Exploration of Novel Technologies: Technological Distance, Betweenness Centrality and Density." *Research Policy* 37 (10): 1717–1731.

Gilsing, V., W. Vanhaverbeke, and M. Pieters. 2014. "Mind the gap: Balancing Alliance Network and Technology Portfolios During Periods of Technological Uncertainty." *Technological Forecasting and Social Change* 81: 351–362.

Graf, H. 2011. "Gatekeepers in Regional Networks of Innovators." *Cambridge Journal of Economics* 35 (1): 173–198.

Guan, J., and H. Wei. 2015. "A Bilateral Comparison of Research Performance at an Institutional Level." *Scientometrics* 104 (1): 147–173.

Houston, M. B., M. Hutt, C. Moorman, P. H. Reingen, A. Rindfleisch, V. Swaminathan, and B. Walker. 2004. "A Network Perspective on Marketing Strategy Performance." *Assessing Marketing Strategy Performance* 12: 247–268.

Hu, D., S. X. Sun, J. L. Zhao, and X. Zhao. 2011. "Strategic Choices of Inter-Organizational Information Systems: A Network Perspective." *Information Systems Frontiers* 13 (5): 681–692.

Jehn, K. A., G. B. Northcraft, and M. A. Neale. 1999. "Why Differences Make a Difference: A Field Study of Diversity, Conflict and Performance in Workgroups." *Administrative Science Quarterly* 44 (4): 741–763.

Katzenbach, J. R., and D. K. Smith. 1993. *The Wisdom of Teams: Creating the High-Performance Organization*. Boston, MA: Harvard Business School Press.

Koka, B. R., and J. E. Prescott. 2008. "Designing Alliance Networks: the Influence of Network Position, Environmental Change, and Strategy on Firm Performance." *Strategic Management Journal* 29 (6): 639–661.

Kumar, P., J. B. Altepeter, and M. A. Hall. 2010. "36th European Conference and Exhibition on Optical Communication, IEEE, 1–6." Quantum communications: present status and future prospects.

Landis, B. 2016. "Personality and Social Networks in Organizations: A Review and Future Directions." *Journal of Organizational Behavior* 37: S107–S121.

Landry, R., N. Amara, and M. Lamari. 2002. "Does Social Capital Determine Innovation? To What Extent?" *Technological Forecasting and Social Change* 69 (7): 681–701.

Lee, D. H., I. W. Seo, H. C. Choe, and H. D. Kim. 2012. "Collaboration Network Patterns and Research Performance: the Case of Korean Public Research Institutions." *Scientometrics* 91 (3): 925–942.

Levin, S. G., and P. E. Stephan. 1991. "Research Productivity Over the Life Cycle: Evidence for Academic Scientists." *The American Economic Review* 81 (1): 114–132.

Lovejoy, W. S., and A. Sinha. 2010. "Efficient Structures for Innovative Social Networks." *Management Science* 56 (7): 1127–1145.

Madsen, P. M., and V. Desai. 2010. "Failing to Learn? The Effects of Failure and Success on Organizational Learning in the Global Orbital Launch Vehicle Industry." *Academy of Management Journal* 53 (3): 451–476.

McFadyen, M. A., and A. A. Cannella, Jr. 2004. "Social Capital and Knowledge Creation: Diminishing Returns of the Number and Strength of Exchange Relationships." *Academy of Management Journal* 47 (5): 735–746.

Mehra, A., M. Kilduff, and D. J. Brass. 2001. "The Social Networks of High and low Self-Monitors: Implications for Workplace Performance." *Administrative Science Quarterly* 46 (1): 121–146.

Newman, M. E. 2004. "Who is the Best Connected Scientist?" *A Study of Scientific Coauthorship Networks. Complex Networks* 650: 337–370.

Oh, W., J. N. Choi, and K. Kim. 2005. "Co-authorship Dynamics and Knowledge Capital: The Patterns of Cross-Disciplinary Collaboration in Information Systems Research." *Journal of Management Information Systems* 22 (3): 265–292.

Otte, E., and R. Rousseau. 2002. "Social Network Analysis: a Powerful Strategy, Also for the Information Sciences." *Journal of Information Science* 28 (6): 441–453.

Perry-Smith, J. E., and C. E. Shalley. 2003. "The Social Side of Creativity: A Static and Dynamic Social Network Perspective." *Academy of Management Review* 28 (1): 89–106.

Podolny, J. M., and J. N. Baron. 1997. "Relationships and Resources: Social Networks and Mobility in the Workplace." *American Sociological Review* 62 (5): 673–693.

Raymer, M. G., and C. Monroe. 2019. "The US National Quantum Initiative." *Quantum Science and Technology* 4 (2): 020504.

Rodan, S., and C. Galunic. 2004. "More Than Network Structure: How Knowledge Heterogeneity Influences Managerial Performance and Innovativeness." *Strategic Management Journal* 25 (6): 541–562.

Rotolo, D., and A. Messeni Petruzzelli. 2013. "When Does Centrality Matter? Scientific Productivity and the Moderating Role of Research Specialization and Cross-Community Ties." *Journal of Organizational Behavior* 34 (5): 648–670.

Schilling, M. A., and C. C. Phelps. 2007. "Interfirm Collaboration Networks: The Impact of Large-Scale Network Structure on Firm Innovation." *Management Science* 53 (7): 1113–1126.

Snijders, T. A., P. E. Pattison, G. L. Robins, and M. S. Handcock. 2006. "New Specifications for Exponential Random Graph Models." *Sociological Methodology* 36 (1): 99–153.

Sparrowe, R. T., R. C. Liden, S. J. Wayne, and M. L. Kraimer. 2001. "Social Networks and the Performance of Individuals and Groups." *Academy of Management Journal* 44 (2): 316–325.

Stuart, T. E., and O. Sorenson. 2005. "Social Networks and Entrepreneurship." In *Handbook of Entrepreneurship Research*, 233–252. Boston: Springer.

Tang, C., and L. Ye. 2015. "Diversified Knowledge, R&D Team Centrality and Radical Creativity." *Creativity and Innovation Management* 24 (1): 123–135.

Tortoriello, M. 2015. "The Social Underpinnings of Absorptive Capacity: The Moderating Effects of Structural Holes on Innovation Generation Based on External Knowledge." *Strategic Management Journal* 36 (4): 586–597.

Valente, T. W., K. Coronges, C. Lakon, and E. Costenbader. 2008. "How Correlated are Network Centrality Measures?" *Connections* 28 (1): 16.

Vanhaverbeke, W., V. Gilsing, and G. Duysters. 2012. "Competence and Governance in Strategic Collaboration: The Differential Effect of Network Structure on the Creation of Core and Noncore Technology." *Journal of Product Innovation Management* 29 (5): 784–802.

Walker, G., B. Kogut, and W. Shan. 1997. "Social Capital, Structural Holes and the Formation of an Industry Network." *Organization Science* 8 (2): 109–125.

Wang, C., S. Rodan, M. Fruin, and X. Xu. 2014. "Knowledge Networks, Collaboration Networks, and Exploratory Innovation." *Academy of Management Journal* 57 (2): 484–514.

Wasserman, S., and K. Faust. 1994. *Social Networks Analysis: Methods and Applications*. Cambridge: Cambridge University Press.

Wu, H., X. Gu, Y. Zhao, and W. Liu. 2020. "Research on the Relationship Between Structural Hole Location, Knowledge Management and Cooperative Innovation Performance in Artificial Intelligence." *Knowledge Management Research & Practice*, 1–10.

Yan, Y., and J. Guan. 2018. "Social Capital, Exploitative and Exploratory Innovations: The Mediating Roles of ego-Network Dynamics." *Technological Forecasting and Social Change* 126: 244–258.

Zucker, L. G., M. R. Darby, M. B. Brewer, and Y. Peng. 1995. *Collaboration Structure and Information Dilemmas in Biotechnology: Organizational Boundaries as Trust Production*. National Bureau of Economic Research.

A bibliometric analysis of quantum computing literature: mapping and evidences from scopus

Jiaxing Wang, Lihua Shen and Wuyuan Zhou

ABSTRACT

Quantum computing is the next-generation technology for future human society. This article aims to give a comprehensive and in-depth analysis of the global development status of quantum computing. First, the latest research hotspots of quantum computing are reviewed. Then multiple bibliometric metrics were used to analyse the current development status, research hotspots, technological trends, and the contribution of authors, institutions, and countries in quantum computing from 2016 to 2020. The results confirm that quantum computing is still under development, with the United States and China in the leading position, from where most critical scholars came. The most important institutions are scattered in the United States, China, and France. The characteristics of international cooperation, research impact, topics with the highest Prominence percentile, distinctive keyphrases, and leading source journals within the field were also analysed. The results may provide a quantitative basis for scientific research and decision-making in quantum computing.

1. Introduction

Quantum information technology is the next-generation technology for future human society and may forever change our economic, industrial, academic, and social landscape (Lekitsch et al. 2017). The field comprises four domains: quantum communication, quantum simulation, quantum computation, and quantum sensing and metrology (Acín et al. 2018). Quantum computing achieves large computational space by orchestrating the superposition, entanglement and interference of quantum bits (qubits), and has the potential to surpass any classical computer (Arute et al. 2019; Harrow and Montanaro 2017; Oliver 2019). It has great potential to solve some of the most challenging computational tasks and explore many possibilities that classical processors cannot handle (Nguyen et al. 2020). A good example is that quantum algorithms and artificial intelligence hold good promise for mutual reinforcement: quantum algorithms can enhance machine learning in data clustering, while machine learning can be used to perform quantum state tomography of highly entangled states with more than a hundred qubits (Palmieri et al. 2020; Torlai et al. 2018). Experimental demonstrations of quantum computing date back to the 1980s, when Charles H. Bennett discussed the logical reversibility of computation (Bennett 1973), Paul Benioff proposed building a quantum mechanical model of computers as represented by Turing machines (Benioff 1980), and Richard P. Feynman proposed the idea of designing computers working according to the laws of quantum mechanics (Feynman 1982). The first theoretical breakthrough with major practical implications in this technology came in 1994 when Shor of AT&T Bell Labs developed a polynomial time algorithm, a quantum algorithm capable of breaking any existing encryption (Shor 1994). Later in 1996, Grover developed a fast quantum mechanical algorithm for unsorted database search (Grover 1996). These two algorithms are now at the core of the entire field of quantum algorithm research.

Scientists have implemented architectures for quantum computing on various material systems such as superconducting circuits, semiconductor quantum wells, single-photon emitters, trapped ions, topological quantum computing elements, and other hybrid quantum systems (Forn-Díaz et al. 2019; Liu and Hersam 2019). Currently, the US and China have achieved quantum of advantage in superconducting and photons architectures, respectively (Arute et al. 2019; Zhong et al. 2021), and the latest effort realised a quantum spin model with tunable interactions for system sizes ranging from 64 to 256 qubits on a programmable quantum simulator (Ebadi et al. 2021). However, even the current state-of-the-art systems have limitations in terms of size and coherence (coherence means the states of electron spin to the right and to the left are correlated, and can be created, manipulated, and measured at the single-quantum level) (DiVincenzo and Loss 1999). What is more, we are still some time away from fault-tolerant quantum computers, which require error correction mechanisms to be incorporated into the computing and storage components to ensure quantum coherence and low error rates (Setia et al. 2020). The latest research has taken a big step forward in this direction by achieving exponential suppression of bit or phase errors through cyclic error correction (Chen et al. 2021). The development of quantum systems capable of performing practical calculations or simulations, like those that implement Shor's algorithm, requires a deep understanding of the dynamics of quantum correlations, entanglement and information scrambling in quantum many-body systems, such as Nash embedding that allows for faultless traversal of the quantum-classical physical divide (Khan and Humble 2019; Lewis-Swan et al. 2019), and the integration of hardware, software, cloud access, benchmarks, and error correction and mitigation (Corcoles et al. 2020).

Many countries are pursuing strategies and research plans in quantum science and technology, such as the US, which announced a massive investment to ensure its global competitiveness (U.S. Department of Energy, 2020). China has proposed fully understanding the importance and urgency of promoting quantum science and technology and strengthening the strategic planning and systematic layout of quantum information technology. IBM promises to achieve a quantum computer with 1000 qubits by 2023, while Google plans to build a quantum computer with one million qubits within ten years (Biamonte, Dorozhkin, and Zacharov 2019). However, the scientific community still has doubts about the prospects of quantum computing. Many believe that quantum computing still has considerable hurdles to overcome before it can be used for some of the most challenging computing tasks, such as 5G communications, power grid management, smart factory optimisation, and drug discovery ('A Precarious Milestone for Quantum Computing,' 2019). For this reason, a comprehensive and in-depth analysis of the current global development status of quantum computing is urgently needed.

Although there have been several bibliometric studies on quantum computing, they are rather outdated and do not reflect the latest academic trends. What is more, the predominant error for these previous studies lies in their flawed search methods, such as using ('quantum computing') as the sole keyword (Dhawan, Gupta, and Bhusan 2018), or a search query of (quantum NEAR/5 comput* or quantum NEAR/15 algorithm* or quantum NEAR/10 simulat* or quantum NEAR/10 error* or 'quantum circuit' or 'quantum Turing machine') (Tian et al. 2020). Another research was confined to four thematic journals in the SCIE database (Terekhov 2020). The limitations of these studies lead to unreliable and incomplete findings that do not truly reflect the development of quantum computing worldwide.

Based on the in-depth understanding of the technical substance of quantum computing, we have made improvements in the search method to comprehensively reflect the global development of quantum computing. Then multiple metrics were used to analyse (i) research trends and hotspots; (ii) the regional distribution of authors, institutions, and countries, and the characteristics of international collaboration, academic-corporate collaboration, and research excellence. The results can provide ideas and suggestions for future researches and policymaking and help promote quantum science development. The main contributions of this paper include four aspects: (1) The global research hotspots of quantum computing have been identified, and the latest development trends of relevant hotspots have been summarised; (2) Determining the academic output pattern in quantum computing, including the distribution of scholars, institutions, and countries/regions, and found that quantum computing is still under development and has not yet become the mainstream hotspot of academic development; (3) The characteristics of international cooperation and research impact of quantum computing were evaluated by multiple metrics; (4) Most active sources journals and top articles with the highest citation count identified.

2. Literature review

Due to the need for research on optical quantum computing, quantum key distribution, quantum metrology, and quantum networks, scientists are vigorously investigating semiconductor quantum dots in various material systems and developing solid state single photon emitters to manipulate single photons (Arakawa and Holmes 2020). In photonics-based quantum computing, photonic qubits are created and manipulated with high precision using interferometry for computational applications and data transmission. Photonic synthetic materials use superconducting qubits and cavities to manipulate the quantum state of microwave photons, thus provide a means of tailoring the interaction between light and matter (Flamini, Spagnolo, and Sciarrino 2019). Tremendous success has been achieved in the ability to generate large numbers of photons, improved light sources and detectors, and novel noise-resistant theoretical approaches. The main issues are optical losses, large scaling, matching of different photonic elements, and near-deterministic generation of the photon as a flying qubit (Carusotto et al. 2020; Elshaari et al. 2020). Integrated quantum photonic circuits are a particularly desirable technology platform. In December 2020, Zhong et al. obtained up to 76-photon coincidence on a photonic quantum computer, yielding a state space dimension of about 10^{30} (Zhong et al. 2021).

Trapped ions are one of the most promising systems for practical quantum computing, in which ions confined in radiofrequency traps serve as qubits, with entanglement achieved by using the shared ion motional modes as a quantum bus (Bruzewicz et al. 2019). Trapped ions have fundamental advantages over superconducting qubits, such as high qubit quality, coherence, and connectivity (Murali et al. 2020). The main challenges for trapped ions are how to generate entanglement between spin and photonic quantum bits efficiently and increase the scale of quantum computers while reducing decoherence and control errors (Gao et al. 2012). An 11-qubit quantum computer in a trapped ion system was developed in 2019, with single-qubit gate fidelities of 99.5%, average two-qubit-gate fidelities of 97.5%, and SPAM errors of 0.7% (Wright et al. 2019). A two-dimensional Penning trap arrays was developed as a scalable platform for quantum computing with trapped atomic ions to allow for fault-tolerant scale devices (Jain et al. 2020). An exact protocol has been devised that simultaneously entangles arbitrary pairs of qubits on a trapped-ion quantum computer and exhibits an exponential improvement in both classical and quantum resources (Grzesiak et al. 2020). The trap sizing, communication topology, and operation implementation methods need to be further improved to realise a 50–100 qubits quantum charge-coupled devices-based trapped ion system (Murali et al. 2020).

Quantum-state engineering in Josephson junction based electronic circuits has shown great promise for quantum computation and communication (Makhlin, Schön, and Shnirman 2001; Nakamura, Pashkin, and Tsai 1999). Superconducting qubits are manipulated by using electromagnetic pulses to control the magnetic flux, the electric charge, or the phase difference across a Josephson junction (Clarke and Wilhelm 2008). Over the past two decades, superconducting quantum circuits have evolved from basic research to the engineering of large-scale superconducting quantum systems, with core concepts and challenges including qubits design, noise properties, qubit control and readout techniques (Krantz et al. 2019). Key experimental breakthroughs have been made in thermal interferometers, diffractors, modulators and routers based on superconducting tunnel junctions (Hwang and Sothmann 2020). Circuit quantum electrodynamics (QED) implements the fundamental requirements of quantum computing in a single architecture. Recent research directions for creating circuit QED based hybrid quantum systems include mechanical oscillators, quantum acoustodynamics with surface acoustic waves, quantum magnonics, and coupling between superconducting circuits and ensembles or single spins (Blais, Girvin, and Oliver 2020; Clerk et al. 2020). Quantum computing platforms based on superconducting qubits have emerged as a leading candidate for scalable high-fidelity quantum processor architectures and achieved the milestone of proving quantum superiority by creating quantum states on 53 qubits for the first time in 2019 (Arute et al. 2019). Experimental efforts towards the large-scale superconducting quantum computer include qubit design, quantum control, readout techniques, and the implementations of error correction and quantum algorithms (Huang et al. 2020).

Further development of quantum computing requires advances in materials science in selecting, synthesis, fabrication, simulation, and characterisation of nanomaterials underlying quantum devices (Richardson et al. 2020). Nanodiamond can be used to fabricate materials with photonic bandgaps with properties to suppress spontaneous light emission and improve light harvesting, which can be used for applications such as optical waveguides, filters, laser resonators, and colour-centered quantum devices (Chia et al. 2021; Kan et al. 2020). Recent researches focus on nanodiamond synthesis, such as the growth of colour centre-rich nanodiamond on prefabricated silicon carbide microdisk resonators to enhance diamond colour-centered light emission (Radulaski et al. 2019), wafer-scale preparation of nanoscale diamond containing optically active silicon vacancy centres (Nelz et al. 2019), and self-assembling colloidal diamond capable of optical properties of photonic bandgaps (He et al. 2020).

3. Search design and data analysis

In this paper, the search strategy is based on the theme of 'quantum computing', using more than 50 sets of keywords to form a search formula (see Table 1). An flowchart of the research process is shown in Figure 1. The search was conducted on 12 July 2021, and a total of 89,777 publications 1996 to present were detected using search query Q1 in Table 1. Data cleaning was then performed, firstly

Table 1. List of search keywords.

Set	Related to	Search keywords in publication title, abstract, and keywords
Q1	Quantum computing	'quantum information', 'quantum computing', 'quantum supercomputer', 'quantum algorithm', 'quantum search', 'quantum machine learning', 'quantum clustering', 'quantum deep learning', 'quantum encoding', 'quantum feedback control', 'quantum acceleration', 'quantum turing', 'quantum error correction', 'quantum simulator', 'quantum data stream', 'quantum chip', 'quantum process', 'quantum information storage', 'quantum memory', 'quantum imaging', 'quantum device', 'quantum sampling', 'quantum signals', 'quantum neural networks', 'quantum circuit', 'quantum internet', 'quantum network', 'quantum router', 'quantum phase estimation', 'quantum tomography', 'quantum cloud', 'quantum gate', 'quantum logic', 'logical quantum instruction', 'quantum assembly language', 'quantum system', 'quantum program', 'quantum resource', 'quantum machine image', 'quantum streaming', 'quantum virtual machine', 'quantum integrated circuit', 'quantum approximate', 'quantum vector machine', 'quantum state generator', 'quantum annealing', 'single photon source', 'Josephson junctions', 'quantum supremacy', 'quantum memory', 'quantum topology', 'quantum teleportation', 'quantum measurement', and others.
Q2	Quantum communication	'quantum telecommunication', 'quantum communication', 'quantum transmission', 'quantum cryptographic', 'quantum cryptography', 'quantum confidential communication', 'quantum stealth transfer', 'quantum key', 'quantum encryption', 'quantum secure encryption', 'quantum relay', and others (such as 'quantum sensing').

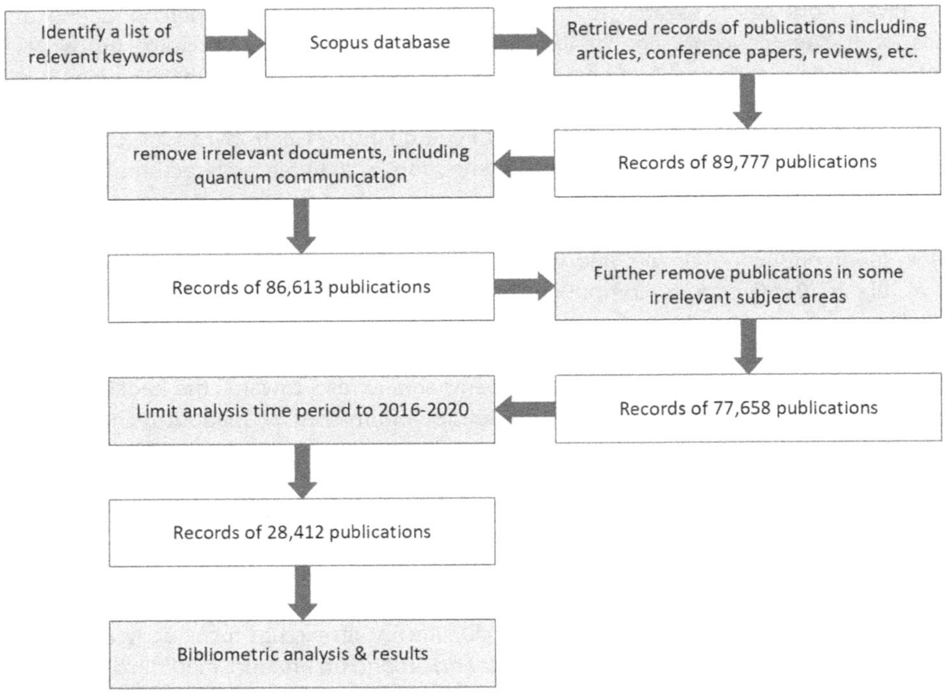

Figure 1. Flowchart illustrating the searching, data cleaning and data selection process.

removing literature on quantum communication (Q2) to obtain 86,613 publications; then removing some irrelevant literature in such subject areas as biochemistry, energy, and medicine to obtain 77,658 publications.

Then, SciVal was used to further analyse the 28,412 peer-reviewed papers from 2016 to 2020, to obtain the current academic output, including the distribution between countries, institutions, and authors, with emphasis on development trends and research hotspots. SciVal is a research management and analysis platform launched by Elsevier, with data sources from Scopus, the world's largest abstract and citation database (Cantú-Ortiz and Fangmeyer 2017). Scopus is more comprehensive in its coverage of computer science publications and has a series of bibliometric metrics that can analyse the current status, hotspots, and trends in the research field, help researchers discover core teams and institutions (Liu et al. 2020; Martín-Martín et al. 2018).

We employed multiple metrics of the Scopus: Scholarly output, Field-Weighted Citation Impact (FWCI), Publications in Top Journal Percentiles, Output in Top Citation Percentiles, Patent-citations per scholarly output, Publications in Top Journal Percentiles. These metrics were extracted from SciVal, and each indicator and its bibliometric significance will be explained below.

The scholarly output indicates the number of publications and measures academic productivity. Scholars publish their research results during their tenure, but the number of publications does not reflect their scientific impact. Other critical dimensions include journal impact, scientific impact, and social popularity (Liu et al. 2016).

Citations vary spatiotemporally and are affected by differences in research fields, and need to be normalised (Gao et al. 2013). As an article-level field-normalised metric, FWCI indicates how the number of citations received by an entity's publications compares with the world average. It benchmarks the comparative research impact of entities regardless of differences in their size, disciplinary profile, age, and publication-type composition (Chang, Phoa, and Nakano 2019; Purkayastha et al. 2019)

Two metrics, publications in top journal percentiles and outputs in top citation percentiles, are often used to illustrate research excellence. As a result of the editors' selection of the best manuscripts, publications in top journal percentiles often show top citation performance within their fields (Bornmann et al. 2011). The metrics used in this study are publications in the top 10% journal percentiles by citescore percentile (%) (abbreviated as JP10%) and output in top 10% citation percentiles (%) (abbreviated as CP10%).

The economic impact indicators can quantify the relationship between science and invention. Patent-citations per scholarly output is the patent citation counts divided by an entity's total scholarly output for that period and multiplied by 1000. It indicates how much, on average, research is being used to create products and provide information about research's economic impact.

There is a positive correlation between the share of academic-corporate collaboration share (abbreviated as ACC%) in a country and the innovation performance indices (Pohl 2021). The effects of international collaboration share (abbreviated as IC%) are positive and statistically significant in enhancing publication impact (Leydesdorff, Bornmann, and Wagner 2019).

4. Results and discussions

4.1. Global quantum computing research hotspots analysis

Distinctive keyphrases within the research area are identified with text mining, which applies various Natural Language Processing techniques to the titles, abstracts, and author keywords of the documents. This technique incorporates a factor that highlights a weighted importance of words that occur frequently or rarely. Thus, the algorithm overcomes the deficiency of calculating research hotspots solely by word frequency. As shown in Figure 2, The critical concepts identified by text mining listed in order of significance as quantum optic, quantum computer, qubit, entanglement, Josephson junction, photon, quantum circuit, particle beam, quantum algorithm, coherence, trapped ion, et al. These keyphrases can be considered as the core concepts of quantum computing.

4.2. Screening of leading topics

The research frontiers of quantum computing are filtered through leading topics. Active topics give insight into the research planning process and help researchers keep up with the latest research

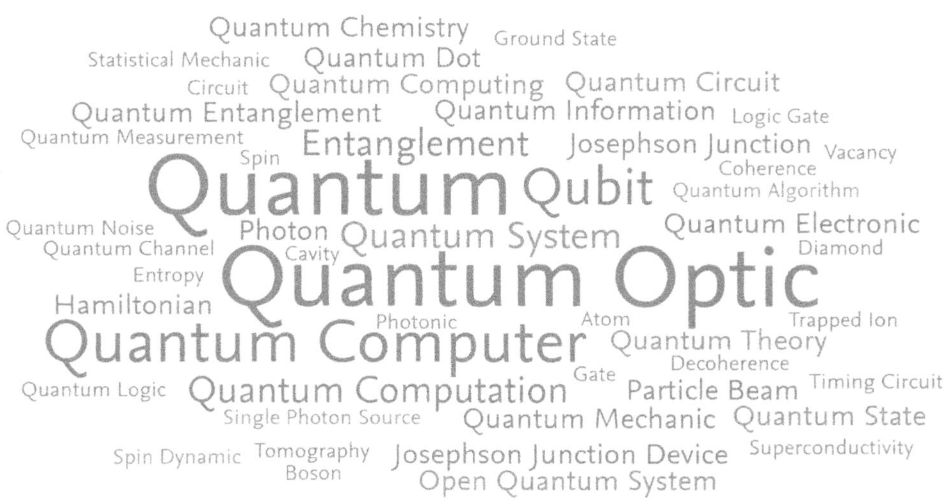

Figure 2. Top keyphrases by relevance 2016–2020.

trends. The Scopus database has approximately 97,000 topics in its citation information and is ranked according to the new metric Prominence percentile. The prominence percentile is calculated from the number of citation count, Scopus view count, and journal CiteScore to determine the topic's popularity and momentum. Topic prominence is positively correlated with research funding and grants; finding topics with a high prominence percentile can help researchers and policymakers.

Table 2 lists topics with the most momentum in quantum computing 2016–2020, such as molybdenum disulfide, topological Insulators, optical vortex, and nanodiamonds. The leading architectures in quantum computing include photonics-based, trapped ions, and superconducting quantum circuits. Quantum materials and other important topics or topics with leading research impact are also listed.

4.3. Global research performance of quantum computing

Table 3 lists the global academic output status of quantum computing using multiple metrics such as scholarly output, citations, FWCI, patent-citations per scholarly output, authors, and outputs in top citation percentiles. The scholarly output shows a successive growth trend during 2011–2020, but there is a significant growth acceleration after 2016. From 2019 on, more than 18,000 scholars have been engaged in quantum computing-related research, and more than 6000 papers have been published each year. Publications in top journal percentiles in quantum computing are significantly low, publications in top 1% most cited from 2011 to 2020 is only 1.6%, and Publications in top 10% most cited is only 13.6%. The average FWCI of quantum computing is 1.26, indicating that the comparative research impact of quantum computing is only slightly better than the global average for similar publications (1.0).

4.4. Research technology fields

As shown in Figure 3, physics and astronomy accounts for 38.7% of the total publications. Materials science accounts for 13.8%, engineering accounts for 13.1%, mathematics accounts for 10.7%, computer science accounts for 11.2%, and chemistry accounts for 4.1%. The multitude of technical fields to which quantum computing's academic output belongs reflects a strongly interdisciplinary nature and necessitates a common language to integrate ideas from quantum materials, electronic structure theory, quantum electrodynamics, algorithm design, and open quantum systems (Head-Marsden et al. 2021).

Table 2. Leading topics in quantum computing 2016–2020.

Topics	Scholarly output	Growth %	FWCI	Prominence percentile
Quantum Computers; Ising; Qubits	1294	10.7	1.93	99.347
Qubits; Josephson Junctions; Superconducting Resonators	867	25.7	1.79	99.288
Color Centers; Vacancies; Nanodiamonds	610	−12.4	1.52	99.545
Quantum Error Correction; MDS Code; Qubits	585	−3.3	1.17	97.562
Reversible Logic; Quantum Circuits; DNA Computing	518	15.6	1.29	93.25
Dynamical Phase Transition; Thermalization (Energy Absorption); Eigenvalues and Eigenfunctions	508	1.3	2.55	99.459
Qubits; Electron Spin; Quantum Computing	483	15.5	1.76	98.548
Origanum; Superconductivity; Josephson Junctions	475	41.1	1.7	99.121
Single Photon Source; Resonance Fluorescence; Quantum Dots	454	1.7	1.3	98.162
Optomechanics; Mechanical Oscillators; Resonators	437	36	2.48	99.437
Trapped Ions; Qubits; Ion Traps (Instrumentation)	400	2.1	1.4	97.259
Open Quantum Systems; Qubits; Master Equation	346	5.2	1.09	93.595
Conformal Field Theory; Entanglement; Ads/Cft Correspondence	263	36.9	2.23	99.087
Quantum Fisher Information; Metrology; Qubits	256	−8.9	1.1	97.279
Topological Insulators; Optical Lattices; Quantum Hall Effect	252	−18.8	2.26	99.834
Optical Vortex; Angular Momentum; Gaussian Beams	190	−25.7	1.3	99.639

Table 3. Overall research performance in quantum computing 2011–2020.

	2011	2012	2013	2014	2015	2016	2017	2018	2019	2020
Scholarly output	3577	3711	3965	4239	4388	4605	4970	5510	6469	6858
Citations	95316	108959	100715	93693	90152	89912	76478	63123	44798	18805
FWCI	1.32	1.35	1.31	1.25	1.25	1.37	1.27	1.28	1.21	1.09
Citations per publication	26.6	29.4	25.4	22.1	20.5	19.5	15.4	11.5	6.9	2.7
Patent-citations per scholarly output	256.9	264.6	295.3	256.4	175.7	148.8	85.7	43.9	13.9	0.1
Authors	8157	8854	9498	10396	11181	12471	13414	15462	18208	20023
Publications in top 1% most cited (%)	1.8	1.9	1.6	1.7	1.9	2.1	1.8	1.4	1.6	-
Publications in top 5% most cited (%)	7.7	7.6	8.5	7.3	7.4	8.5	7.4	7.2	7.1	5.8
Publications in top 10% most cited (%)	14.1	13.9	15.1	14	13.6	14.5	13.3	13.3	12.9	12.9
Publications in top 25% most cited (%)	30.4	30.7	32	29.4	31	31.4	29.5	29.9	29.2	30.2

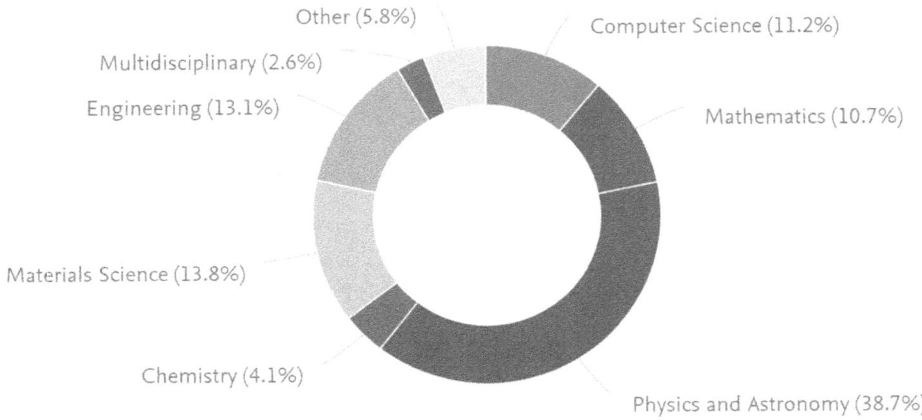

Figure 3. Analysis of technical areas of scholarly output.

4.5. Global geographical distribution

The geographical distribution of quantum computing research 2016–2020 is shown in Table 4. The United States ranks first in scholarly output, with 7272, and has an FWCI of 1.84. China's scholarly output reaches 6272, with the FWCI being 1. They were followed by Germany and the United Kingdom, whose scholarly outputs reach 3209 and 2585, respectively, and their FWCI is similarly high. The scholarly output of Japan, France, Russian Federation, Italy, Canada and India is very similar, all around 1500. However, the FWCI of Russian Federation and India is far below 1, indicating its lower research impact, while Switzerland, the Netherlands, and Austria enjoy high research impact, with their FWCI exceeding 2.

For other research performances, Germany, the UK, Australia, Spain, Switzerland, Austria, and Singapore have their publications in top 10% journal percentiles by CiteScore percentile (JP10%) exceed 50%, while the US is 49.9%, and China merely at 28.8%. Countries with high JP10% also show high CP10% of above 20%. The US, Japan, Canada, Switzerland, and the Netherlands have nearly 10% of academic-corporate corporations, while China has merely 2.3%. It is noteworthy that the proportion

Table 4. Top 20 countries in terms of scholarly output.

Country/region	Scholarly output	Citation count	FWCI	JP10%	CP10%	ACC%	IC%
United States	7272	121942	1.84	49.9	24.8	9.8	48.2
China	6272	54940	1	28.8	13.3	2.3	33.5
Germany	3209	52490	1.65	51.8	22.9	4.3	69.9
United Kingdom	2585	44165	1.7	55.5	25.1	6.5	69.5
Japan	1966	24589	1.36	40.4	18.6	10	48
France	1550	24263	1.67	46.7	23.2	5.6	68.4
Russian Federation	1536	10206	0.85	24.4	9.5	3.2	47.8
Italy	1519	19059	1.37	41.8	19.2	2.8	63.3
Canada	1444	23757	1.75	46.7	23.6	9.2	69.9
India	1394	7330	0.82	20.1	6.9	0.9	28
Australia	1160	16436	1.47	55.5	21.6	6.6	72.1
Spain	1123	18077	1.59	50.3	23.3	2.7	76
Switzerland	843	17760	2.39	58.7	32.1	15.3	76.2
Netherlands	725	13186	2.92	48.2	29.5	13.2	75.4
Brazil	648	4878	0.89	36.8	9.9	0.8	51.9
Austria	631	11619	2.88	58.9	30.6	4.9	78.4
Poland	603	6681	1.21	38.2	15.3	2.3	56.6
Singapore	578	7959	1.57	50	22.1	4.3	82.9
South Korea	570	5187	1.08	43.5	15.8	4.4	53.9
Iran	547	2866	0.72	16.1	6.6	0.4	28.3

of international cooperation for quantum computing research in European countries is generally high up to 70%, while that in Asian and South American countries is significantly low, usually less than 50%.

4.6. Contribution of leading institutions

The ranking of institutions during 2016–2020, as shown in Table 5, was obtained using the selection criteria of Citation Count >6000 and FWCI >1, and listed according to their citation count. Among the top 20 institutions, seven are from the US, seven from Europe, and two from Japan, China, and Australia each. CNRS ranks first, followed by MIT, Chinese Academy of Sciences, Harvard University, University of Oxford, University of Maryland, College Park, National Institute of Standards and Technology, University of Science and Technology of China, California Institute of Technology. They all have a citation count of over 10,000. CNRS and Chinese Academy of Sciences have a scholarly output of more than 1000.

For research impact, as reflected by FWCI, US and European institutions are among the highest, while the two Chinese institutions are the lowest. University of California at Santa Barbara, Delft University of Technology, and Swiss Federal Institute of Technology Zurich have the highest academic-corporate collaborations. This collaboration rate was not seen in institutions of the UK, France, Italy, Australia, Japan, and China.

In terms of international collaboration, European countries, Japan and Australia all seek cooperation with the United States at high rates. The US has a low rate of international cooperation due to its strong R&D capabilities. China, on the other hand, is less likely to cooperate internationally.

4.7. Contribution of leading authors

Table 6 lists scholars according to the citation count, and it is evident that these highly cited scholars display a high research impact represented by their FWCI. In terms of citation count, Jianwei Pan of

Table 5. Top institutions in the field of quantum computing 2016–2020.

Institution	Country	Scholarly output	Citation count	FWCI	JP10%	CP10%	ACC %	IC%
CNRS	France	1094	18721	1.7	50	23.9	3.9	66.5
Massachusetts Institute of Technology	US	535	16719	2.77	64.5	40.6	12.7	49.9
Chinese Academy of Sciences	China	1105	14085	1.33	43	20.5	5.2	40.7
Harvard University	US	363	13060	3.09	66.1	43.8	13.5	65.3
University of Oxford	UK	509	10403	2.05	59.3	27.7	5.7	67.8
University of Maryland, College Park	US	482	10307	2.08	60	30.5	11.6	40
National Institute of Standards and Technology	US	486	10195	2.08	61.8	31.9	6.6	45.5
University of Science and Technology of China	China	744	10140	1.36	46	21.5	4.4	36.6
California Institute of Technology	US	307	9408	3.11	63.8	38.1	13.4	52.4
Australian National University	Australia	539	8561	1.6	63.2	24.7	4.8	70.1
National Research Council of Italy	Italy	531	8423	1.52	47.8	22.6	2.4	63.1
Princeton University	US	244	8308	3.54	64.3	39.3	13.1	52.5
The University of Tokyo	Japan	331	8137	2.05	56.4	26	4.5	46.8
Delft University of Technology	Netherlands	319	8021	4.42	61.5	39.8	20.1	75.2
Université Paris-Saclay	France	396	7991	1.92	46.7	22.5	5.8	60.1
University of Technology Sydney	Australia	417	7852	1.85	60.6	27.8	5.8	72.9
University of California at Santa Barbara	US	200	7258	3.62	60.6	44	28.5	42
Swiss Federal Institute of Technology Zurich	Switzerland	315	7002	2.18	67	37.5	17.5	76.5
RIKEN	Japan	266	6724	2.23	62.5	38.7	4.5	73.7
University of Copenhagen	Denmark	210	6481	2.47	68.1	37.6	9.5	87.1

Table 6. Top scholars in the field of quantum computing 2016–2020.

Author	Affiliation	Country	Scholarly output	Citation count	FWCI	JP10%	CP10%	ACC %	IC10%
Pan, Jianwei	University of Science and Technology of China	China	70	3521	4.11	84.4	48.6	28.6	52.9
Lukin, Mikhail D.	Harvard University	US	46	3293	5.21	81.8	65.2	8.7	71.7
Babbush, Ryan	Alphabet Inc.	US	30	3275	9.9	82.8	80	80	56.7
Lu, Chaoyang	University of Science and Technology of China	China	44	2917	5.27	91.7	52.3	29.5	56.8
Neven, Hartmut	Alphabet Inc.	US	29	2846	9.8	78.6	72.4	82.8	44.8
Englund, Dirk R.	Massachusetts Institute of Technology	US	75	2734	2.49	72.2	42.7	22.7	36
McClean, Jarrod R.	Alphabet Inc.	US	25	2713	10.12	79.2	80	76	44
Martinis, John M.	University of California at Santa Barbara	US	23	2603	11.1	90.9	69.6	95.7	30.4
Marcus, Charles M.	University of Copenhagen	Denmark	27	2269	5.5	88.9	66.7	29.6	92.6
Fowler, Austin G.	Alphabet Inc.	US	26	2220	8.12	72	57.7	100	57.7
Barends, Rami	Alphabet Inc.	US	19	2178	10.97	88.9	73.7	100	26.3
Roushan, Pedram	Alphabet Inc.	US	17	2169	12.14	87.5	82.4	100	23.5
Kelly, Julian	Alphabet Inc.	US	18	2163	11.45	88.2	72.2	100	22.2
Megrant, Anthony Edward	Alphabet Inc.	US	19	2162	10.88	88.9	68.4	100	31.6
Mutus, Joshua Y.	Alphabet Inc.	US	18	2152	11.37	82.4	72.2	94.4	22.2
Sank, Daniel Thomas	Alphabet Inc.	US	17	2148	12	81.2	76.5	94.1	17.6
Jeffrey, Evan R.	Alphabet Inc.	US	17	2148	12	81.2	76.5	94.1	17.6
Nori, Franco	RIKEN	Japan	73	2053	2.31	65.8	45.2	4.1	97.3
Monroe, Christopher R.	University of Maryland, College Park	US	38	2052	4.08	77.4	60.5	26.3	23.7
Smelyanskiy, Vadim N.	Alphabet Inc.	US	18	2018	10.73	88.2	61.1	83.3	33.3

the University of Science and Technology of China was cited 3521, Mikhail D. Lukin of Harvard University was cited 3293, and Ryan Babbush of Alphabet Inc. was cited 3275. 12 out of the top 20 cited scholars are from Alphabet Inc, among which Ryan Babbush and Hartmut Neven ranked on the top. The rest of the highly cited scholars include Chaoyang Lu of the University of Science and Technology of China, John M. Martinis of the University of California at Santa Barbara, Charles M. Marcus of the University of Copenhagen, Franco Nori of RIKEN, and Christopher R. Monroe of University of Maryland, College Park. From the perspective of international collaboration, it is significantly higher for scholars from universities and institutions than from corporates, suggesting that corporations might be concerned about intellectual property protection and lack motivation in international cooperation.

A rank based on scholarly output would be much different. Scholars from Universities are more prolific than their corporate counterparts. Chuanfeng Li of the University of Science and Technology of China (117 publications) and Guangcan Guo of the Chinese Academy of Sciences (97 publications) would be among the most prolific scholars. However, their citation counts are relatively low, and their FWCI is 1.11 and 1.18, respectively.

4.8. Most cited research articles after 2016

To provide a clear vision of the recent works, we list the top 10 cited research articles related to quantum computing published after 2016 in Table 7. Nature has played an essential role in

Table 7. Most cited sources worldwide in quantum computing since 2016.

Title	Author	Year	Source	Citation
Quantum supremacy using a programmable superconducting processor	Arute F. et al.	2019	Nature	948
Single-molecule strong coupling at room temperature in plasmonic nanocavities	Chikkaraddy R. et al.	2016	Nature	811
Probing many-body dynamics on a 51-atom quantum simulator	Bernien H. et al.	2017	Nature	670
Exponential protection of zero modes in Majorana islands	Albrecht S.M.et al.	2016	Nature	613
Quantum emission from hexagonal boron nitride monolayers	Tran T.T. et al.	2016	Nature Nanotechnology	563
Near-optimal single-photon sources in the solid state	Somaschi N. et al.	2016	Nature Photonics	556
Integrated lithium niobate electro-optic modulators operating at CMOS-compatible voltages	Wang C. et al.	2018	Nature	531
Hardware-efficient variational quantum eigensolver for small molecules and quantum magnets	Kandala A. et al.	2017	Nature	522
Proximate Kitaev quantum spin liquid behaviour in a honeycomb magnet	Banerjee A. et al.	2016	Nature Materials	465
Many-body localisation in a quantum simulator with programmable random disorder	Smith J. et al.	2016	Nature Physics	394

publishing scientific research on quantum computing and fueling its technological advances in publishing many high-impact original studies.

From the technical perspective, architectures for quantum computing on various material systems have been studied in these highly-cited articles. Solid-state architecture is the leading physical system for quantum computing. In 2019, Google achieved a quantum of advantage in superconducting architecture, which was the first milestone in quantum computing in recent years, evidenced in its 948 citations (Arute et al. 2019). Prior studies developed room-temperature, polarised and ultrabright single-photon emission from a colour centre in two-dimensional hexagonal boron nitride (Tran et al. 2017), a bright source generating near-unity indistinguishability and pure single photons made of quantum dots in electrically controlled cavities (Somaschi et al. 2016), and plasmonic nanocavities providing single-molecule strong coupling at room temperature (Chikkaraddy et al. 2016). Other architectures include 51 qubits programmable Ising-type quantum spin model (Bernien et al. 2017), and proximate Kitaev quantum spin liquid, which generated Marajona fermions that could be used as the basic material for quantum computers (Banerjee et al. 2016). Many-body localisation, which is an important phenomenon in superconducting quantum field, has been studied in a quantum simulator with programmable random disorder (Smith et al. 2016).

New quantum algorithms have been the focus of research. A quantum algorithm on superconducting quantum devices has been developed to determine the ground-state energy for molecules (Kandala et al. 2017). Another article focuses on new quantum materials, monolithically integrated lithium niobate electro-optic modulators, which are useful in photonic circuits (Wang et al. 2018).

4.9. *Top sources in terms of publications, citation, and FWCI*

Table 8 lists top sources by research impact, as indicated by FWCI. The highest publications are Nature, Nature Photonics, Science, Nature Physics, Nature Nanotechnology, Physical Review X, and npj Quantum Information.

Citation count is another indicator of the quality of the journal. The journals with more than 10,000 citations are: Physical Review Letters, Physical Review A, Nature, Physical Review B, Science, and Physical Review X.

As for the number of publications published, Physical Review A has the highest number of publications, with 2935 publications published since 2016. Both Physical Review Letters and Physical Review B have more than 1000 publications. They were followed by Quantum Information

Table 8. Top sources in quantum computing since 2016.

Journal title	Publications	Citation	FWCI
Nature	222	18383	7.89
Nature Photonics	78	5128	6.1
Science	142	10361	5.77
Nature Physics	182	7799	4.94
Nature Nanotechnology	66	2690	4.69
Physical Review X	264	10224	3.84
npj Quantum Information	290	4000	2.93
Journal of High Energy Physics	148	3393	2.73
Nature Communications	455	12706	2.43
Optica	131	2737	2.38
ACS Nano	81	1589	2.32
Journal of Statistical Mechanics: Theory and Experiment	134	2022	2.3
Physical Review Letters	1416	29039	2.18
Communications in Mathematical Physics	61	713	2.15
Nano Letters	215	4731	2.11
Proceedings of the National Academy of Sciences of the United States of America	63	1711	2.04
Science advances	151	3794	1.97
Quantum Science and Technology	269	2851	1.91
Quantum	257	2440	1.82
ACS Photonics	112	1798	1.81

Processing (829 publications), Scientific Reports (692 publications), and New Journal of Physics (687 publications).

5. Conclusions

This article aims to give a comprehensive and in-depth analysis of the global development status of quantum computing. To achieve this aim, we reviewed the current development status, analysed research hotspots and technological trends, and the contribution of authors, institutions, and countries in quantum computing from 2016 to 2020. We found that quantum computing is still under development, with the US and China in the leading position, from where most critical scholars came. The most important institutions are scattered in the United States, China, and France. Topics with the highest Prominence percentile, distinctive keyphrases, and leading source journals were also analysed. The research findings are expected to provide ideas and suggestions for future researches and policymaking and help promote quantum science development.

Despite the meaningful contributions that have been made in this study, there are several limitations. First, the data analysis in this study was based on Scopus, and the analysis was performed in SciVal. The research findings can be validated by comparison with other databases and bibliometric analysis tools. Second, the review section of this study is limited to only a few of the current hotspots, which is not comprehensive enough. In future works, the development status, research fronts, knowledge flow, and technology transfer and transformation within quantum computing can be further explored by citation network analysis and science paper-patent integration analysis.

The results show that although the age of quantum computing has not yet arrived, it already promises some exciting things, and many important milestones have been achieved. Noting the interdisciplinary nature of quantum science, scholars and research institutions worldwide should pay more attention to international cooperation to promote the growth of this discipline. Continual funding and investment in quantum computing are also essential. The FWCI of quantum computing indicates a relatively low research impact in the science community. By focusing on research and funding on the hotspots, promoting the cooperation between academia and corporate, and laying out the critical technologies in advance, the next generation of quantum computing technology will be developed even faster.

In conclusion, the scientific community needs further breakthroughs in quantum computing and more in-depth cooperation and communication between universities, national laboratories, companies, and governments to promote the development and fabrication of quantum hardware and software and the production of quantum control materials. This paper presents a clear blueprint of the quantum computing field in the past five years, which will help researchers and policymakers to develop a more explicit strategy for the development of quantum computing.

Acknowledgements

The authors gratefully acknowledge the support of the China Postdoctoral Science Foundation (Grant number 2019M660145).

Disclosure statement

The authors have declared no conflict of interest.

Funding

This work was supported by the China Postdoctoral Science Foundation under [grant number: 2019M660145].

ORCID

Jiaxing Wang http://orcid.org/0000-0002-7672-6911
Wuyuan Zhou http://orcid.org/0000-0001-5506-3373

References

A Precarious Milestone for Quantum Computing. 2019. *Nature* 574 (7779): 453–454.

Acín, A., I. Bloch, H. Buhrman, T. Calarco, C. Eichler, J. Eisert, D. Esteve, et al. 2018. "The Quantum Technologies Roadmap: A European Community View." *New Journal of Physics* 20 (8). doi:10.1088/1367-2630/aad1ea.

Arakawa, Y., and M. J. Holmes. 2020. "Progress in Quantum-Dot Single Photon Sources for Quantum Information Technologies: A Broad Spectrum Overview." *Applied Physics Reviews* 7 (2). doi:10.1063/5.0010193.

Arute, F., K. Arya, R. Babbush, D. Bacon, J. C. Bardin, R. Barends, R. Biswas, … J. M. Martinis. 2019. "Quantum Supremacy Using a Programmable Superconducting Processor." *Nature* 574 (7779): 505–510. doi:10.1038/s41586-019-1666-5.

Banerjee, A., C. A. Bridges, J.-Q. Yan, A. A. Aczel, L. Li, M. B. Stone, G. E. Granroth, M. D. Lumsden, Y. Yiu, J. Knolle, D. G. Mandrus, and S. E. Nagler. 2016. "Proximate Kitaev Quantum Spin Liquid Behaviour in a Honeycomb Magnet." *Nature Materials* 15: 733–740. doi:10.1038/nmat4604.

Benioff, P. 1980. "The Computer as a Physical System: A Microscopic Quantum Mechanical Hamiltonian Model of Computers as Represented by Turing Machines." *Journal of Statistical Physics* 22 (5): 563–591. doi:10.1007/BF01011339.

Bennett, C. H. 1973. "Logical Reversibility of Computation." *IBM Journal of Research and Development* 17 (6): 525–532. doi:10.1147/rd.176.0525.

Bernien, H., S. Schwartz, A. Keesling, H. Levine, A. Omran, H. Pichler, S. Choi, A. S. Zibrov, M. Endres, M. Greiner, V. Vuletic, and M. D. Lukin. 2017. "Probing Many-Body Dynamics on a 51-Atom Quantum Simulator." *Nature* 551: 579–584. doi:10.1038/nature24622.

Biamonte, J. D., P. Dorozhkin, and I. Zacharov. 2019. "Keep Quantum Computing Global and Open." *Nature* 573 (7773): 190–191. doi:10.1038/d41586-019-02675-5.

Blais, A., S. M. Girvin, and W. D. Oliver. 2020. "Quantum Information Processing and Quantum Optics with Circuit Quantum Electrodynamics." *Nature Physics* 16 (3): 247–256. doi:10.1038/s41567-020-0806-z.

Bornmann, L., R. Mutz, W. Marx, H. Schier, and H. D. Daniel. 2011. "A Multilevel Modelling Approach to Investigating the Predictive Validity of Editorial Decisions: Do the Editors of a High Profile Journal Select Manuscripts That Are Highly Cited After Publication?" *Journal of the Royal Statistical Society: Series A (Statistics in Society)* 174 (4): 857–879. doi:10.1111/j.1467-985X.2011.00689.x.

Bruzewicz, C. D., J. Chiaverini, R. McConnell, and J. M. Sage. 2019. "Trapped-ion Quantum Computing: Progress and Challenges." *Applied Physics Reviews* 6 (2). doi:10.1063/1.5088164.

Cantú-Ortiz, F. J., and J. Fangmeyer. 2017. "University Performance in the Age of Research Analytics." In *Research Analytics: Boosting University Productivity and Competitiveness Through Scientometrics*. doi:10.1201/9781315155890

Carusotto, I., A. A. Houck, A. J. Kollár, P. Roushan, D. I. Schuster, and J. Simon. 2020. "Photonic Materials in Circuit Quantum Electrodynamics." *Nature Physics* 16 (3): 268–279. doi:10.1038/s41567-020-0815-y.

Chang, L. L. H., F. K. H. Phoa, and J. Nakano. 2019. "A New Metric for the Analysis of the Scientific Article Citation Network." *IEEE Access* 7: 132027–132032. doi:10.1109/ACCESS.2019.2937220.

Chen, Z., K. J. Satzinger, J. Atalaya, A. N. Korotkov, A. Dunsworth, D. Sank, C. Quintana, … J. Kelly. 2021. "Exponential Suppression of Bit or Phase Errors with Cyclic Error Correction." *Nature* 595 (7867): 383–387. doi:10.1038/s41586-021-03588-y.

Chia, C., B. Machielse, B. Pingault, M. Chalupnik, G. Joe, E. Cornell, S. W. Ding, et al. 2021. "Diamond Quantum Nanophotonics and Optomechanics." *Semiconductors and Semimetals* 104: 219–251. doi:10.1016/bs.semsem.2020.08.005

Chikkaraddy, R., B. De Nijs, F. Benz, S. J. Barrow, O. A. Scherman, E. Rosta, A. Demetriadou, P. Fox, O. Hess, and J. J. Baumberg. 2016. "Single-molecule Strong Coupling at Room Temperature in Plasmonic Nanocavities." *Nature* 535: 127–130. doi:10.1038/nature17974.

Clarke, J., and F. K. Wilhelm. 2008. "Superconducting Quantum Bits." *Nature* 453 (7198): 1031–1042. doi:10.1038/nature07128.

Clerk, A. A., K. W. Lehnert, P. Bertet, J. R. Petta, and Y. Nakamura. 2020. "Hybrid Quantum Systems with Circuit Quantum Electrodynamics." *Nature Physics* 16 (3): 257–267. doi:10.1038/s41567-020-0797-9.

Corcoles, A. D., A. Kandala, A. Javadi-Abhari, D. T. McClure, A. W. Cross, K. Temme, P. D. Nation, M. Steffen, and J. M. Gambetta. 2020. "Challenges and Opportunities of Near-Term Quantum Computing Systems." *Proceedings of the IEEE* 108 (8): 1338–1352. doi:10.1109/JPROC.2019.2954005.

Dhawan, S. M., B. M. Gupta, and S. Bhusan. 2018. "Global Publications Output in Quantum Computing Research: A Scientometric Assessment During 2007–16." *Emerging Science Journal* 2 (4): 228–237. doi:10.28991/esj-2018-01147.

DiVincenzo, D. P., and D. Loss. 1999. "Quantum Computers and Quantum Coherence." *Journal of Magnetism and Magnetic Materials* 200 (1–3): 202–218. doi:10.1016/S0304-8853(99)00315-7.

Ebadi, S., T. T. Wang, H. Levine, A. Keesling, G. Semeghini, A. Omran, D. Bluvstein, et al. 2021. "Quantum Phases of Matter on a 256-Atom Programmable Quantum Simulator." *Nature* 595 (7866): 227–232. doi:10.1038/s41586-021-03582-4.

Elshaari, A. W., W. Pernice, K. Srinivasan, O. Benson, and V. Zwiller. 2020. "Hybrid Integrated Quantum Photonic Circuits." *Nature Photonics* 14 (5): 285–298. doi:10.1038/s41566-020-0609-x.

Feynman, R. P. 1982. "Simulating Physics with Computers." *International Journal of Theoretical Physics* 21 (6–7): 467–488. doi:10.1007/BF02650179.

Flamini, F., N. Spagnolo, and F. Sciarrino. 2019. "Photonic Quantum Information Processing: A Review." *Reports on Progress in Physics* 82: 016001. doi:10.1088/1361-6633/aad5b2.

Forn-Díaz, P., L. Lamata, E. Rico, J. Kono, and E. Solano. 2019. "Ultrastrong Coupling Regimes of Light-Matter Interaction." *Reviews of Modern Physics* 91 (2). doi:10.1103/RevModPhys.91.025005.

Gao, W. B., P. Fallahi, E. Togan, J. Miguel-Sanchez, and A. Imamoglu. 2012. "Observation of Entanglement Between a Quantum Dot Spin and a Single Photon." *Nature* 491 (7424): 426–430. doi:10.1038/nature11573.

Gao, S., Y. Hu, K. Janowicz, and G. McKenzie. 2013. "A Spatiotemporal Scientometrics Framework for Exploring the Citation Impact of Publications and Scientists." *GIS: Proceedings of the ACM International Symposium on Advances in Geographic Information Systems*, 204–213.

Grover, L. K. 1996. "A Fast Quantum Mechanical Algorithm for Database Search." In *Proceedings of the Annual ACM Symposium on Theory of Computing*, Part F1294, 212–219. doi:10.1145/237814.237866.

Grzesiak, N., R. Blümel, K. Wright, K. M. Beck, N. C. Pisenti, M. Li, V. Chaplin, et al. 2020. "Efficient Arbitrary Simultaneously Entangling Gates on a Trapped-ion Quantum Computer." *Nature Communications* 11 (1). doi:10.1038/s41467-020-16790-9.

Harrow, A. W., and A. Montanaro. 2017. "Quantum Computational Supremacy." *Nature* 549 (7671): 203–209. doi:10.1038/nature23458.

He, M., J. P. Gales, É Ducrot, Z. Gong, G. R. Yi, S. Sacanna, and D. J. Pine. 2020. "Colloidal Diamond." *Nature* 585 (7826): 524–529. doi:10.1038/s41586-020-2718-6.

Head-Marsden, K., J. Flick, C. J. Ciccarino, and P. Narang. 2021. "Quantum Information and Algorithms for Correlated Quantum Matter." *Chemical Reviews* 121 (5): 3061–3120. doi:10.1021/acs.chemrev.0c00620.

Huang, H. L., D. Wu, D. Fan, and X. Zhu. 2020. "Superconducting Quantum Computing: A Review." *Science China Information Sciences* 63 (8). doi:10.1007/s11432-020-2881-9.

Hwang, S. Y., and B. Sothmann. 2020. "Phase-coherent Caloritronics with Ordinary and Topological Josephson Junctions." *The European Physical Journal Special Topics* 229 (4): 683–705. doi:10.1140/epjst/e2019-900094-y.

Jain, S., J. Alonso, M. Grau, and J. P. Home. 2020. "Scalable Arrays of Micro-Penning Traps for Quantum Computing and Simulation." *Physical Review X* 10 (3), doi:10.1103/PhysRevX.10.031027.

Kan, Y., S. K. H. Andersen, F. Ding, S. Kumar, C. Zhao, and S. I. Bozhevolnyi. 2020. "Metasurface-Enabled Generation of Circularly Polarized Single Photons." *Advanced Materials* 32 (16). doi:10.1002/adma.201907832.

Kandala, A., A. Mezzacapo, K. Temme, M. Takita, M. Brink, J. M. Chow, and J. M. Gambetta. 2017. "Hardware-Efficient Variational Quantum Eigensolver for Small Molecules and Quantum Magnets." *Nature* 549: 242–246. doi:10.1038/nature23879.

Khan, F. S., and T. S. Humble. 2019. "Nash Embedding and Equilibrium in Pure Quantum States." In *Lecture Notes in Computer Science (Including Subseries Lecture Notes in Artificial Intelligence and Lecture Notes in Bioinformatics)*. Vol. 11413: *LNCS*. doi:10.1007/978-3-030-14082-3_5.

Krantz, P., M. Kjaergaard, F. Yan, T. P. Orlando, S. Gustavsson, and W. D. Oliver. 2019. "A Quantum Engineer's Guide to Superconducting Qubits." *Applied Physics Reviews* 6 (2). doi:10.1063/1.5089550.

Lekitsch, B., S. Weidt, A. G. Fowler, K. Mølmer, S. J. Devitt, C. Wunderlich, and W. K. Hensinger. 2017. "Blueprint for a Microwave Trapped ion Quantum Computer." *Science Advances* 3 (2). doi:10.1126/sciadv.1601540.

Lewis-Swan, R. J., A. Safavi-Naini, A. M. Kaufman, and A. M. Rey. 2019. "Dynamics of Quantum Information." *Nature Reviews Physics* 1 (10): 627–634. doi:10.1038/s42254-019-0090-y.

Leydesdorff, L., L. Bornmann, and C. S. Wagner. 2019. "The Relative Influences of Government Funding and International Collaboration on Citation Impact." *Journal of the Association for Information Science and Technology* 70 (2): 198–201. doi:10.1002/asi.24109.

Liu, Xiaolong, and M. C. Hersam. 2019. "2D Materials for Quantum Information Science." *Nature Reviews Materials* 4 (10): 669–684. doi:10.1038/s41578-019-0136-x.

Liu, Y., D. Lin, J. Li, and S. Shan. 2016. "Scholarly Output Graph: A Graphical Article-Level Metric Indicating the Impact of a Scholar's Publications." In *Lecture Notes in Computer Science (Including Subseries Lecture Notes in Artificial Intelligence and Lecture Notes in Bioinformatics)*. Vol. 10086: *LNAI*. doi:10.1007/978-3-319-49586-6_40.

Liu, Xiaohong, R. Sun, S. Wang, and Y. J. Wu. 2020. "The Research Landscape of Big Data: A Bibliometric Analysis." *Library Hi Tech* 38 (2): 367–384.

Makhlin, Y., G. Schön, and A. Shnirman. 2001. "Quantum-state Engineering with Josephson-Junction Devices." *Reviews of Modern Physics* 73 (2): 357–400. doi:10.1103/RevModPhys.73.357.

Martín-Martín, A., E. Orduna-Malea, M. Thelwall, and E. Delgado López-Cózar. 2018. "Google Scholar, Web of Science, and Scopus: A Systematic Comparison of Citations in 252 Subject Categories." *Journal of Informetrics* 12 (4): 1160–1177. doi:10.1016/j.joi.2018.09.002.

Murali, P., D. M. Debroy, K. R. Brown, and M. Martonosi. 2020. "Architecting Noisy Intermediate-Scale Trapped Ion Quantum Computers." *Proceedings – International Symposium on Computer Architecture*, 529–542. doi:10.1109/ISCA45697.2020.00051.

Nakamura, Y., Y. A. Pashkin, and J. S. Tsai. 1999. "Coherent Control of Macroscopic Quantum States in a Single-Cooper-Pair box." *Nature* 398 (6730): 786–788. doi:10.1038/19718.

Nelz, R., J. Görlitz, D. Herrmann, A. Slablab, M. Challier, M. Radtke, M. Fischer, et al. 2019. "Toward Wafer-Scale Diamond Nano- and Quantum Technologies." *APL Materials* 7 (1). doi:10.1063/1.5067267.

Nguyen, N. H., E. C. Behrman, M. A. Moustafa, and J. E. Steck. 2020. "Benchmarking Neural Networks for Quantum Computations." *IEEE Transactions on Neural Networks and Learning Systems* 31 (7): 2522–2531.

Oliver, W. D. 2019. "Quantum Computing Takes Flight." *Nature* 574 (7779): 487–488. doi:10.1038/d41586-019-03173-4.

Palmieri, A. M., E. Kovlakov, F. Bianchi, D. Yudin, S. Straupe, J. D. Biamonte, and S. Kulik. 2020. "Experimental Neural Network Enhanced Quantum Tomography." *Npj Quantum Information* 6 (1). doi:10.1038/s41534-020-0248-6.

Pohl, H. 2021. "Internationalisation, Innovation, and Academic–Corporate co-Publications." *Scientometrics* 126 (2): 1329–1358. doi:10.1007/s11192-020-03799-6.

Purkayastha, A., E. Palmaro, H. J. Falk-Krzesinski, and J. Baas. 2019. "Comparison of Two Article-Level, Field-Independent Citation Metrics: Field-Weighted Citation Impact (FWCI) and Relative Citation Ratio (RCR)." *Journal of Informetrics* 13 (2): 635–642. doi:10.1016/j.joi.2019.03.012.

Radulaski, M., J. L. Zhang, Y. K. Tzeng, K. G. Lagoudakis, H. Ishiwata, C. Dory, K. A. Fischer, et al. 2019. "Nanodiamond Integration with Photonic Devices." *Laser and Photonics Reviews* 13 (8). doi:10.1002/lpor.201800316.

Richardson, C. J. K., V. Lordi, S. Misra, and J. Shabani. 2020. "Materials Science for Quantum Information Science and Technology." *MRS Bulletin* 45 (6): 485–497. doi:10.1557/mrs.2020.147.

Setia, K., R. Chen, J. E. Rice, A. Mezzacapo, M. Pistoia, and J. D. Whitfield. 2020. "Reducing Qubit Requirements for Quantum Simulations Using Molecular Point Group Symmetries." *Journal of Chemical Theory and Computation* 16 (10): 6091–6097. doi:10.1021/acs.jctc.0c00113.

Shor, P. W. 1994. "Polynomial Time Algorithms for Discrete Logarithms and Factoring on a Quantum Computer." In *Lecture Notes in Computer Science (Including Subseries Lecture Notes in Artificial Intelligence and Lecture Notes in Bioinformatics)*. Vol. 877: *LNCS*. doi:10.1007/3-540-58691-1_68.

Smith, J., A. Lee, P. Richerme, B. Neyenhuis, P. W. Hess, P. Hauke, M. Heyl, D. A. Huse, and C. Monroe. 2016. "Many-body Localization in a Quantum Simulator with Programmable Random Disorder." *Nature Physics* 12 (10): 907–911. doi:10.1038/nphys3783.

Somaschi, N., V. Giesz, L. De Santis, J. C. Loredo, M. P. Almeida, G. Hornecker, S. L. Portalupi, T. Grange, C. Antón, J. Demory, L. Lanco, and P. Senellart. 2016. "Near-optimal Single-Photon Sources in the Solid State." *Nature Photonics* 10: 340–345. doi:10.1038/nphoton.2016.23.

Terekhov, A. I. 2020. "Bibliometric Trends in Quantum Information Processing." *Scientific and Technical Information Processing* 47 (2): 94–103. doi:10.3103/S0147688220020021.

Tian, Q., L. Wang, C. Tang, J. Zhang, J. Xu, Q. Tian, L. Wang, C. Tang, J. Zhang, and J. Xu. 2020. "International Development Trend of Quantum Computing Research Based on Bibliometric Analysis." *Science Focus* 14 (6): 1–9.

Torlai, G., G. Mazzola, J. Carrasquilla, M. Troyer, R. Melko, and G. Carleo. 2018. "Neural-network Quantum State Tomography." *Nature Physics* 14 (5): 447–450. doi:10.1038/s41567-018-0048-5.

Tran, T. T., S. Choi, J. A. Scott, Z. Q. Xu, C. Zheng, G. Seniutinas, A. Bendavid, M. S. Fuhrer, M. Toth, and I. Aharonovich. 2017. "Room-Temperature Single-Photon Emission from Oxidized Tungsten Disulfide Multilayers. *Advanced Optical Materials* 5: 1600939. doi:10.1002/adom.201600939.

U.S. Department of Energy. 2020. "White House Office of Technology Policy, National Science Foundation and Department of Energy Announce Over $1 Billion in Awards for Artificial Intelligence and Quantum Information Science Research Institutes." Accessed 9 July 2021. https://www.energy.gov/articles/white-house-office-technology-policy-national-science-foundation-and-department-energy.

Wang, C., M. Zhang, X. Chen, M. Bertrand, A. Shams-Ansari, S. Chandrasekhar, P. Winzer, and M. Lončar. 2018. "Integrated Lithium Niobate Electro-optic Modulators Operating at CMOS-compatible Voltages." *Nature* 562: 101–104. doi:10.1038/s41586-018-0551-y.

Wright, K., K. M. Beck, S. Debnath, J. M. Amini, Y. Nam, N. Grzesiak, J. S. Chen, … J. Kim. 2019. "Benchmarking an 11-Qubit Quantum Computer." *Nature Communications* 10 (1). doi:10.1038/s41467-019-13534-2.

Zhong, H. Sen, H. Wang, Y. H. Deng, M. C. Chen, L. C. Peng, Y. H. Luo, J. Qin, … J. W. Pan. 2021. "Quantum Computational Advantage Using Photons." *Science* 370 (6523): 1460–1463.

OPEN ACCESS

Asleep at the wheel? Responsible Innovation in quantum computing

Philip Inglesant, Carolyn Ten Holter, Marina Jirotka and Robin Williams

ABSTRACT

Quantum computing is an emerging set of technologies which promise to transform aspects of computing in ways that, though increasingly defined, are still largely theoretical. Responsible Innovation (RI) asserts that technologies with potentially transformative capacity on society should be approached with care and forethought; this paper is based on applying RI in one of the UK's National Quantum Technology Hubs.

Quantum computing is at a key juncture as it emerges from the laboratory to be of interest commercially. This provides an opportunity to observe and influence the trajectory of this technology. Quantum computing is widely envisioned to have major impacts on computing and society; there are, however, great uncertainties about development timescales and the scope and impact of applications.

From experiences with a major quantum computing project in the UK, we discuss the challenges in applying RI to quantum computing. Existing RI practices struggle to address the societal implications of such a complex and innovative technology. We argue that uncovering the visions and sociotechnical imaginaries that inform the development this technology enables RI to make valuable insights into future societal implications of quantum computing. This provides lessons for RI in emerging technologies more widely.

Introduction

The Promethean powers of modern technology are expanding at an ever-increasing rate. Quantum computing promises to be one of these powers. Even if society is not, as some fear, '*asleep at the wheel*' (Khan 2021), experience with other emerging science and technology shows that social control of technologies faces a dilemma: potentially harmful outcomes cannot easily be anticipated and controlled in the earliest stages of development, but it is difficult to change the trajectory later once outcomes are more evident (Collingridge 1980).

How, then, is Responsible Innovation (RI) to understand and react to the choices made available by an emerging technology, when so little can be known about the implications? Despite the profoundly uncertain early stages of emerging science and technology, we believe that it is possible to discern, and potentially to intervene in the *meanings* (van der Burg 2014), visions, and sociotechnical imaginaries (Jasanoff 2015) which drive and shape new technologies.

Quantum computing aims to harness the phenomena of quantum mechanics – such as entanglement and superposition – to do things which cannot be done by current 'classical' (non-quantum)

computing methods (Montanaro 2016), such as efficient searching through unordered data, optimisation, simulating the behaviour of molecules, and factorisation. Already there is interest in exploiting existing or soon-to-exist devices using quantum methods for applications that can address difficult and useful real-world computing problems (Preskill 2018). Quantum computing in some forms, therefore, is already with us; now is an appropriate moment at which to consider the implications of these new technologies. It is at this stage, when the processes and products are becoming discernible but not yet established, that we can consider what sort of futures we want these new technologies to engender.

This paper draws evidence from interviews and workshops in the application of RI in a major UK project in quantum computing: Networked Quantum Information Technologies (NQIT), one of four quantum technology Hubs in the UK National Quantum Technologies Programme (UKNQTP) (UK Research and Innovation 2021). The process of RI in NQIT included one-to-one semi-structured interviews with key researchers and directors of NQIT, a series of workshops at NQIT events and other UKNQTP Hubs, and case studies of quantum machine learning and defence and national security implications of quantum technologies (Inglesant, Hartswood, and Jirotka 2016; Inglesant, Jirotka, and Hartswood 2018).

Responsible Innovation

There are several currents and themes in Responsible Innovation (RI) (also sometimes known as Responsible *Research and* Innovation (RRI); for a useful discussion of these two linked discourses, see Owen and Pansera (2019)). RI emphasises proactive and anticipatory responses, in contrast to retrospective risk-based regulation of the outcomes. RI proposes '*a transparent, interactive process*' to address '*the (ethical) acceptability, sustainability, and societal desirability of the innovation process and its marketable products … to allow a proper embedding … in our society*' (von Schomberg 2013).

One approach to RRI has been developed by the European Commission and focusses around five themes: public engagement, open access, gender equality, ethics, and science education, plus, in various versions, governance and institutional change.[1]

In the UK, the Engineering and Physical Sciences Research Council (EPSRC) has adopted the AREA Framework - Anticipate, Reflect, Engage, Act,[2] based on work by Stilgoe, Owen, and Macnaghten (2013) (Table 1). Jirotka et al. (2017) added a second range of attributes: the '4 P's': the Products, Processes, People, and Purpose, to articulate its practical application as the AREA Plus Framework.

Fundamentally, RI questions the framings which surround science and innovation (Williams and Edge 1996; Grunwald 2011; Stilgoe and Guston 2017; Özdemir 2019). We draw on these insights to uncover attributed meanings and to dig more deeply into opportunities for assessment and intervention (Williams 2006). We consider the '*sociotechnical imaginaries*' (Jasanoff 2015) which shape actually-existing and still-emerging technologies, and show how, by reflecting on these, the trajectory of *innovation* may be changed.

These visions and imaginaries are not fixed but are continually negotiated in dialogue — a dialogue in which some voices will be heard more loudly than others. Certain technologies, because of their perceived immense potential, come to be viewed in the context of national strategy and as part of '*the design and fulfilment of nation-specific … projects*' (Jasanoff and Kim 2009) in the national

Table 1: The AREA Framework

Anticipation	Anticipation means preparedness rather than prediction in the face of novel technologies (Collingridge 1980; Guston 2014).
Reflection	Holds a mirror to value systems, assumptions and framings that inform our own activities; questions the 'moral division of labour' (Swierstra and Rip 2007).
Engagement	'Opening up' (Stirling 2008) processes of research and innovation to wider participatory deliberation.
Action	'Responsiveness' (Stilgoe, Owen, and Macnaghten 2013) is the capacity to change trajectory where necessary; for example, midstream modulation (Fisher, Mahajan, and Mitcham 2006), or Stage-Gates (Stilgoe, Owen, and Macnaghten 2013).

collective imagination. Quantum computing is particularly rich in such visions. Indeed, the work on which this paper is based is part of a national strategy (UK National Quantum Technologies Programme Strategic Advisory Board 2015a), geared towards 'a new era for the UK' and promising '*the next generation of products with exciting and astounding properties that will affect our lives profoundly*'.

The emergence of 'revolutionary' new technologies is often accompanied by claims about their transformatory potential (Rayner 2004). However, the ultimate technical and social outcomes of a technology are usually far removed from these initial visions (Williams 2006). These visions anticipate and influence the future but they cannot predict it; they reflect, rather, our *current* ideas — we cannot envision the world as future generations will see it (Grunwald 2014).

This is a challenge but also an opportunity for Responsible Innovation. Rather than understanding innovation as simply '*whatever happens to emerge from incumbent structures of interest, privilege, and power*' (Genus and Stirling 2018, 62), RI calls into question the '*narrative of inevitability*' (Stilgoe 2013) in the development trajectory of new science and technology and its societal impacts, good or bad. RI builds on an extensive body of enquiry showing that the technical and social outcomes of an emerging technology are not intrinsic but are patterned by a succession of choices as the technology is developed and adopted and becomes embedded in society (Williams and Edge 1996).

RI has been articulated around nanotechnology (Fisher and Rip 2013; Kjølberg and Strand 2011), artificial intelligence (Brundage 2016), information technologies (Jirotka et al. 2017), and synthetic biology (Macnaghten, Owen, and Jackson 2016). But beyond the generic lessons identified in retrospective studies of earlier technologies, there is a need to tackle the sociomaterial specificities surrounding quantum computing. Despite considerable uncertainty, it is possible to discern the outline of quantum computing on the horizon through the visions which define and shape it. The following sections explore these visions and framings, which we then unpack to discuss the implications for RI.

Quantum computing

There are many excellent expositions of quantum computing (see for example: (Aaronson 2013; Bernhardt 2019)); here we seek simply to give sufficient explanation to examine what quantum computing may imply for society. Briefly:

1. Quantum computing applies quantum phenomena, such as superposition and entanglement, to computation (DiVincenzo 2000; Ambainis 2014). Quantum computing holds the promise of speeding up or making possible solutions to *certain kinds* of computing problem, but is not *in general* faster than classical computing, except for specific computational problems (Aaronson 2008).
2. There is not one single form of quantum computer. Many physical systems showing controllable quantum effects, each with its own advantages and disadvantages, could enable quantum computing and its fundamental unit, the 'qubit' or quantum bit. Some of the most promising are: ion traps (the main approach adopted by NQIT), superconductors, photons, and qubits in solid-state materials (DiVincenzo 2000).
3. However, most physical qubits are vulnerable to environmental 'noise' and errors; building quantum computers for some of the most high-profile expected applications will require large numbers of error-corrected qubits. This is still far from being achieved and is a major research area in its own right.
4. Although large-scale, fault-tolerant 'universal', gate-based quantum computers may be years away, there is increasing interest in problems which might be solved by small quantum computers that already exist, or soon will do. These ideas have coalesced around what is known as 'Noisy Intermediate-Scale Quantum Computing' (NISQ), from an article by Preskill (2018).
5. The term 'quantum computer' is somewhat misleading. Computers are familiar artefacts as laptops, servers, smartphones etc. Quantum comput*ing*, our preferred term, will not replace

these forms of computer, at least as far as we can foresee. Quantum computing might be developed as 'Quantum Processing Units' (QPUs) co-processors (Britt and Humble 2017), and/or accessed over cloud-style services (Preskill 2018) — already possible in a limited way with the IBM Quantum Experience and its competitors.[3]

Meanwhile, non-quantum, 'classical' computing continues to develop in sophistication and speed (Bleicher 2018; Preskill 2018). This is not only a continuation of the increasing miniaturisation predicted by Moore's Law (Moore 2006) – but also through new models of computation, specialised architectures, and new kinds of materials and devices (Shalf 2020).

Visions of Quantum Computing

We identify three visions of quantum computing. In the first vision, we are on the threshold of an era of computing more powerful than anything that has gone before (Khan 2021). The second vision tries to identify practical implications of quantum computing in the short term (Preskill 2018). Thirdly, the discourse of 'quantum supremacy' is concerned with increases in speed for specialised problems, irrespective of real-world use-cases; the demonstration of quantum supremacy is said to herald a new era of quantum computing (Arute et al. 2019).

Capabilities far beyond the most powerful classical computers

There are classes of problem which even the most powerful, fastest classical computers cannot solve in a reasonable timeframe; quantum computing is expected to be able to help solve *a subset* of these problems (Aaronson 2008). Some quantum computing developers suggest that this will lead to '*a new computer technology era more powerful than anything that preceded it*' (Khan 2021), first in areas such as materials and drug development, and, later, transforming areas including machine learning[4] (Lloyd, Mohseni, and Rebentrost 2013; Biamonte et al. 2017; Dunjko and Wittek 2019) and natural language processing. This could have applications to defence, for example for improved target identification (Congressional Research Service 2021), and in many other application areas.

One capability which has drawn much attention is the potential to perform certain mathematically difficult tasks such as factorisation, impossible in a practicable timescale with large numbers using classical methods, but possible for quantum computing using methods such as Shor's algorithm (Shor 1999; Aaronson 2007). This requires capabilities far beyond what is currently available, but which, if implemented, would render many existing forms of encrypted communications insecure.[5] This would present an immediate problem for very high-value data communications or root-level public keys that must remain secure over many decades (National Cyber Security Centre 2020). However, researchers are already developing new forms of what is known as post-quantum cryptography (Bernstein 2009), seeking to develop cryptographic systems which are believed to be not vulnerable to this attack.

Quantum computing can be useful now, or soon will be

Despite important advances, however, flexible quantum computers on the scale of tens of thousands of qubits remain at least some years from achievement; the timescale, and whether it is even possible in principle, remains highly uncertain (Pritchard and Till 2016; Dyakonov 2019). Since such large-scale, error-corrected 'universal', gate-based quantum computers may be decades away, there is increasing interest in useful applications of quantum computing that are expected to be available in the near future (for example, (Wecker, Hastings, and Troyer 2015)). One example is 'Noisy Intermediate-Scale Quantum Computing' (NISQ) (Preskill 2018). These devices are of the order of 50–100 qubits and are 'noisy': not fully error-corrected and are limited in the size of quantum circuits, or algorithms, that they can execute. (For a recent overview of progress, see (Bharti et al. 2021)). An innovator working with NQIT suggested that:

> *'there is an assumption that these devices would have to be very polished and very commercialised before they'd be able to be sold. ... [but] there could be a market for this thing which is very unstable and very difficult to work with, but ... is just about able to solve a problem which a normal computer couldn't.'* – *Interviewee LI5*

Useful tasks that such computing may be able to address near-term include:

Optimisation

Optimisation — such as the maximum or minimum value of some function[6] — in many cases is hard to do using classical computers (Mohseni et al. 2017). Optimisation underlies many practical applications and is also a key part of machine learning algorithms (Sra, Nowozin, and Wright 2012).

Quantum computing is not expected to be able to solve 'NP-Hard'[7] combinatorial optimisation problems such as the 'travelling salesperson' problem,[8] but is possible that they might be able to find good *approximate* solutions more quickly for some problems (Preskill 2018). However, it is by no means trivial to identify the optimisation problems for which quantum methods will provide an advantage over known non-quantum methods (Moussa, Calandra, and Dunjko 2020) – a reminder, again, of the uncertainty that surrounds quantum computing.

Quantum simulation

Another class of applications which may be amenable to NISQ or other early quantum computing methods is the wide field of quantum simulation (Johnson, Clark, and Jaksch 2014; Nielsen 2015). Simulation is an echo of Feynman's (1981) initial insight that to model quantum processes requires quantum mechanical devices. Modelling, or simulating, many physical processes at the sub-atomic level is a very difficult problem for classical computers that physicists have struggled with for decades, but seems to be a natural fit for quantum computing.

Simulation has important applications in areas such as atomic physics, quantum chemistry and cosmology ((Georgescu, Ashhab, and Nori 2014) provide a good review). Quantum chemistry has been mooted as the 'killer application' for quantum computing, including, possibly, efficient nitrogen fixation for fertiliser production; this occurs naturally and efficiently in nature but known industrial processes are energy-intensive (Reiher et al. 2017). Such quantum-enabled advances in chemistry are not likely to be reached in the 'NISQ era', but physicists do hope to use NISQ technology to learn interesting things about quantum dynamics, reminiscent of the way in which chaos theory developed rapidly from classical simulations with early computers in the 1960s and 70s (Preskill 2018).

But, in a resonant phrase, Preskill suggests that we '*probably lack the imagination to anticipate the most transformative discoveries which will flow from more powerful quantum simulators*' (Preskill 2018, 13) – expressing, in a form of 'de-facto' Responsible Innovation, the interplay of imagination and anticipation.

Quantum supremacy

The promise of quantum computing has recently been thrown into high profile by Google's announcement of a claim to 'quantum supremacy': the demonstration of a calculation on a quantum computer which would be beyond the capability of any classical computer (Harrow and Montanaro 2017; Arute et al. 2019). Google's quantum processor performed in 200 seconds tasks that their researchers estimate could take 10,000 years using a state-of-the-art supercomputer (Arute et al. 2019). The moment of 'quantum supremacy', assuming this is what has been achieved, has been said to be nothing less than '*a privileged time in the history of our planet*' (Preskill 2019); it has been demonstrated that quantum computing can do things that classical computers cannot

(Aaronson 2019), and — the most challenging part — can be controlled and made to do things as predicted by their designers.

Aside from unfortunate historical connotations of the word (Wiesner 2017), claims around 'quantum supremacy' have been contested ('*the gloves are off*' (Aaronson 2019)): researchers at IBM calculated that the world's most powerful high-powered conventional computers could do similar calculations to Google's quantum computer in 2.5 days, much faster than Google's (Arute et al. 2019) estimate. Moreover, the calculation in this case is (probably) not very useful; it has been carefully chosen as something that quantum computing can do well but which is hard for non-quantum. Recall that quantum computing is not expected to replace or to be 'supreme' over non-quantum computing in general; meanwhile, non-quantum computers are also getting faster, partly as a response to advances in quantum computing; classical can 'fight back', but the direction of travel seems clear (Aaronson 2019).

From Visions to Responsible Innovation

These debates — about quantum supremacy, Google's claim and IBM's response; about what might be done with NISQ computing; and what might be possible with universal quantum computing and when — have largely been conducted in highly technical terms, and the trajectories towards universal quantum computing framed in terms of solving scientific and engineering problems.

However, the '*character and implications*' (Williams 2006) of technologies are always open to question. This is clear in quantum computing, which requires not only advanced technology but also highly trained practitioners and has potential applications beyond what can currently be perceived. Despite the demonstration of 'quantum supremacy' for specialised tasks, the shape of future quantum computing performing 'useful' tasks at scale is still being formed. Part of NQIT's role, participants in an RI workshop argued, was to participate actively in this discourse as a '*trusted source of information*'.

Even in technologies where the implementation is more advanced and apparently more certain, there are tensions between expectations of how a technology might be used and its intended sphere of operation. Fleck, Webster, and Williams (1990) analyse how 1980s visions of general-purpose robots as direct replacements for manual workers unhelpfully constrained understanding of their potential application in manufacturing; the anticipated development trajectory petered out or failed in the face of diverging user requirements.

It is easy in retrospect to identify trajectories from initial concept to adoption and widespread use, but this clarity is apparent only in hindsight (Pinch and Bijker 1984). Visions which attempt to project forwards not only risk being wide of the mark in practice but reify preconceived notions of what a technology 'is' and what it is 'for' — expectations which are the '*cause and consequence*' of the ways in which technologies are developed, supported, and adopted (Borup et al. 2006).

Opening up visions

While the claims made for quantum computing need to be tempered by an understanding of the difficulties of realising it in practice, we expect in the medium- to long-term that at least some of its promises will be borne out, but — this is a crucial point for RI — probably not in the ways that we currently foresee. There are multiple visions and competing dynamics, opening up (Stirling 2008) different challenges and considerations. Major companies, research institutions, and nation-states vie for dominance. Choices throughout the development pathways of innovation are made in conditions of uncertainty and tension.

Applying an RI lens and building on these visions, in the terms of the Anticipate-Reflect-Engage-Act framework, it might be thought that we are still very much in the 'Anticipation' dimension, with perhaps a little scope for Reflection on what we know currently. Until quantum computing is in widespread use, it remains a '*social experiment*' (van de Poel 2016). The already-difficult task of anticipating social consequences is obscured by layers of uncertainty; it is '*doubly fictional*' (Rip and Te Kulve 2008) still-imagined technical achievements from which plausible societal outcomes are then extrapolated.

Engagement is complex because of the conceptual challenges. It is hard for non-specialists to understand what quantum computing might actually be able to do (DiVincenzo 2017; Aaronson 2021b). Even for specialists, this is a subject of considerable debate. A public dialogue exercise in 2017 (Kantar Public 2018) found wide public familiarity with the word 'quantum', but little understanding of its application to quantum technologies: unsurprisingly, participants were most positive about applications with potential to benefit individuals and society and were wary of a quantum technologies 'arms race'. Dialogue remains essential to RI, however, both as '*the right thing to do*' (Stirling 2008) and to avert the risk that some compelling conception of quantum, positive or negative, will take hold and fill this space in the public imagination (Wagner et al. 2006).

The uncertainty and difficulties in anticipating the future potential and specific applications of quantum computing do not mean that RI has nothing to say or that there is nothing that can be done in the 'Act' dimension. The aim of RI is not to 'tick box' instrumental issues which might be raised by quantum computing but to engage in the process of anticipating and reflecting on the shape and framings of these technologies as they emerge. In our view, RI can make valuable contributions, not based on any attempt at *predicting* the future trajectory but from analysing these visions as '*sociotechnical imaginaries*' (Jasanoff 2015) which shape the emerging forms of quantum computing.

Imaginaries of quantum computing

One vision of quantum computing is of a new industrial revolution '*at an even larger scale than anything we have previously experienced*' (Khan 2021). A recent prospectus for a quantum computing company public offering suggests: '*Computers that utilise the power of quantum mechanics could provide revolutionary breakthroughs in human health and longevity, climate change and energy production, artificial intelligence, and more*' (IonQ 2021).

We could call this the 'heroic' early vision; at the current stage of knowledge, it is hard to draw a line between '*defensible optimism*' and exaggeration (Aaronson 2021a). The strong claims of quantum computing as the 'next big thing' (Rayner 2004) are counterbalanced by acknowledgements that the list of mathematically intractable problems currently known to be solvable by quantum computing is not a long one (DiVincenzo 2017). Unfulfilled early promises could lead to a 'quantum winter' (The Economist 2018). In either eventuality – or some more nuanced, complex mix of outcomes – these visions shape the '*assemblages of materiality, meaning, and morality*' (Jasanoff 2015) and are constitutive of, as well as reflective of, forms of social life. RI might explore how these visions may mobilise large investments and direct them towards some fields rather than others.

A more negatively figured potential of quantum computing is the risk of 'breaking the Internet' — rendering vulnerable existing forms of encryption — using Shor's algorithm or similar (Biever 2013) (alternatively, '*giving governments more power to surveil their citizens*' (Aaronson 2021a)). This risk is real, but should be an in-principle solvable problem, although not without continuing challenges. Nevertheless, this does have a significant interest for RI: we suggest that post-quantum cryptography (Bernstein, 2019), by anticipating and responding to a problem, is implementing 'de-facto' anticipatory governance elements of RI.

However, actually building a quantum computer that presents this risk — or that solves more socially-useful problems — is still very challenging, as we have repeatedly emphasised. These challenges are framed more as 'engineering' than as 'science' by a senior NQIT researcher:

> *'my take on it is, the physics, the science, has largely been done, so, as far as the physicists would believe, it's engineering' – LD2*

but, as we have stated, simply 'scaling up' is uncertain and with plenty of potential surprises; some argue that it is impossible (Dyakonov 2019) or, possibly, according to an NQIT researcher, failure could call into question quantum mechanics as a scientific paradigm:

> *'although we have absolutely no reason to think that at some point as you try and build a bigger and bigger version of a quantum computer anything should go wrong, like you should just be able to scale it up, … it's very difficult to be totally sure … if it didn't work out, that would mean something in the foundations of quantum theory was wrong … we're really putting that to the test' – LR8*

Conversely, quantum computing has important implications for physics:

> *'if one builds a quantum computer, not only can you solve societal problems, but you can also start to study new regimes of physics which you cannot do in any other way' – LD4*

Meanwhile, the discourse of NISQ is raising hopes of what might be possible with quantum computing in the near- to mid-term. What is interesting as a sociotechnical imaginary is the way in which the 'material' (Jasanoff 2015) — algorithms as well as hardware — is slowly coming together with 'the social'. If/when NISQ devices are adopted outside the specialised quantum research communities, it can be expected that the set of real-world applications will deepen as users adapt, appropriate, and try things out with the available technology in practices of mutual shaping or *innofusion* (Fleck 1993; Williams and Edge 1996). Indeed, Preskill (2018) suggests that NISQ might provide testbeds to in turn accelerate the development of quantum algorithms.

Arms race or the common good

Debates about the achievement of quantum supremacy, technically defined and demonstrated experimentally though not particularly useful outside quantum computing research, sit alongside broader visions of what supremacy in QC might entail. 'Supremacy' in other contexts is framed in terms of military superiority or economic dominance by nation states, tending to orient scientific and technological advances towards national or company goals rather than the common good of humanity.

Similar discourses surrounded, for example, the Japanese Fifth Generation Computer Systems Project (FGCS) in the 1980s. Intended for AI as a public good, FGCS provoked fears in the United States of Japanese technological world domination (Feigenbaum and McCorduck 1983). Widely seen as a failure in *Western,* commercial terms, re-framed as a contest between nations (Garvey 2020), neither FGCS nor competing national initiatives succeeded in their broader aims of Artificial Intelligence (AI). In a pertinent turn of history, the subsequent 'AI Winter' has now given way to a new AI 'arms race', this time with China as the antagonist to the USA.

We see parallels between the history of FGCS and the emerging history of quantum computing. Following the logic of supremacy, quantum technologies are becoming a central part of national and supra-national economic strategies.[9] Narratives of new technologies are largely formed through strategy documents and roadmaps which produce and reproduce established framings (Marris and Calvert 2020); examples such as the UK National Strategy and the Roadmap for quantum technologies (UK National Quantum Technologies Programme Strategic Advisory Board 2015b, 2015a) are not passive descriptions, but performatively construct the concept of quantum technologies and what they are 'for'.

Conclusions

The increasing emphasis on Responsible Innovation as a core aspect of scientific and technological development makes this a privileged time to consider RI applied to a core emerging technology.

When the research on which this paper is based commenced, quantum computing was expected to be several years, possibly decades, from realisation. The NQIT Hub aimed to progress the underlying elements of scalable quantum computing, and to contribute to quantum information theory and other quantum technologies. Production of a large-scale, fault-tolerant quantum computer was not expected in a near-term timescale and is still some years distant. However, quantum comput*ing*, using quantum effects to do interesting and useful computation, has developed in other ways, with new insights and new framings, so that the shape of the technology envisaged at the start of our research is somewhat different from the ways it is understood now.

This shift – in a relatively short space of time – demonstrates the importance of RI's iterative, responsive approach. Applying RI through the AREA Plus framework is not once-and-for-all: the parameters are changing even as we attempt to delineate them.

The trajectories of these technologies are hard to perceive: some are near-term, some are barely visible on the horizon, others are speculative. Solutions to some specific computing and optimisation problems, quantum machine learning, new forms of simulation of drugs and materials, and risks and opportunities for secure communications, with applications in fields such as medicine, logistics, and finance: any and all of these, and others that have not yet been imagined, are likely to engender social transformations. These transformations arise not only from specific affordances of the technology, but from the interplay of society and technology, from the ways in which the technology is imagined, adopted, and co-designed in use, from its governance and its availability.

Faced with this complex web of interests and a highly uncertain trajectory of innovation (Fleck, Webster, and Williams 1990), RI seeks to contribute to a '*proper embedding*' (von Schomberg 2013) of quantum computing in society, recognising its anticipated applications as '*sociotechnical imaginaries*' (Jasanoff 2015). Responsible Innovation can actively engage in these framings, anticipating and reflecting on possible futures. The point is not to predict or only interpret the future in various ways, but to explore, prepare and respond to it.

Notes

1. https://ec.europa.eu/programmes/horizon2020/en/h2020-section/responsible-research-innovation
2. https://epsrc.ukri.org/research/framework/area/
3. https://quantum-computing.ibm.com/
4. https://www.quantummachinelearning.org/qtml2021-program.html
5. https://en.wikipedia.org/wiki/Shor%27s_algorithm
6. https://en.wikipedia.org/wiki/Mathematical_optimization
7. https://en.wikipedia.org/wiki/NP-hardness
8. https://en.wikipedia.org/wiki/Travelling_salesman_problem
9. The UK press release about the recent 'New Atlantic Charter', which is notably less global in outlook than the original of 1941, specifically mentions quantum technologies alongside AI as part of a USA-UK science and technology partnership: https://www.gov.uk/government/news/uk-and-us-agree-to-strengthen-ties-in-science-and-technology

Acknowledgements

This work was funded as part of UK Quantum Technology Hub: Networked Quantum Information Technologies EPSRC grant number EP/M013243/1.

Disclosure statement

No potential conflict of interest was reported by the author(s).

Funding

This work was supported by Engineering and Physical Sciences Research Council: [Grant Number EP/M013243/1].

ORCID

Philip Inglesant http://orcid.org/0000-0002-5265-8707
Carolyn Ten Holter http://orcid.org/0000-0001-8739-3211
Marina Jirotka http://orcid.org/0000-0002-6088-3955
Robin Williams http://orcid.org/0000-0002-9044-4611

References

Aaronson, S. 2007. "Shor, I'll do it: Explanation for the Man in The Street" Blog: Shtetl-Optimized 24/02/2007. https://www.scottaaronson.com/blog/?p=208 Accessed: 27/09/2021.

Aaronson, S. 2008. "The Limits of Quantum Computers." *Scientific American* 298, 62–69.

Aaronson, S. 2013. *Quantum Computing Since Democritus*. Cambridge, UK: Cambridge University Press.

Aaronson, S. 2019. "Quantum Supremacy: The Gloves are off" Blog: Shtetl-Optimized. https://www.scottaaronson.com/blog/?p=4372 Accessed: 27/09/2021.

Aaronson, S. 2021a. "QC Ethics and Hype: The Call is Coming from Inside the House" Blog: Shtetl-Optimized 20/03/2021. https://www.scottaaronson.com/blog/?p=5387 Accessed: 27/09/2021.

Aaronson, S. 2021b. "What Makes Quantum Computing So Hard to Explain?" *Quantamagazine* 08/06/2021 (June 8, 2021). https://www.quantamagazine.org/why-is-quantum-computing-so-hard-to-explain-20210608/# Accessed: 27/09/2021.

Ambainis, A. 2014. "What Can We Do with a Quantum Computer?" *The Institute Letter* Spring 2014 Princeton, NJ, USA: Institute of Advanced Study https://www.ias.edu/ideas/2014/ambainis-quantum-computing Accessed: 27/09/2021.

Arute, F., K. Arya, R. Babbush, D. Bacon, J. C. Bardin, R. Barends, … J. M. Martinis. 2019. "Quantum Supremacy Using a Programmable Superconducting Processor." *Nature* 574 (7779): 505–510. https://doi.org/10.1038/s41586-019-1666-5.

Bernhardt, C. 2019. *Quantum Computing for Everyone*. Cambridge, MA, USA: MIT Press.

Bernstein, D. J. 2009. "Introduction to Post-Quantum Cryptography." In *Post-quantum Cryptography*, edited by D. J. Bernstein, J. Buchmann, and E. Dahmen 1–14. Berlin, Germany: Springer. https://pqcrypto.org/www.springer.com/cda/content/document/cda_downloaddocument/9783540887010-c1.pdf Accessed: 08/09/2021.

Bharti, K., A. Cervera-Lierta, T. H. Kyaw, T. Haug, S. Alperin-Lea, A. Anand, … T. Menke. 2021. "Noisy Intermediate-Scale Quantum (NISQ) Algorithms." Preprint arXiv:2101.08448 https://arxiv.org/abs/2101.08448v1 Accessed: 08/09/2021.

Biamonte, J., P. Wittek, N. Pancotti, P. Rebentrost, N. Wiebe, and S. Lloyd. 2017. "Quantum Machine Learning." *Nature* 549 (7671): 195–202. https://doi.org/10.1038/nature23474.

Biever, C. 2013. "Don't Worry, my Algorithm Won't Break the Internet … yet." *New Scientist* 220 (2944): 29. https://doi.org/10.1016/S0262-4079(13)62741-4.

Bleicher, A. 2018. "Quantum Algorithms Struggle Against Old Foe: Clever Computers." *Quanta Magazine* February 1, 2018. https://www.quantamagazine.org/quantum-computers-struggle-against-classical-algorithms-20180201/# Accessed: 08/09/2021.

Borup, M., N. Brown, K. Konrad, and H. Van Lente. 2006. "The Sociology of Expectations in Science and Technology." *Technology Analysis & Strategic Management* 18 (3-4): 285–298. https://doi.org/10.1080/09537320600777002.

Britt, K. A., and T. S. Humble. 2017. "High-performance Computing with Quantum Processing Units." *ACM Journal on Emerging Technologies in Computing Systems (JETC)* 13 (3): 39. https://doi.org/10.1145/3007651.

Brundage, M. 2016. "Artificial Intelligence and Responsible Innovation." In *Fundamental Issues of Artificial Intelligence*, edited by V. C. Müller, 543–554. Cham, CH: Springer. https://doi.org/10.1007/978-3-319-26485-1_32.

Collingridge, D. 1980. *The Social Control of Technology*. London: Pinter.

Congressional Research Service. 2021. "Defense Primer: Quantum Technology." https://crsreports.congress.gov/product/pdf/IF/IF11836 Accessed: 13/09/2021.

DiVincenzo, D. P. 2000. "The Physical Implementation of Quantum Computation." *Fortschritte der Physik* 48 (9-11): 771–783. https://doi.org/10.1002/1521-3978(200009)48:9/11<771::AID-PROP771>3.0.CO;2-E.

DiVincenzo, D. P. 2017. "Scientists and Citizens: Getting to Quantum Technologies." *Ethics and Information Technology* 19 (4): 247–251. https://doi.org/10.1007/s10676-017-9435-3.

Dunjko, V., and P. Wittek. 2019. "A non-Review of Quantum Machine Learning: Trends and Explorations." *Quantum: The Open Journal for Quantum Science* 4: 32. https://doi.org/10.22331/qv-2020-03-17-32.

Dyakonov, M. I. 2019. "When Will we Have a Quantum Computer?" *Solid-State Electronics* 155: 4–6. https://doi.org/10.1016/j.sse.2019.03.004.

The Economist. 2018. "Quantum spring: The Race is on to Dominate Quantum Computing." *The Economist* Aug 18th 2018. https://www.economist.com/business/2018/08/18/the-race-is-on-to-dominate-quantum-computing Accessed: 08/09/2021.

Feigenbaum, E. A., and P. McCorduck. 1983. *The Fifth Generation: Artificial Intelligence and Japan's Computer Challenge to the World*. Boston, MA, USA: Addison-Wesley Longman Publishing Co. https://dl.acm.org/doi/book/10.5555/4565.

Feynman, R. P. 1981. "Simulating Physics with Computers." *International Journal of Theoretical Physics* 21 (6): 467–488. https://doi.org/10.1007/BF02650179.

Fisher, E., and Rip, A. 2013. "Responsible Innovation: Multi-Level Dynamics and Soft Intervention Practices." In *Responsible Innovation: Managing the Responsible Emergence of Science and Innovation in Society*, edited by R. Owen, J. R. Bessant, and M. Heintz. Chapter 9, 165–185. Chichester, UK: John Wiley & Sons Ltd. https://doi.org/10.1002/9781118551424.ch9

Fisher, E., R. L. Mahajan, and C. Mitcham. 2006. "Midstream Modulation of Technology: Governance from Within." *Bulletin of Science, Technology & Society* 26 (6): 485–496. https://doi.org/10.1177%2F0270467606295402.

Fleck, J. 1993. "Innofusion: Feedback in the Innovation Process." In *Systems Science*, edited by F. A. Stowell, D. West, and J. G. Howell, 169–174. Boston, MA, USA: Springer. https://doi.org/10.1007/978-1-4615-2862-3_30.

Fleck, J., J. Webster, and R. Williams. 1990. "Dynamics of Information Technology Implementation: a Reassessment of Paradigms and Trajectories of Development." *Futures* 22 (6): 618–640. https://doi.org/10.1016/0016-3287(90)90131-Z.

Garvey, C. S. 2020. "AI for Social Good" and The First AI Arms Race Lessons from Japan's Fifth Generation Computer Systems (FGCS) Project. Paper presented at the The 34th Annual Conference of the Japanese Society for Artificial Intelligence (2020).

Genus, A., and A. Stirling. 2018. "Collingridge and the Dilemma of Control: Towards Responsible and Accountable Innovation." *Research Policy* 47 (1): 61–69. https://doi.org/10.1016/j.respol.2017.09.012.

Georgescu, I., S. Ashhab, and F. Nori. 2014. "Quantum Simulation." *Reviews of Modern Physics* 86 (1): 153. https://doi.org/10.1103/RevModPhys.86.153.

Grunwald, A. 2011. "Responsible Innovation: Bringing Together Technology Assessment, Applied Ethics, and STS Research." *Enterprise and Work Innovation Studies* 31: 10–19. http://hdl.handle.net/10362/7944.

Grunwald, A. 2014. "The Hermeneutic Side of Responsible Research and Innovation." *Journal of Responsible Innovation* 1 (3): 274–291. https://doi.org/10.1080/23299460.2014.968437.

Guston, D. H. 2014. "Understanding 'Anticipatory Governance'." *Social Studies of Science* 44 (2): 218–242. https://doi.org/10.1177%2F0306312713508669.

Harrow, A. W., and A. Montanaro. 2017. "Quantum Computational Supremacy." *Nature* 549 (7671): 203–209. https://doi.org/10.1038/nature23458.

Inglesant, P., M. Hartswood, and M. Jirotka. 2016. "Thinking Ahead to a World with Quantum Computers: The Landscape of Responsible Research and Innovation in Quantum Computing." https://nqit.ox.ac.uk/content/responsible-research-and-innovation-landscape-report.html Accessed: 25/06/2021.

Inglesant, P., M. Jirotka, and M. Hartswood. 2018. "Responsible Innovation in Quantum Technologies Applied to Defence and National Security." https://nqit.ox.ac.uk/content/responsible-innovation-defence-briefing-note.html Accessed: 25/06/2021.

IonQ. 2021. "Investor Presentation." https://static1.squarespace.com/static/5e33152a051d2e7588f7571c/t/60459578b8c075444a656357/1615173012167/IonQ+Investor+Presentation+030721+vFF.pdf Accessed: 22/06/2021.

Jasanoff, S. 2015. "Future Imperfect: Science, Technology, and the Imaginations of Modernity." In *Dreamscapes of Modernity: Sociotechnical Imaginaries and the Fabrication of Power*, edited by S. Jasanoff, and S.-H. Kim, 1–33. Chicago, IL, USA: University of Chicago Press. Chapter One, https://doi.org/10.7208/chicago/9780226276663.003.0001.

Jasanoff, S., and S.-H. Kim. 2009. "Containing the Atom: Sociotechnical Imaginaries and Nuclear Power in the United States and South Korea." *Minerva* 47 (2): 119–146. https://doi.org/10.1007/s11024-009-9124-4.

Jirotka, M., B. Grimpe, B. Stahl, G. Eden, and M. Hartswood. 2017. "Responsible Research and Innovation in the Digital age." *Communications of the ACM* 60 (5): 62–68. https://doi.org/10.1145/3064940.

Johnson, T. H., S. R. Clark, and D. Jaksch. 2014. "What is a Quantum Simulator?" *EPJ Quantum Technology* 1: 10. https://doi.org/10.1140/epjqt10.

Kantar Public. 2018. "Quantum Technologies: Public Dialogue Report." https://nqit.ox.ac.uk/content/quantum-technologies-public-dialogue-report.html Accessed: 27/09/2021.

Khan, I. 2021. "Will Quantum Computers Truly Serve Humanity?" *Scientific American* 17/02/2021 February 17, 2021. https://www.scientificamerican.com/article/will-quantum-computers-truly-serve-humanity/ Accessed: 27/09/2021.

Kjølberg, K. L., and R. Strand. 2011. "Conversations About Responsible Nanoresearch." *NanoEthics* 5 (1): 99–113. https://doi.org/10.1007/s11569-011-0114-2.

Lloyd, S., M. Mohseni, and P. Rebentrost. 2013. "Quantum algorithms for supervised and unsupervised machine learning." Preprint arXiv:1307.0411v2 https://arxiv.org/abs/1307.0411v2 Accessed: 08/09/2021.

Macnaghten, P., R. Owen, and R. Jackson. 2016. "Synthetic Biology and the Prospects for Responsible Innovation." *Essays in Biochemistry* 60 (4): 347–355. https://doi.org/10.1042/ebc20160048.

Marris, C., and J. Calvert. 2020. "Science and Technology Studies in Policy: the UK Synthetic Biology Roadmap." *Science, Technology, & Human Values* 45 (1): 34–61. https://doi.org/10.1177/0162243919828107.

Mohseni, M., P. Read, H. Neven, S. Boixo, V. Denchev, R. Babbush, … J. Martinis. 2017. "Commercialize Quantum Technologies in Five Years." *Nature News* 543 (7644): 171–174. https://doi.org/10.1038/543171a.

Montanaro, A. 2016. "Quantum Algorithms: An Overview." *npj Quantum Information* 2 (1): 15023. https://doi.org/10.1038/npjqi.2015.23.

Moore, G. E. 2006. "Cramming More Components onto Integrated Circuits, Reprinted from Electronics, 38(8), April 19, 1965, pp. 114 ff." *IEEE Solid-State Circuits Society Newsletter* 11 (3):33-5. doi: https://doi.org/10.1109/N-SSC.2006.4785860.

Moussa, C., H. Calandra, and V. Dunjko. 2020. "To Quantum or not to Quantum: Towards Algorithm Selection in Near-term Quantum Optimization." Preprint arXiv:2001.08271v2 https://arxiv.org/abs/2001.08271v2 Accessed: 08/09/2021.

National Cyber Security Centre. 2020. "Preparing for Quantum-safe Cryptography." https://www.ncsc.gov.uk/whitepaper/preparing-for-quantum-safe-cryptography Accessed: 08/09/2021.

Nielsen, M. 2015. "The Physical Origin of Universal Computing." *Quanta Magazine* 07/12/2015. https://www.scientificamerican.com/article/the-physical-origin-of-universal-computing/ Accessed: 08/09/2021.

Owen, R., and M. Pansera. 2019. "Chapter 2 - Responsible Innovation and Responsible Research and Innovation." In *Handbook on Science and Public Policy*, edited by D. Simon, S. Kuhlmann, J. Stamm, and W. Canzler, 26–48. Cheltenham, UK: Edward Elgar Publishing. https://doi.org/10.4337/9781784715946.

Özdemir, V. 2019. "Chapter 5 - Towards an Ethics-of-Ethics for Responsible Innovation." In *International Handbook on Responsible Innovation*, edited by R. v. Schomberg, and J. Hankins, 70–82. Cheltenham, UK: Edward Elgar Publishing. https://doi.org/10.4337/9781784718862.00011.

Pinch, T. J., and W. E. Bijker. 1984. "The Social Construction of Facts and Artefacts: Or how the Sociology of Science and the Sociology of Technology Might Benefit Each Other." *Social Studies of Science* 14 (3): 399–441. https://doi.org/10.1177%2F030631284014003004.

Preskill, J. 2018. "Quantum Computing in the NISQ era and Beyond." *Quantum* 2: 79. https://doi.org/10.22331/q-2018-08-06-79.

Preskill, J. 2019. "Why I Called It 'Quantum Supremacy'." *Quanta Magazine* 02/10/2019. https://www.quantamagazine.org/john-preskill-explains-quantum-supremacy-20191002 Accessed: 27/09/2021.

Pritchard, J., and S. Till. 2016. "UK Quantum Technology Landscape 2016: A perspective of UK Quantum Technology prepared by and for the UK Quantum Technology Community." Porton Down, UK: https://uknqt.ukri.org/files/ukquantumtechnologylandscape2016/ Accessed: 13/09/2021.

Rayner, S. 2004. "The Novelty Trap: Why Does Institutional Learning About New Technologies Seem So Difficult?" *Industry and Higher Education* 18 (6): 349–355. https://doi.org/10.5367%2F0000000042683601.

Reiher, M., N. Wiebe, K. M. Svore, D. Wecker, and M. Troyer. 2017. "Elucidating Reaction Mechanisms on Quantum Computers." *Proceedings of the National Academy of Sciences* 114 (29): 7555–7560. https://doi.org/10.1073/pnas.1619152114.

Rip, A., and H. Te Kulve. 2008. "Constructive Technology Assessment and Socio-Technical Scenarios." In *Presenting Futures. The Yearbook of Nanotechnology in Society, vol 1*, edited by E. Fisher, C. Selin, and J. M. Wetmore, 49–70. Dordrecht, NL: Springer. https://doi.org/10.1007/978-1-4020-8416-4_4.

Shalf, J. 2020. "The Future of Computing Beyond Moore's law." *Philosophical Transactions of the Royal Society A: Mathematical, Physical and Engineering Sciences* 378 (2166): 20190061. https://doi.org/10.1098/rsta.2019.0061.

Shor, P. W. 1999. "Polynomial-Time Algorithms for Prime Factorization and Discrete Logarithms on a Quantum Computer." *SIAM Review* 41 (2): 303–332. https://doi.org/10.1137/S0097539795293172.

Sra, S., S. Nowozin, and S. J. Wright. 2012. "Chapter 1 - Introduction." In *Optimization for Machine Learning*, edited by S. Sra, S. Nowozin, and S. J. Wright, 1–17. Cambridge, MA, USA: MIT Press.

Stilgoe, J. 2013. "Foreword: Why Responsible Innovation?" In *Responsible Innovation: Managing the Responsible Emergence of Science and Innovation in Society*, edited by R. Owen, J. R. Bessant, and M. Heintz, xi–xv. Chichester, UK: John Wiley & Sons Ltd. https://onlinelibrary.wiley.com/doi/pdf/10.1002/9781118551424.fmatter Accessed: 08/09/2021.

Stilgoe, J., and D. H. Guston. 2017. "Responsible Research and Innovation." In *The Handbook of Science and Technology Studies, Fourth Edition*, edited by U. Felt, R. Fouché, C. A. Miller, and L. Smith-Doerr, 853–880. Cambridge, MA, USA: The MIT Press.

Stilgoe, J., R. Owen, and P. Macnaghten. 2013. "Developing a Framework for Responsible Innovation." *Research Policy* 42 (9): 1568–1580. https://doi.org/10.1016/j.respol.2013.05.008.

Stirling, A. 2008. ""Opening up" and "Closing Down": Power, Participation, and Pluralism in the Social Appraisal of Technology." *Science, Technology & Human Values* 33 (2): 262–294. https://doi.org/10.1177%2F0162243907311265.

Swierstra, T., and A. Rip. 2007. "Nano-ethics as NEST-Ethics: Patterns of Moral Argumentation About new and Emerging Science and Technology." *NanoEthics* 1 (1): 3–20. https://doi.org/10.1007/s11569-007-0005-8.

UK National Quantum Technologies Programme Strategic Advisory Board. 2015a. "National Strategy for Quantum Technologies: A New Era for the UK." Engineering and Physical Sciences Research Council https://www.gov.uk/government/publications/national-strategy-for-quantum-technologies Accessed: 08/09/2021.

UK National Quantum Technologies Programme Strategic Advisory Board. 2015b. "A Roadmap for Quantum Technologies in the UK." Engineering and Physical Sciences Research Council https://epsrc.ukri.org/newsevents/pubs/quantumtechroadmap/ Accessed: 08/09/2021.

UK Research and Innovation. "UK National Technologies Programme." https://uknqt.ukri.org/ Accessed: 03/03/2021.

van de Poel, I. 2016. "An Ethical Framework for Evaluating Experimental Technology." *Science and Engineering Ethics* 22 (3): 667–686. https://doi.org/10.1007/s11948-015-9724-3.

van der Burg, S. 2014. "On the Hermeneutic Need for Future Anticipation." *Journal of Responsible Innovation* 1 (1): 99–102. https://doi.org/10.1080/23299460.2014.882556.

von Schomberg, R. 2013. "A Vision of Responsible Research and Innovation." In *Responsible Innovation: Managing the Responsible Emergence of Science and Innovation in Society*, edited by R. Owen, J. R. Bessant, and M. Heintz, 51–74. Chichester, UK: John Wiley & Sons Ltd. Chapter 3. https://doi.org/10.1002/9781118551424.ch3.

Wagner, W., N. Kronberger, S. F. Berg, and H. Torgersen. 2006. "Chapter Ten - The Monster in the Public Imagination." In *Genomics and Society: Legal, Ethical, and Social Dimensions*, edited by G. Gaskell, and M. W. Bauer, 150–168. London, UK: Routledge. https://doi.org/10.4324/9781849773867.

Wecker, D., M. B. Hastings, and M. Troyer. 2015. "Progress Towards Practical Quantum Variational Algorithms." *Physical Review A* 92 (4): 042303. https://doi.org/10.1103/PhysRevA.92.042303.

Wiesner, K. 2017. "The careless use of Language in Quantum Information." Preprint arXiv:1705.06768 https://arxiv.org/abs/1705.06768 Accessed: 11/09/2021.

Williams, R. 2006. "Compressed Foresight and Narrative Bias: Pitfalls in Assessing High Technology Futures." *Science as Culture* 15 (4): 327–348. https://doi.org/10.1080/09505430601022668.

Williams, R., and D. Edge. 1996. 'The Social Shaping of Technology.' *Research Policy* 25 (6): 865–899. https://doi.org/10.1016/0048-7333(96)00885-2.

OPEN ACCESS

Reading the road: challenges and opportunities on the path to responsible innovation in quantum computing

Carolyn Ten Holter, Philip Inglesant and Marina Jirotka

University of Oxford, Oxford, UK

ABSTRACT

Novel technologies such as quantum computing present new opportunities to support societal needs, but societal engagement is vital to secure public trust. Quantum computing technologies are at a pivotal point in their journey from foundational research to deployment, creating a moment for society to investigate, reflect, and consult on their implications. Responsible Innovation (RI) is one method for considering impacts, engaging with societal needs, reflecting on any concerns, and influencing the trajectory of the innovation in response. This paper draws on the empirical work of the RI team embedded in the Networked Quantum Information Technologies Hub. The team investigated researchers' perceptions of RI and their understanding of societal impacts of quantum technologies, and sought to gauge the challenges of embedding RI across a multi-disciplinary, large-scale enterprise such as the UK quantum programme. The work demonstrated some of the difficulties involved in embedding RI approaches, and in creating a dialogue between innovators and societies. Finally, the authors offer recommendations to policymakers, researchers, and industrial organisations, for better practice in responsible quantum computing, and to ensure that societal considerations are discussed alongside commercial motivations. Applying RI to quantum computing at this pivotal point has implications for RI in other emerging technologies.

1. Introduction

The social, legal, economic, and practical landscape of quantum computing is changing fast. Advances and breakthroughs that five years ago seemed relatively remote are now discussed as imminent possibilities (e.g. Cookson 2021; Waters 2021). Although it is difficult to identify the precise 'tipping point'[1] of a technology whilst it develops, there is now increasing research, development, and investment in quantum computing – examples include: the development of Noisy, Intermediate-Scale Quantum Computing (Preskill 2018); investment by major corporations (Castellanos 2021); and the announcement of so-called 'quantum supremacy' (Arute et al. 2019).

Digital systems such as quantum computing can work to support the needs of society; many innovations have potential benefits for societies and individuals. However, technology can also have outcomes that do not benefit all of society – therefore, innovations that potentially impact societies in profound ways should have questions asked of them through the innovation lifecycle – questions such as: *who benefits? who's in control?* (Stilgoe 2013).

Technologies such as quantum computing are highly likely to develop as just such impactful innovations that can affect society in significant ways (Inglesant, Hartswood, and Jirotka 2016). The process of such influential innovations moving from the research laboratory into practical use provides society with a 'window' during which technologies can be interrogated on questions around societal impact. It is therefore important that during this trajectory of development and deployment, issues concerning risks, responses, and responsibilities should be investigated. As use-cases become clearer there are opportunities to review possible effects that may raise concerns, and potentially to alter the trajectory of development and innovation, ensure accountability, and consolidate the rights of individuals and communities. If such opportunities are ignored, they may not recur until the technology is embedded in everyday use and potentially undesirable effects have occurred.

This paper draws on the empirical work carried out by the Responsible Innovation $(RI)^2$ initiative within the UK Quantum Technology Hubs. This work examined challenges and opportunities in using anticipatory, prospective approaches such as RI to help secure societally responsive quantum technologies in the UK. Section 2 briefly outlines the history of RI and its embedding into funders and funding calls, as well as why we consider the concept of 'quantum ethics' to be a necessary foundational component, but operationally insufficient. In Section 3, we outline the genesis of the quantum Hubs and the RI work carried out in them, before setting out some of our key findings from the work in Section 4. In Section 5, we discuss our findings, and suggest better practices for responsible quantum computing, and pathways to explore in the future, before concluding with Section 6.

2. Responsible innovation

The history of RI initiatives is now well-documented (e.g. Boenink and Kudina 2020; Owen et al. 2021). These initiatives emerged over a decade ago, with the aim of identifying and addressing uncertainties and risks associated with novel areas of research. They began in nanotechnology (Murphy 2010), expanded to geo-engineering (Stilgoe 2015) and synthetic biology (Frow and Calvert 2013), before widening to include computer science, robotics, informatics, and ICT more generally (Jirotka et al. 2017). A comprehensive definition comes from the RRI Tools project:

> RRI is a way to do research that takes a long-term perspective on the type of world in which we want to live … [RRI means] involving society in science and innovation 'very upstream' in the processes of R&I to align its outcomes with the values of society. (RRI Tools n.d.)

In the UK, the Engineering and Physical Sciences Research Council (EPSRC) committed to RI across its portfolio of ICT research grants (Owen 2014). RI in this context has a number of dimensions, brought together by EPSRC in an interpretation known as the Anticipate-Reflect-Engage-Act (AREA) Framework (Stilgoe, Owen, and Macnaghten 2013). Since 2013, EPSRC has developed its commitment to embedding RI in funding calls. This commitment has been more emphatic at some times than others (Owen et al. 2021), but overall the trend is towards greater embedding of RI in UK research and innovation.

2.1. Embedding RI in UK funding; towards institutionalisation

Randles and Laasch (2016) describe 'institutionalisation' as a process of 'stabilisation of norms' (Randles and Laasch 2016, 54). They distinguish between formal adoption of such norms into policy and procedure (top-down), and a *de facto* process whereby behaviours are seen in practice regardless of 'official' procedures (ground-upwards). EPSRC as a locus for institutionalisation of RI in the UK, its promulgation of the AREA Framework, and inclusion of RI as a mandatory component of funding proposals (for example, Centres for Doctoral Training (EPSRC 2018)) indicate the top-down type of institutionalisation. Genus and Iskandarova (2018) critique the institutionalisation of

RI in the EU and US as 'partial', citing motivations for the inclusion of RI as rooted in 'the need to secure desirable outcomes from scientific research and promising innovations'.

However, a case study with interesting parallels for quantum technologies is to be found in Pansera et al. (2020)'s tracking of RI within a synthetic-biology research centre. Pansera et al. (2020) analysed some of the challenges of carrying out funder-embedded RI activities over the course of several years, arguing that with an essentially interpretive framework such as RI, it is critical to examine its operation 'in situated practice'. The researchers track a trajectory of understanding in the project's RI activity, beginning with a 'public engagement' conceptualisation based on 'deficit model' concepts (Wynne 1993) and shifting towards a much more 'deliberative and dialogic' approach, in a learning arc. Signs such as these are encouraging from an RI perspective; however, these developments may also be influenced by wider discussions in some fields of the ethical implications of novel technologies.

2.2. RI and 'quantum ethics'

Discussions of the ethical implications around technologies such as computing are not a new phenomenon – the comprehensive review by Stahl, Timmermans, and Mittelstadt (2016) of nearly 600 sources demonstrates roots dating back to the earliest computers – but have come to the fore again relatively recently in fields such as artificial intelligence (e.g. Leslie 2019). The concept of 'quantum ethics' has also recently appeared in the field (Khan 2021; Perrier 2021). These contributions often build on the ethical discourses of computing that, as noted above, have a deep history of questioning the impacts of these technologies.

These interesting contributions are necessary to foundational understandings of RI but are not sufficient; we argue that discussion of the ethics of quantum computing does not provide concrete guidance to the researchers and industrial start-ups grappling with the technical and engineering challenges of building a quantum computer. This is not to downplay the value or importance of drawing on ethical approaches, but the focus of a Responsible Innovation approach is based on the actions and day to day decisions of those working to create the technology (Pansera et al. 2020). Such an approach is rooted in ethics but has a very practical application. Ethics is necessary but not sufficient; it does not ask the questions that we believe must be embedded in the development of these technologies – *what will be the impacts on societies? who will benefit? And who will lose?*

3. Methodology

As part of the UK's national investment in a quantum technologies programme, four Hubs were funded for an initial five-year period starting in late 2014 totalling £270 m (EPSRC 2020). The Hubs were based in Birmingham, Oxford, York and Glasgow, and comprised large consortia of universities and companies. The aim was to exploit the potential of quantum science to develop technologies that would benefit UK business, government, and society (EPSRC 2020).

RI was incorporated into the entirety of the Quantum Technologies Programme and in the call for the Hubs from the outset. Each of the Hubs was required to commit to RI, though the means of doing this was left up to the leadership of each Hub. In three of the Hubs – echoing the synthetic biology case study discussed in 2.1 above – the RI work was largely framed as a type of public engagement or public communication and was carried out by the Hub's researchers. However, the quantum computing Hub included funding for an RI team within its proposal and consequently was able to sustain an RI effort throughout the five-year project. The work detailed below is therefore mainly focused on the work of the NQIT Hub – the project entitled NQIT-RRI.

3.1. Research methods

NQIT-RRI adopted qualitative methodologies to conduct the research; quantum technologies fields are interdisciplinary, highly specialised, and relatively small, meaning that qualitative work was judged to be more appropriate for the questions the research sought to investigate. What the project examined in depth was not just the state-of-the-art in technical terms and how this might relate to societal impacts, but also the positions of the researchers and engineers themselves in relation to societal concerns and the technologies they were progressing in their work.

It was clear from the outset that within the NQIT Hub, familiarity with RI methods was limited, and so a portion of the RI work was directed towards explaining and embedding RI approaches and working with developers to broaden their understanding of RI frameworks and methodologies. This included training (for example on 'anticipatory' techniques) so that developers and researchers were empowered to undertake this type of work themselves.

The research was multi-stranded, using interviews, case-study-focused workshops, and ultimately a series of 'RI roadshows' that used an 'action research' modality to demonstrate and disseminate the work around all four Hubs. The focus of the NQIT-RRI team was not to be responsible for all the RI activity in the Hubs, but rather to act as sources of expertise, generators of discussion, and facilitators of RI-focused conversations.

3.1.1. Strand 1: interviews

Semi-structured interviews were carried out with academic researchers at all levels in the programme, including directors of the NQIT Hub as well as researchers working directly in the laboratory and advanced theory, and with people from industry and companies related to the programme. These were an opportunity to hear views and in-depth opinions on the technologies, participants' own approaches, and their views on how the innovations they were developing related to society. The semi-structured approach permits wide-ranging discussions that can investigate areas of particular interest in depth, while retaining the structure of a parallel set of questions for each participant, enabling comparative analysis.

3.1.2. Strand 2: case studies

Case studies were designed on the basis of the interviews and used as the focus for workshops and further interviews. The workshops and interviews encouraged broad-ranging discussions between co-researchers and developers, who in many cases may have been considering some of the questions for the first time. Drawing-together of specialists from different fields in workshops generated productive and creative analysis and insight around potential challenges and impacts from technologies.

The case studies developed analyses of particular use-cases where quantum technologies were identified by researchers and other stakeholders as particular areas of expected future application. These case studies investigated quantum for machine learning, and for defence and national security.

3.1.2.1. Case study 1. Quantum machine learning. The prospect of Quantum Machine-Learning (QML) has been widely discussed by researchers at the Hubs and in literature as an emerging field of research for quantum computing (Biamonte et al. 2018). The ability to parse large numbers of variables and vast quantities of data in relatively short timeframes or in ways which are otherwise intractable might enable applications for ML that could be highly commercialisable or help to solve important social challenges. For RI, questions around such a use case include:

(1) Skills shortages, because expertise-overlaps between ML and quantum technologies are rare.
(2) The difficulties of carrying out academic work in such an interdisciplinary area; this emerging field of research has, so far, been dominated by quantum experts, raising the risk that quantum methods for ML will lag behind the fast-changing applications of classical ML.
(3) Quantum is unlikely to replace classical-computing ML but may be complementary to it. However, the emergence of 'quantum ML' as a distinct field may divide ML between methods that are amenable to quantum and those that are not.

(4) Clearly, if quantum computing were to enlarge significantly the range or scale of ML, this could expand the already large societal impact of these technologies. But at the same time, there remains uncertainty about the viability and timescale.
(5) Responsible use of language to discourage hype. Many of the suggested techniques for quantum ML are years from achievement; however, some more generally applicable quantum computing methods for optimisation may be achievable sooner.

The discussions and literature review generated by the case study found that there is a large theoretical base to this emerging field of interest, but still a great deal of uncertainty about timescales and when, if at all, it will be implemented at scale for real-world applications. Perhaps, for this reason, there was a reluctance to engage with possible impacts and meanings – QML remains very theoretical and anticipatory work can seem remote from the day-to-day technical challenges.

The interdisciplinary nature of QML research is also a challenge for applying RI. The point around the responsible use of language in order to manage expectations shows an awareness of the need to represent quantum technologies carefully and in a non-hyperbolic way to stakeholders, which includes funders and policymakers as well as general publics. However, as classical ML demonstrates, real-world impacts and ethical challenges can be highly significant, and so QML should be the subject of focused reflection in order to try to address some of the problematic impacts, which may be extensions or entirely different from those seen in classical ML (e.g. Edwards and Veale 2017).

The QML case study, with its highly theoretical focus, served as a useful contrast with the second study, which examined the possible impacts on defence and national security.

3.1.2.2. Case study 2. Defence and national security. The investigatory workshop on responsible innovation in quantum technologies applied to defence and national security drew out themes and issues around dual-use, bad actors, state investment, and other issues. This is a field in which quantum technologies more broadly, as well as quantum computing specifically, are of interest for applications including quantum-enhanced navigation, sensing, imaging, and quantum secure communications. Although many of the potential applications remain theoretical in practice, their possible impacts were more readily discerned due to the already anticipatory modality of much defence work. Presentations voiced challenges from perspectives related to international relations, government, and RI. The discussions focused on:

(1) Whether the challenges raised by quantum technology are in some way different from those of other technologies; are their capabilities qualitatively different, or incremental improvements to existing functionality?
(2) Ethical challenges specific to quantum technologies – including the potential use of quantum technologies by terrorists, the enhanced encryption capabilities, and the potential violations of privacy.
(3) Responsible use of language to prevent a build-up of hype around quantum technologies.
(4) Potential regulatory frameworks.
(5) The importance of public dialogue, to learn the public's hopes and fears and to balance overstated or incorrect claims.

RI was identified as an opportunity for the research community to imagine possible and desirable futures together with different stakeholders. Overall, the workshop demonstrated that there is demand for a more structured conversation at the intersection of responsible research and innovation, quantum technologies, and the national security and defence sectors.

As with the QML case study, responsible use of language also appears here as necessary for keeping expectations at a realistic level. This awareness of the field's responsibility to stakeholders can be regarded as *de facto* RI, discussed further in Finding 5 below. The role of public engagement will also be discussed at greater length in Section 4. Both workshops formed part of the RI fieldwork that was made available to all the Hubs.

3.1.3. Strand 3: roadshows

The RI work in the NQIT Hub was significantly different from the RI approaches of the other three Hubs, so the NQIT-RRI team created 'Roadshows' – workshops at each of the Hubs, covering quantum imaging, quantum sensing, and quantum communications, as well as quantum computing – to demonstrate the NQIT RI work, generate greater awareness of, and discussion around, RI, and disseminate some of their findings. The Roadshows were productive of useful insights into the RI approaches in the other Hubs, as well as aiming to encourage adoption of the NQIT vision of RI around the other Hubs and to establish a collective RI strategy that could build on the commonalities between the technologies and activities of the Hubs.

3.1.4. Strand 4: public dialogue

A key aspect of RI approaches is engagement with stakeholders, and this was a core focus of the RI work in all the Hubs. However, there was very little previous data on public views, understanding, and attitudes to quantum technologies. A report by 'Sciencewise' in 2014, timed to coincide with the start of the first phase of the quantum technologies programme, was unable to find any direct data on public opinion about quantum technologies and instead drew its evidence from media reports and blog entries (Sciencewise 2014).

EPSRC, therefore, commissioned a one-off public dialogue exercise to create a two-way process of engagement by opening a channel between the public and experts/researchers, in order to:

- inform the public about the technology, services and devices which may emerge from the UKNQTP and the wider community;
- inform the quantum research community of the public's views (through the dialogue and its outputs) about the social and ethical implications of quantum research and technologies.

Participants were recruited from around the UK to represent a mix of participants in terms of gender, ethnicity, age, and background, around 25 in each of the locations of the Hubs and were paid for their time.

4. Results

The NQIT-RRI work threw into relief the challenges and opportunities that lie ahead for the development of responsible quantum technologies. RI within ICT fields requires interdisciplinary understandings, and utilising methods that may be entirely unfamiliar to physicists and mathematicians, therefore deepening familiarity with these methods formed a significant part of the work, as explained in Section 3.1 above.

The data collected through the various strands outlined in Section 3.1 was gathered into NVivo qualitative analysis software[3] and analysed inductively to discern trends and themes (Braun and Clarke 2006). The results detailed in Sections 4.1–4.6 below represent some of the key themes that emerged from the interviews, workshops, public dialogue, and roadshows.

4.1. Finding 1: public engagement considerations

Prior to the Kantar public dialogue (EPSRC 2017), there was very little evidence of public views on quantum technologies. The dialogue found wide familiarity with the term 'quantum' but little knowledge about what that meant in practice. Participants were – unsurprisingly – positive about the potential upsides of quantum technologies, particularly in healthcare and humanitarian fields, while also being concerned about potential misuse of these technologies. Their most significant concerns related to the broader and less predictable aspects of the rollout of quantum technologies, including: uneven access to the technologies; quantum as a profit-driven exercise at the expense of the public interest; and possible job losses from automation.

Participants in the NQIT-RRI interviews had different levels of experience with public engagement. There were some, particularly at the more foundational end of the research spectrum, who displayed scepticism about the value of explaining quantum processes so that non-specialists could form an educated view.

> it would be a mistake to imagine that ... even a very alert and engaged individual is in a position to contribute ... thoughts about the ... direction a researcher can go in, because you are just ultra-simplifying things ... so that they can make decisions. LD3

However, echoing Pansera et al. (2020), more often there was agreement that researchers had frequently been surprised by the level of self-education and interest among the general public.

> they're often coming up with detailed high-tech questions because they already know about ... programming or computers or quantum ... and often they're surprisingly interested in the details. LS1

> It's amazing actually how big the general population's appetite for popular science is and how well informed many of them are. LS3

In particular, several interviewees wanted more public engagement at earlier stages of education. They expressed frustration that basic quantum physics is not included in the National Curriculum and students commence their University courses with no quantum grounding.

> One of the big problems is that ... even though quantum physics is more than 100 years old, schoolchildren don't learn about it. LI1

> These are absolutely basic concepts in the quantum world and students who have got to age 18 or 19 ... don't know them. LS8

There was also understanding of the role of public engagement as creating a connection between science and society, and the resultant impact on society's ability to make broad decisions about how science and innovation should be directed.

> if you're working on that thing which might ... change society, ... the duty is ... for a sort of communication from researchers to the wider public, so that everyone can then discuss that thing. LS9

4.2. Finding 2: policy drivers and routes to action

A clear finding from the Roadshows and interviews was a need to broaden the pathways between research and policy, and create more accessible tracks for both sides. Currently, consultation mechanisms most frequently draw on the expertise of very senior academics, who are often invited to give evidence to parliamentary groups and sit on panels.

> as scientists reach a more senior stage in their career they're more and more likely to be involved in committees and panels ... and those committees and panels feed into the decision-making processes, along with political views and so on. LD4

However, not only may these views represent just a fraction of the views of the project, but they will inevitably be 'filtered' through a number of competing priorities. Individual scientists, or the project as a group, may perceive wider policy implications from their research, but there is currently no easy mechanism for passing these insights to research policymakers who would be able to act on them. An example is the need identified in the section above for quantum to be taught as part of the UK's National Curriculum – at present, the routes for researchers to pass insights such as these back into policy-formation mechanisms are weak and un-coordinated, so important perceptions may be entirely lost or insufficiently weighted.

4.3. Finding 3: the (non-)neutrality of technology

Our findings here support conclusions from *A Framework for Responsible Research and Innovation in ICT* (FRRIICT) (Jirotka et al. 2017), which found that several factors can combine to make it difficult for researchers to connect their work to societal impacts. The more foundational the research, and the further it is from applications, the less immediate is its 'impact'. Researchers at this level often see their work as 'neutral' research, carried out for its intrinsic fascination. In NQIT-RRI we also found that researchers were more likely to be motivated by intense interest than by ultimate applications. There was a tendency to view end-uses as relatively divorced from the foundational research that had led to those uses – this led to a range of views on the responsibility to consider possible consequences.

> maybe I wouldn't feel wholly responsible since ... people ... can do bad things with many things. LS4

> I'm building the device. So how it's being used is a secondary question. LS6

The view of technology as necessarily 'value-neutral' in and of itself is frequently underpinned by years of training that promote this idea. At the same time, there is a dearth of input from interdisciplinary fields that might draw on wider or different perspectives that could be incorporated into the design of these innovations.[4]

However, we also found that – when equipped with the appropriate tools, such as training in RI – researchers do look forward and imagine possible futures, while accepting that future applications will emerge which cannot yet be predicted.

> that's the continual lesson ... how impossible it is to predict what's going to make the ... biggest changes to society. LS4

> we do talk, what is the best way to move forward and what would be the best mode of operation ... these are important issues to discuss. LS5

RI work can also increase understandings of 'who are stakeholders' – for example, the concept of 'stakeholders' is not limited to ultimate users, and during early-stage development 'stakeholders' might be peers within the research team, or those in similar fields. RI training can increase these understandings.

4.4. Finding 4: the difficulty of anticipation

A further point to emerge from the discussions around stakeholders and the uses of technology is the challenge of identifying the appropriate juncture at which anticipatory work can be most effective.

> it's so difficult to predict what effect basic research done now is going to have far in the future. LS1

Although an RI approach argues for a consistently anticipatory and reflective mindset, there are key decision-making points at which such activities become more than usually critical. Stilgoe, Owen, and Macnaghten (2013) discussed the use of 'stage-gates' in the development of technology. Stage-gates are built-in pause-points at which a technology under development should be reviewed to ensure it could pass through the gate to the next stage – but these key stages can also be difficult to identify in practice (e.g. Edwards et al. 2019). However, comments such as the quote above demonstrate that participants who may be unfamiliar with specific RI concepts are often articulating what may be termed *de facto* RI (Randles et al. 2016).

4.5. Finding 5: **de facto** *RI*

The concept of *de facto* RI is 'in-practice' behaviour that may not be framed as RI but that has the hallmarks of RI approaches, and is well-recognised (e.g. Lindner et al. 2016; Porcari et al. 2021). It was clear from the discussions with some participants that RI-type processes were familiar, even if they had not previously considered them as 'responsible innovation'.

> we need to communicate where ... fundamental science impacts society. LS5

> we've identified something, what procedures should we put in place? LS3

> Almost every decision that is made has to have risk associated with it. LS8

These thoughts are well-aligned with such RI concepts as public engagement, anticipation, and reflection, respectively, but the next step is to draw these threads together more consciously into a cohesive set of considerations that inform each other and, ultimately, a response. These grassroots understandings align with the Randles and Laasch (2016) description of the 'ground-upwards' type of RI institutionalisation described in Section 2.1. Also in 2.1, at the other end of the RI institutionalisation scale are high-level 'top-down' questions of policy, which characterised the discussions around the nation-state impacts of quantum computing in Case Study 2 (Defence).

4.6. Finding 6: national and global impacts

A strong thread in the Defence Case Study was the potential impact on international politics and the balance of power globally, should one country develop scalable and error-corrected quantum computing before others (Inglesant, Jirotka, and Hartswood 2018). As one interview participant put it, 'whoever gets there last pays a price' (LS4). For example, if one nation or non-state actor was able to intercept encrypted Internet communications – a known possible application of quantum computing, albeit far beyond the capabilities of existing quantum computers – it would gain a strategic advantage and would probably not announce its capability (Schneier 2015)

Signs of national sensitivity around research in areas such as quantum computing are seen in protocols such as the UK's National Security And Investment Act,[5] which gives the UK government powers to investigate and potentially repudiate investment into a UK company for national security reasons. Such protectionist impulses – seen also in the multi-state Wassenaar Arrangement,[6] and the US's ITAR regulations[7] – can be understood as an expression of uncertainty around the global impact of novel technologies such as quantum computing. As our Defence workshop showed, there are multiple variables and high-level sensitivities influencing this space, and thus a need for a careful and measured approach. In Section 5, we draw this understanding together with our other findings to offer recommendations to policymakers, industrial organisations, and researchers.

5. Discussion and recommendations for practice

As outlined at the beginning of this paper, based on the numerous research strands of the NQIT-RRI project detailed in Section 3, we have identified several areas of challenge and opportunity for quantum computing as well as broader quantum-based technological development. We have developed these challenges and opportunities into recommendations for better practice.

5.1. R1: Create clearer, more direct pathways from researchers to policymakers

Informal pathways could provide appropriate mechanisms for researchers to express concerns or issues and for policymakers to access information from the 'coalface'. The absence of clear lines of communication between scientists and policymakers and guidance as to how to construct these dialogues in a mutually comprehensible way creates the 'filtration' effect described above in Section 4 (*Finding 2: Policy drivers and routes to action*). In this mode, an issue may be channelled through several layers of mediated intervention before it reaches a relevant recipient, by which time its immediacy and possibly matters of contextual significance may have been lost. In this respect,

EPSRC, research councils and other funders can have an important role to play not only as motivators for RI but also potentially as intermediaries between researchers and policymakers.

5.2. R2: Generate more frequent, more detailed conversations with society

Public acceptance of quantum is unlikely to be smooth unless there are efforts to support consultation and two-way conversation – it is as important for researchers to listen to the public as it is for the public to learn about quantum technologies and therefore **increased public engagement is indicated**. The Kantar dialogue demonstrated that public understanding of quantum technologies is not keeping step with innovations in quantum fields. The public dialogue took place in 2017, and the pace of development in quantum has accelerated considerably since. This is also supported by the recognition from the case studies in defence and QML that projects and researchers have a responsibility to manage expectations through careful use of language and the avoidance of hype. There is not currently a high degree of knowledge in the public domain about quantum technologies and their possibilities – an **RI-driven public engagement programme**, aimed at addressing questions on governance, access, and other matters of public concern, would anticipate and pre-empt societal concern by engaging with citizens.

5.3. R3: Support interdisciplinary dialogue between fields to empower researchers

It is not reasonable to expect researchers to be able to apply techniques and methods from unfamiliar interdisciplinary fields without training, resourcing, and support. As quantum technologies move from the lab to the marketplace, **input from other disciplines becomes not only desirable but essential** to add richness of understanding to possible impacts. Lack of interdisciplinarity and support from more social-science grounded fields can create narrow views and definitions of 'success' within technological fields, as well as an attitude that technology is value-neutral. Presumptions around the limits of researcher responsibility create a hurdle that must be overcome when embedding more broad-based approaches such as RI. It is important to start these conversations early so that there is time and scope to influence trajectories where necessary. Ensuring access to such support will, therefore, be essential to ongoing RI work.

5.4. R4: Ensure wide, democratic access to technologies

De Wolf (2017) and others have suggested that inequity of access may well be a significant impact from quantum computing, and argue that **governments must ensure that citizens are able to access quantum computing** – that it must not be restricted to deep-pocketed corporations. There are broad political challenges for quantum technologies around questions of access: if states have access but deny it to citizens, what would this mean for the balance of power between the state and the individual? If corporations can analyse big data in new ways, will individuals demand tighter controls over their personal information? Market responses may also be seen – for instance, the access to AWS's Braket service[8] – that will influence these discussions.

5.5. R5: Participate in efforts for global co-operation

The 'national' approaches seen in the Defence workshop and discussed in interviews demonstrate an awareness that, although the UK has a depth of expertise in quantum technologies and in the application of RI techniques in quantum, there is nation-state level sensitivity to global competitiveness. This suggests a need to participate in worldwide discussion with partners and collaborators to ensure that **ethical concerns around fairness, access, and equity are not subsumed into technology arms races**.

5.6. R6: Expand the scope of responsible innovation

The application of RI within quantum fields is also an **opportunity to expand and verify the methodology of RI**, which is sometimes critiqued for being difficult to apply in real-world projects. This is a crucial moment as these technologies move from basic research into industrial application. The questions identified in this project, such as the precise timing of interventions – how 'upstream' is it reasonable to start looking at impacts? – can be further researched and field-tested. Additionally, the ongoing process of institutionalisation of RI can be further embedded in quantum technologies as understandings and practice mature.

5.7. R7: Widen the pool of stakeholders consulted

This is also an opportune time to **incorporate the views of wider groups of stakeholders.** There is a need to develop understanding, within all channels and levels of the policy-industry-academia model, of the possible effects and impacts of quantum-based technologies. As the work from Pansera et al. (2020) and our NQIT work has shown, not only are citizens and professionals able to bring insight and new perspectives to the research questions, but undertaking such dialogic activities can serve to mature RI understandings that in turn may inform the direction of the work. Good levels of understanding are currently restricted to relatively narrow groups and teams – engagement needs to happen not only with publics, but with all types of interested stakeholder including regulators, contingent industries, and other branches of the academy.

6. Conclusions

We have argued that we may be seeing a 'tipping point' for quantum computing, and that this is therefore an opportune moment to take a step back and reflect on what can be learned from the work of the NQIT-RRI project. Although the quantum technology Hubs varied in the readiness of the innovations they were investigating, these novel technologies are collectively at an important juncture in terms of both their ability to contribute to economic life and the need for a meaningful public conversation. Although to some degree quantum fields of enquiry and development have a 'blank sheet' in public perception, it is important to maintain this public acceptability, pre-empting the social and ethical challenges seen in other novel technological fields such as artificial intelligence. It was partly to that end that RI was included in the quantum technologies Hubs.

However, the RI work that was done in the Hubs is not complete (insofar as responsible development can ever be considered 'complete') and there is a need, identified throughout this research, not only for more granular understandings and embedding of RI concerns on a day-to-day basis, but also more in-depth policy responses that can provide an overarching structure to the development of the field. An infrastructure of 'responsibility' is required that understands the complexity of the landscape. RI can operate as both a 'top-down' structure and a 'bottom-up' methodology – seen in some of the 'de facto' RI work being carried out in the NQIT Hub – but there needs to be both an understanding and an overarching view of these different perspectives and levels of granularity.

Vermaas (2017)'s call for us to pay 'good attention' to these questions could be interpreted simply as 'close' attention but could also refer to the need for 'high-quality' attention, a call that we echo here. Although this call for a 'responsibility' infrastructure is a broader interpretation of RI than hitherto, it is our contention, based upon the NQIT-RRI work, that a narrow view of RI cannot be sufficient when incorporated into such a wide-ranging and potentially impactful field as quantum technologies. In order both to act responsibly and be seen to be acting responsibly, a cohesive and comprehensive approach is required.

Notes

1. Here used in a combination of the physics and sociological senses to indicate incremental changes that accumulate to then form a cascade beyond which there is no return to the former state.

2. RI and RRI are sometimes used interchangeably. In this paper we will use the former except where referring to the project name.
3. https://www.qsrinternational.com/nvivo-qualitative-data-analysis-software/home.
4. For example, Winner (1980) on whether artefacts can be inherently political.
5. https://www.legislation.gov.uk/ukpga/2021/25/contents/enacted.
6. https://en.wikipedia.org/wiki/Wassenaar_Arrangement.
7. https://en.wikipedia.org/wiki/International_Traffic_in_Arms_Regulations.
8. https://aws.amazon.com/braket/.

Disclosure statement

No potential conflict of interest was reported by the author(s).

Funding

This work was supported by Engineering and Physical Sciences Research Council [grant number EP/M013243/1].

Notes on contributor

Carolyn Ten Holter is a social scientist by training, and is part of the Human Centred Computing research group in the Department of Computer Science at the University of Oxford. She has over twenty years' experience in the private sector and is currently investigating responsible innovation in quantum technologies.

ORCID

Carolyn Ten Holter http://orcid.org/0000-0001-8739-3211
Philip Inglesant http://orcid.org/0000-0002-5265-8707
Marina Jirotka http://orcid.org/0000-0002-6088-3955

References

Arute, F., K. Arya, R. Babbush, D. Bacon, J. C. Bardin, R. Barends, and J. M. Martinis. 2019. "Quantum Supremacy Using a Programmable Superconducting Processor." *Nature* 574 (7779): 505–510. doi:10.1038/s41586-019-1666-5.

Biamonte, J., P. Wittek, N. Pancotti, P. Rebentrost, N. Wiebe, and S. Lloyd. 2018. *Quantum Machine Learning*.

Boenink, M., and O. Kudina. 2020. "Values in Responsible Research and Innovation: From Entities to Practices." *Journal of Responsible Innovation* 7 (3): 450–470. doi:10.1080/23299460.2020.1806451.

Braun, V., and V. Clarke. 2006. "Using Thematic Analysis in Psychology." *Qualitative Research in Psychology* 3 (2): 77–101. doi:10.1191/1478088706qp063oa.

Castellanos, S. 2021. *Google Aims for Commercial-Grade Quantum Computer by 2029*. Accessed June 24, 2021, from https://www.wsj.com/articles/google-aims-for-commercial-grade-quantum-computer-by-2029-11621359156?mod=pls_whats_news_us_business_f.

Cookson, C. 2021. *PsiQuantum Expects Commercial Quantum Computer by 2025*. Accessed August 16, 2021, from https://www.ft.com/content/a5af3039-abbf-4b25-92e2-c40e5957c8cd.

De Wolf, R. 2017. "The Potential Impact of Quantum Computers on Society." *Ethics and Information Technology* 19: 271–276. doi:10.1007/s10676-017-9439-z.

Edwards, K., R. G. Cooper, T. Vedsmand, and G. Nardelli. 2019. "Evaluating the Agile-Stage-Gate Hybrid Model: Experiences from Three SME Manufacturing Firms." *International Journal of Innovation and Technology Management* 16: 8. doi:10.1142/S0219877019500482.

Edwards, L., and M. Veale. 2017. "Slave to the Algorithm? Why a Right to Explanation is Probably Not the Remedy You are Looking for." *SSRN Electronic Journal*. doi:10.2139/ssrn.2972855.

EPSRC. 2017. *Quantum Technologies Public Dialogue Report*. https://www.nqit.ox.ac.uk/sites/www.nqit.ox.ac.uk/files/2018-07/Quantum Technologies Public Dialogue Full Report_0.pdf.

EPSRC. 2018. 2018 CDT Exercise – EPSRC Website. Accessed June 20, 2021, from https://epsrc.ukri.org/skills/students/centres/2018-cdt-exercise/.

EPSRC. 2020. UK National Quantum Technologies Programme. https://uknqt.epsrc.ac.uk/.

Frow, E., and J. Calvert. 2013. "Opening up the Future(s) of Synthetic Biology." *Futures* 48: 32–43. doi:10.1016/j.futures.2013.03.001.

Genus, A., and M. Iskandarova. 2018. "Responsible Innovation: Its Institutionalisation and a Critique." *Technological Forecasting and Social Change* 128: 1–9. doi:10.1016/j.techfore.2017.09.029.

Inglesant, P., M. Hartswood, and M. Jirotka. 2016. *Thinking Ahead to a World with Quantum Computers the Landscape of Responsible Research and Innovation in Quantum Computing.*

Inglesant, P., M. Jirotka, and M. Hartswood. 2018. *Responsible Innovation in Quantum Technologies Applied to Defence and National Security.* https://nqit.ox.ac.uk/sites/www.nqit.ox.ac.uk/files/2018-11/Responsible Innovation in Quantum Technologies applied to Defence and National Security PDFNov18.pdf.

Jirotka, M., B. Grimpe, B. Stahl, G. Eden, and M. Hartswood. 2017. "Responsible Research and Innovation in the Digital Age." *Communications of the ACM* 60 (5): 62–68. doi:10.1145/3064940.

Khan, I. 2021. Will Quantum Computers Truly Serve Humanity? Accessed March 15, 2021, from https://www.scientificamerican.com/article/will-quantum-computers-truly-serve-humanity/.

Leslie, D. 2019. *Understanding Artificial Intelligence Ethics and Safety: A Guide for the Responsible Design and Implementation of AI Systems in the Public Sector.* doi:10.5281/zenodo.3240529.

Lindner, R., S. Kuhlmann, S. Randles, B. Bedsted, G. Gorgoni, E. Griessler, and N. Mejlgaard. 2016. *Navigating Towards Shared Responsibility in Research and Innovation.*

Murphy, P. 2010. *Nanotechnology: Public Engagement with Health, Environmental and Social Issues. STRIVE Report (2007-FS-EH-1-M5).* STRIVE Report Series No.61. Retrieved from www.epa.ie.

Owen, R. 2014. "The UK Engineering and Physical Sciences Research Council's Commitment to a Framework for Responsible Innovation." *Journal of Responsible Innovation* 1 (1): 113–117. doi:10.1080/23299460.2014.882065.

Owen, R., M. Pansera, P. Macnaghten, and S. Randles. 2021. "Organisational Institutionalisation of Responsible Innovation." *Research Policy* 50 (1): 104132. doi:10.1016/j.respol.2020.104132.

Pansera, M., R. Owen, D. Meacham, and V. Kuh. 2020. "Embedding Responsible Innovation Within Synthetic Biology Research and Innovation: Insights from a UK Multi-Disciplinary Research Centre." *Journal of Responsible Innovation*, 384–409. doi:10.1080/23299460.2020.1785678.

Perrier, E. 2021. *Ethical Quantum Computing: A Roadmap.* www.aaai.org.

Porcari, A., D. Pimponi, E. Borsella, P. Klaassen, M. Maia, and E. Mantovani. 2021. "Supporting RRI Uptake in Industry: A Qualitative and Multi-Criteria Approach to Analysing the Costs and Benefits of Implementation." In *Assessment of Responsible Innovation: Methods and Practices*, edited by E. Yaghmaei, and I. van de Poel. Abingdon: Routledge.

Preskill, J. 2018. *Quantum Computing in the NISQ Era and Beyond.* https://doi.org/10.22331/q-2018-08-06-79.

Randles, S., and O. Laasch. 2016. "Theorising the Normative Business Model." *Organization and Environment* 29 (1): 53–73. doi:10.1177/1086026615592934.

Randles, S., P. Laredo, A. Loconto, B. Walhout, and R. Lindner. 2016. "Framings and Frameworks: Six Grand Narratives of de facto RRI." In *Navigating Towards Shared Responsibility in Research and Innovation: Approach, Process and Results of the Res-AGorA Project*, 31–36.

RRI Tools. n.d. Accessed March 22, 2021, from https://rri-tools.eu/.

Schneier, B. 2015. *NSA Plans for a Post-Quantum World.* Accessed June 24, 2021, from https://www.schneier.com/blog/archives/2015/08/nsa_plans_for_a.html.

Sciencewise. 2014. *Public Attitudes to Quantum Technology.* https://webarchive.nationalarchives.gov.uk/20170110123807/http://www.sciencewise-erc.org.uk/cms/public-attitudes-to-quantum-technology.

Stahl, B. C., J. Timmermans, and B. D. Mittelstadt. 2016. "The Ethics of Computing." *ACM Computing Surveys* 48 (4): 1–38. doi:10.1145/2871196.

Stilgoe, J. 2013. "Why Responsible Innovation?" In *Responsible Innovation: Managing the Responsible Emergence of Science and Innovation in Society*, edited by R. Owen, J. R. Bessant, and M. Heintz, 306. Oxford: Wiley.

Stilgoe, J. 2015. *Experiment Earth: Responsible Innovation in Geoengineering.* Abingdon: Routledge.

Stilgoe, J., R. Owen, and P. Macnaghten. 2013. "Developing a Framework for Responsible Innovation." *Research Policy* 42 (9): 1568–1580. doi:10.1016/j.respol.2013.05.008.

Vermaas, P. E. 2017. "The Societal Impact of the Emerging Quantum Technologies: A Renewed Urgency to Make Quantum Theory Understandable." *Ethics and Information Technology* 19 (4): 241–246. doi:10.1007/s10676-017-9429-1.

Waters, R. 2021. *Goldman Sachs Predicts Quantum Computing 5 Years Away From Use in Markets.* Accessed August 16, 2021, from https://www.ft.com/content/bbff5dfd-caa3-4481-a111-c79f0d38d486.

Winner, L. 1980. "Do Artifacts Have Politics?" *Daedalus* 109 (1): 121–136.

Wynne, B. 1993. "Public Uptake of Science: A Case for Institutional Reflexivity." *Public Understanding of Science* 2 (4): 321–337. doi:10.1088/0963-6625/2/4/003.

Afterword

Faisal Shah Khan and Davide La Torre

As we conclude this exploration into the fascinating realm of quantum information technology, it's evident that we are at the beginning of a transformative era. The journey through these pages has unveiled the profound potential of quantum computing to revolutionize the way we process, store, and transmit information. From quantum computing's promise of solving complex problems at unprecedented speeds to quantum cryptography's ability to secure communications with unbreakable encryption, the possibilities are limitless. This book has also unveiled the importance and significance of quantum for business leaders and managers.

As with any disruptive technology, the integration of quantum information technology into business practices comes with its own set of challenges and considerations, from technical feasibility and scalability to regulatory compliance and ethical implications, navigating the quantum business landscape requires strategic vision, collaboration, and adaptability.

The future of quantum information technology holds immense promise. The journey ahead is boundless, and it is through the collective efforts of researchers, entrepreneurs, and business leaders that we will unlock the full potential of quantum information technology to shape a more prosperous and sustainable future for all.

Index

Note: **Bold** page numbers refer to tables; *italic* page numbers refer to figures and page numbers followed by "n" denote endnotes.

For Product Safety Concerns and Information please contact our EU representative GPSR@taylorandfrancis.com
Taylor & Francis Verlag GmbH, Kaufingerstraße 24, 80331 München, Germany

www.ingramcontent.com/pod-product-compliance
Lightning Source LLC
LaVergne TN
LVHW080657011026
849160LV00014B/1461
9781032835747